Working with Young People

Working with Young People

This Reader forms part of the Open University course *Introduction to Working with Young People* (E131). This is a 30 point course and is part of the Foundation Degree in Working with Young People.

Details of this and other Open University courses can be obtained from the Student Registration and Enquiry Service, The Open University, PO Box 197, Milton Keynes MK7 6BJ, United Kingdom: tel. +44 (0)870 333 4340, e-mail general-enquiries@open.ac.uk

Alternatively, you may visit the Open University website at http://www.open.ac.uk where you can learn more about the wide range of courses and packs offered at all levels by The Open University.

To purchase a selection of Open University course materials visit www.ouw.co.uk, or contact Open University Worldwide, Michael Young Building, Walton Hall, Milton Keynes MK7 6AA, United Kingdom for a brochure tel. +44 (0)1908 858785; fax +44 (0)1908 858787; e-mail ouwenq@open.ac.uk

Working with Young People

edited by
Roger Harrison
and
Christine Wise

The Open University in association with $SAGE Publications

Los Angeles • London • New Delhi • Singapore

First published 2005
Reprinted 2006, 2007 (twice), 2008

SAGE Publications Ltd
1 Oliver's Yard
55 City Road
London EC1Y 1SP

SAGE Publications Inc.
2455 Teller Road
Thousand Oaks, California 91320

SAGE Publications India Pvt Ltd
B 1/I 1 Mohan Cooperative Industrial Area
Mathura Road, New Delhi 110 044
India

SAGE Publications Asia-Pacific Pte Ltd
33 Pekin Street #02-01
Far East Square
Singapore 048763

British Library Cataloguing in Publication data

A catalogue record for this book is available from the British Library

ISBN 978-1-4129-1945-6
ISBN 978-1-4129-1946-3 (pbk)

Library of Congress Control Number: 2005926978

Typeset by C&M Digitals (P) Ltd., Chennai, India
Printed on paper from sustainable resources
Printed in Great Britain by The Cromwell Press Ltd, Trowbridge, Wiltshire

Contents

Acknowledgements

Every effort has been made to trace all the copyright holders, but if any have been inadvertently overlooked the publishers will be pleased to make the necessary arrangement at the first opportunity.

Chapter 1 is a revised version of the original text which appeared as Chapter 4 in *Delivering Good Youth Work* by Gina Ingram and Jean Harris. First published in 2001 by Russell House Publishing Ltd. www.russellhouse.co.uk

Chapter 2 is a revised version of the original text which appeared in the statement of values and principles from The National Youth Agency.

Chapter 3 is a revised version of the original text which appeared in the DfES Common Core prospectus.

Chapter 4 is a newly commissioned chapter from Jean Spence.

Chapter 5 is a newly commissioned chapter from Simon Bradford.

Chapter 6 is a newly commissioned chapter from Howard Williamson.

Chapter 7 is a revised version of the original text which appeared as Chapter 5 in *Delivering Good Youth Work* by Gina Ingram and Jean Harris. First published in 2001 by Russell House Publishing Ltd. www.russellhouse.co.uk

Chapter 8 is a revised version of the original text which appeared as Chapter 4 in *Principles & Practice of Informal Education* edited by Linda Deer Richardson and Mary Wolfe. First published in 2001 by RoutledgeFalmer.

Chapter 9 is a newly commissioned chapter by Jane Westergaard.

Chapter 10 is a revised version of the original text which appeared as Chapter 15 in *People Skills, second edition* by Neil Thompson. First published in 2002 by Palgrave Macmillan. Reproduced with permission of Palgrave Macmillan.

Chapter 11 is a revised version of the original text which appeared as Chapter 15 in *Principles & Practice of Informal Education* edited by Linda Deer Richardson and Mary Wolfe. First published in 2001 by RoutledgeFalmer.

Chapter 12 is a revised version of the original text which appeared as 3–17 in *Communities of Practice* by Etienne Wenger. First published in 1998 by Cambridge University Press. Reproduced with permission.

Chapter 13 is a revised version of the original text which appeared in *Youth and Policy, the journal of critical analysis* edited by Ruth Gilchrist, Tony Jeffs and Jean Spence. Published by The National Youth Agency.

Chapter 14 is a revised version of the original text which appeared as Chapter 17 in *People Skills, second edition* by Neil Thompson. First published in 2002 by Palgrave Macmillan. Reproduced with permission of Palgrave Macmillan.

Chapter 15 is a revised version of the original text which appeared as Chapter 4 in *Local Education* by Mark Smith. Published in 1994 by Open University Press. Reproduced with the kind permission of the Open University Press/McGraw-Hill Publishing Company.

Chapter 16 is a revised version of the original text which appeared as Chapter 24 in *People Skills, second edition* by Neil Thompson. First published in 2002 by Palgrave Macmillan. Reproduced with permission of Palgrave Macmillan.

Chapter 17 is a newly commission chapter by Stan Tucker.

Chapter 18 is a revised version of the original text which appeared as Chapter 18 in *Principles & Practice of Informal Education* edited by Linda Deer Richardson and Mary Wolfe. First published in 2001 by RoutledgeFalmer.

Introduction

Roger Harrison and Christine Wise

This book is a collection of writing about the practices of working with young people. These practices are not only extensive and diverse, they are also in transition; continuously realigning themselves with changes in the social and political landscape. From this shifting and ambiguous field of practice emerge different kinds of writing, reflecting different perspectives on the field. In this Introduction we attempt to identify some of these different kinds of writing about work with young people, and provide an outline of the professional terrain we are seeking to address through the selections we have made.

First we need to be clear about the origins of the book, since as colleagues elsewhere have noted, 'All books have a history, a reason for being written' (Richardson and Wolfe, 2001: xi). In our case it was to produce a volume of readings to support students studying the Open University's Foundation Degree in 'Working with Young People'. The title of the degree, and also the title of this book, were chosen to signal to both students and readers that we are seeking to address practitioners working with young people in a range of contexts and roles. As a reader you might be a youth worker, a learning mentor, a Scouts/ Guides leader, a sports or after-school club leader, or a specialist advisor working with young people at risk. You might be working with a young men's group in Belfast or young black women in Leicester. You might be working from an established centre or as a detached worker. You might also be a teacher or researcher in this or a related field of practice. Taken together these practices form a complex pattern of provision which is increasingly recognised by government as a highly significant force in the lives of young people (DfES, 2001).

We are also using the phrase 'work with young people' to signal a particular kind of intervention; one in which the participation of young people is voluntary and the aims are broadly educational. This definition is crucial, since it helps to distinguish the kind of work we have in mind from many other sorts of professional interventions, such as probation work or formal programmes of study, which commit young people to attendance. Alongside this 'voluntary principle' is the aim of promoting learning and personal development. Writers on youth work often refer to 'informal education', making a distinction between this kind of work and the more formal instruction which might occur at school or on a training course. It is the kind of work which emphasises responsiveness to the situation and needs of young people, rather than the completion of a syllabus or the realisation of pre-determined outcomes. Learning and development emerge through collaboration between worker, young person and the possibilities inherent in the situation. Whilst the contingencies of actual practice often reveal these principles as more complex and ambiguous than they might seem, it is the commitment of workers to voluntary and participatory relationships with young people which characterises the kind of 'work' we have in mind.

Some chapters in the book have been specially commissioned, some are edited versions of texts which have been previously published in books or journals, and some are recent policy statements from national agencies. They have been selected from a diverse and vibrant literature, first to give a sense of the different issues which are currently being debated in this field, and second to present some of the different kinds of writing through which work with young people is being described and discussed. Some of these issues, such as the nature and scope of youth work, have a long history but are now brought into sharper focus by national policies which emphasise targets and link funding to measurable outcomes. Others, such as the role of counselling skills in supporting and advising young people, have emerged more recently in the wake of the Connexions programme. Some are analytical pieces which reflect the concerns of academic researchers, probing and questioning the assumptions which often lie behind notions of 'community', 'youth', 'supporting and advising' or 'learning'. Some are explanatory 'how-to' texts which aim to distil the wisdom of experienced practitioners in the form of advice and guidance to others. Some are policy statements which seek to establish norms for the values, purposes and practices of work in this field. All are persuasive in their own ways, representing particular views or interpretations of what it means to work with young people at this time. They are certainly not representative in the sense of covering all the issues or kinds of writing which are available, but are selected to give a flavour of the issues and debates which are current in the field.

The book is divided into three unequal and overlapping parts. Part 1 covers debates around the meanings of 'youth' and 'youth work'. These debates are important in attempts to delineate what is different and distinctive about this kind of work with young people. Part 2 covers issues which emerge from the actual practices of this work. These reveal what Simon Bradford describes, in Chapter 5, as an 'infinitely fluid, flexible, and mobile' set of practices, represented and discussed here by committed and reflective practitioners. Part 3 covers issues of learning and continuing professional development. Taking responsibility for one's own professional development is seen as crucial to maintaining professional standards in practice. In these chapters the development of professional capability is discussed in terms of reflection, reflexivity and supervision.

Part 1, 'Defining the field', begins with Gina Ingram and Jean Harris's succinct characterisation of youth work. Whilst describing the breadth and diversity of the work undertaken, and the subtle nature of the skills required, the authors also focus on what good youth work so often comes back to: the quality of the relationship between worker and young person. It is on this that the potency of youth work depends. The National Youth Agency's statement of ethical conduct is a very different kind of text. Developed in consultation with a wide range of practitioners, this is an attempt to capture and codify the core values and principles of youth workers. Whilst the NYA addresses predominantly those practitioners who identify themselves as youth workers, their ethical framework is equally relevant to a much wider set of practices. The 'common core' of skills and knowledge produced by the Department for Education and Skills (DfES) represents a much more ambitious and far reaching project. Emerging from the 2003 Green Paper 'Every Child Matters' it marks a policy move towards integrating those practitioners who work with children and young people within a single set of occupational standards with the aim of increasing levels of cooperation between them. Here we see an important difference of approach, moving from a framework of ethics which leaves practitioners with the responsibility for interpreting what these mean in particular settings, to a specification of competences which can be taught, measured and accredited.

Defining 'youth' in a way which clearly separates this group of people from others has been a recurrent theme in the literature and a crucial component in the case for a separate youth service. Jean Spence's chapter explores the shifting meanings of youth, identifying the close relationship these have with historical, social and economic circumstances, and the diversity of experience available to young people depending on the accidents of their birth. Identifying youth as 'a highly complex notion' she warns that it needs to be used 'critically and carefully' in attempts to explain and understand the lives of particular groups and individuals.

The chapters by Simon Bradford and Howard Williamson both describe and discuss the position of youth work in the current policy climate, but do so in quite different ways. Bradford's is a sophisticated analysis of the historically shifting accounts of youth work as contributing to the social good, acknowledging the humanistic ideals on which it is based but also recognising the element of social control inherent in these professional interventions in the lives of others. Howard Williamson takes a more personal stance as a youth worker, aware of the policy agendas which threaten to undermine those forms of work to which he is committed, but willing to explore practical strategies for challenging and also working alongside current priorities.

Part 2, 'Issues in practice', is the largest section in the book, reflecting a preoccupation in the literature with the challenges presented by the practical business of working with young people. Once again we start with Gina Ingram and Jean Harris, this time presenting a process model, illustrated with case study examples, of a needs based approach to work with young people. Whilst set in the context of youth work this is an approach which will be equally familiar to those engaged in various forms of community work and informal education. The chapter by Mary Crosby reinforces this last point by using the term 'informal educator' in exploring in rather more depth what it means to operate a needs based approach. Her account emphasises the importance of paying attention to our own feelings, perceptions and experiences, as well as those of others, in work of this nature. She describes this process as 'extending ourselves', relying less on method (of the kind presented in the previous chapter) and more on a creative, interactive and less certain approach 'where the worker's chief concern is to discover and work with the client's meanings'. It is a challenging form of practice, one which demands much more of the practitioner than the successful implementation of a generic method, and offers instead the possibility of 'an approach to practice which respects the uniqueness of people and the validity of their experiences'.

Whilst Mary Crosby inspires with a sense of the developmental possibilities of working with young people, Jane Westergaard brings us face to face with the real pressures experienced by many practitioners as they seek to balance a client-centred, needs based approach with the requirements of externally imposed performance targets. Drawing on research with Connexions Personal Advisers she provides graphic evidence of the demands on practitioners of providing help and support to young people and the importance of good quality training and supervision. Her focus on the role of counselling skills also serves as a reminder of the hybrid and overlapping practices which come together in different forms of work with young people.

In his book *People Skills* (2002) Neil Thompson identifies the common ground between a range of professions – including health and social care staff, social workers, counsellors, personnel officers and youth workers – as the skills of dealing with people. People skills are conceptualised in terms of three dimensions: 'thinking' (the cognitive dimension), 'feeling' (the affective dimension), and 'doing' (the behavioural dimension). This 'Think-Feel-Do' framework is used as a helpful device for understanding the complex and composite nature of people work, suggesting that each aspect has a role to play in most forms of effective practice. In the first of three chapters from the book,

'Handling feelings' focuses on the affective dimension, drawing attention to the importance of practitioners being aware of their own feelings as well as those of their clients.

Working with groups is a familiar context for most practitioners and is recognised as an important setting for developing self-awareness, social skills and practical knowledge. In his chapter 'Working with groups' Malcolm Payne draws on experience from across the helping professions to argue for group work as an essential component of informal education. As he puts it, 'For some, working with groups is a – or even *the* – primary means of encouraging learning, because those with whom we work are able to learn from and with one another, rather than simply from us as the worker'. Whilst the benefits of this mutual and democratic form of education might be convincing, creating the conditions in which it will flourish is not straightforward. Payne's thoughtful analysis, supported by case study examples, examines the roles played by workers, the agendas they bring to the work and the ways in which learning might be organised and developed in a group context.

The central position given to learning as a valued outcome of work with young people raises the question of what exactly we mean by the term 'learning'. Most of our everyday understandings suggest that learning is an individual enterprise involving the mental processing of new experience and the accumulation of knowledge in the mind of the learner. Drawing on research which used observation of people learning practical skills in real life contexts (Lave and Wenger, 1991) Etienne Wenger summarises the idea of learning as primarily a social rather than an individual activity. This idea of learning as inseparable from social participation in what he terms 'communities of practice' has significant implications for anyone working to promote learning, especially in informal settings. Learning, within this frame of understanding, is not something which can be organised or regulated as a separate activity, but is embedded in our everyday lives. The role of the practitioner becomes one of setting up and facilitating situations which are rich in learning opportunities, rather than attempting to achieve pre-arranged learning outcomes.

'Community' is another term which has received much attention in the fields of youth work, community and social work. In the chapter 'Trouble and Tribes' Jeremy Brent dares to ask the question 'What is community, anyway?' Drawing on his own in-depth research into the community in Bristol where he works, Brent is able to disturb the rather cosy view of community as necessarily 'a good thing'. Whilst adults might view young people's actions as a threat to their communities, these actions can equally be viewed as communal, community building activities in their own right. His careful uncovering of the subtle dynamics of communities, and the unequal distribution of power within them, provides a useful counter to policies which seek to impose a singular kind of order in local communities.

It is the issue of discrimination against less powerful groups in society which Neil Thompson addresses in his chapter on 'Anti-discriminatory practice'. Moving to the action part of his 'Think-Feel-Do' framework, he identifies why anti-discriminatory practice is an essential part of good practice in all forms of people work, and outlines a practical approach to dealing with the discrimination and oppression associated with diversity. Thompson's approach takes account not only of work with individuals, but also the role of organisational context and the wider societal context in which we live and work.

So far in this part we have heard from a number of writers engaging with a range of themes, and approaching these from different professional standpoints – as informal educators, youth workers, people workers, practitioners and theorists. In the final chapter we hear from Mark Smith, a youth worker and researcher, who encourages us to think about the worker's relationship with their client in terms of conversation, since, 'In conversation we can never be sure of the way things will turn out'. Smith's goal of 'creative participation' brings to mind Wenger's idea of learning as 'social participation', and also Crosby's emphasis on 'working with' people. Each of them rejects the idea of planning for linear and progressive development as incompatible with the more fluid and open ended interactions experienced in their work. Smith goes on to explore how these interactions might be understood, from the practitioner's perspective, as more than just happy accidents. Drawing on the experience of other practitioners he is able to build up a framework of ideas which helps to answer the questions 'what guides our thinking and acting?' and 'how do we make decisions about the directions that encounters are taking?'

Part 3 'Professional development' acknowledges the importance attached to continuous professional development in current discourses of professional competence. Learning and development are seen as essential if practitioners are to adapt to ever accelerating social, economic and technological changes in society and in their fields of practice. The NYA's 'Ethical Conduct in Youth Work' (Chapter 2 in this book) includes the injunction to 'Develop and maintain the skills and competences required to do the job', and the DfES common core (Chapter 3 in this book) includes the requirement, 'Know how to use theory and experience to reflect upon, think about and improve your practice'. The generally accepted model for how this might be achieved is through reflection on the experience of practice. Neil Thompson's chapter on 'Reflective practice' provides a clear account of the basis of this idea, and explores the role of theory in any reflective evaluation of practice. The reflective practitioner has been widely adopted as the underpinning model for professional formation in, among others, teaching, nursing, social work and youth work. It is attractive at least in part because it puts the practitioner at the centre of the picture, taking responsibility for her/his own development and taking control of decisions made in the practice setting. However, this has been undermined by the experience of many practitioners as they become subject to various forms of targeting and auditing of their work, leaving little space or time for the exercise of professional autonomy (Harrison, 2003).

It is this last point which is picked up and developed by Stan Tucker. He explores some of the influences: social, economic, educational, political and occupational, which shape the identities of those engaged in what he terms 'youth working'. Tucker identifies a wide agenda of change to the conditions in which this work takes place, with profound effects on the kinds of work, and the kind of workers, which then become possible. What he suggests is not that change is simply imposed from above, although government departments and professional agencies do hold considerable power, but that work is a 'site of struggle' in which different interests and agendas are played out. It is within these struggles that worker identities are constructed, organised and developed. His analysis provides a useful counter to the individualistic notion of the reflective practitioner and reminds us of the wider social and political context in which practice is embedded.

In the final chapter in the book, 'Using line management', Annmarie Turnbull looks at supervision and how it can contribute towards the professional development of workers. She identifies the potential of the supervisory relationship in enabling the organisation to get the best out of its staff, and also for the individual worker to benefit from support and guidance. This kind of support can be particularly important in the often isolating conditions and stressful interactions in which many informal educators, or people workers, are engaged – as we saw from Jane Westergaard's account of personal advisors in Chapter 9. As well as offering practical advice to supervisors and supervisees on how to conduct their relationship, Turnbull also points towards the role of the organisational context and culture in influencing the outcomes of these interactions.

What we have attempted in this book, is to provide a selection of some of the writing emerging from this complex, ambiguous and dynamic field of work with young people. The selection aims to cover what we see as key themes which are being discussed in the field, and to represent some of the different kinds of writing through which the field is currently being constituted. As such it seeks to construct its own account of what constitutes the field, an account which is necessarily partial, personal and located in a particular time and place. Nevertheless, we hope you find it a useful collection.

References

Department for Education and Skills (2001) *Transforming Youth Work*, London: The Stationery Office.

Harrison, R. (2003) 'Learning for Professional Development', in L. Kydd, L. Anderson and W. Newton (eds) *Leading People and Teams in Education*. London: Sage.

Lave, J. and Wenger, E. (1991) *Situated Learning: legitimate peripheral participation*, Cambridge: Cambridge University Press.

Richardson, L. and Wolfe, M. (2001) (eds) *Principles and Practice of Informal Education: Learning through life*. London: RoutledgeFalmer.

Thompson, N. (2002) *People Skills*. Basingstoke: Palgrave Macmillan.

Defining the field

Defining good youth work

Gina Ingram and Jean Harris

There is a story that may or may not have its origins in truth:

> Matt had been going to the local youth centre for six months. His mother decided that she ought to go and see what they did there. She called at about 8.30 p.m. It was a busy night. Two young people welcomed her and took her to see George, the full-time worker in charge. She explained why she had come and George asked two young people to show her around. They took her through the coffee bar where a group was planning a visit to Hungary. They pointed out the murals done by members over a number of years. She saw the arts and craft room where the women's group were working on entertainment for a local hospital. In the yard she saw where the young men and women had set out an outdoor training circuit. She returned via the counselling room: she couldn't enter of course, but her guides explained to her about the help-line that the youth council had established. The young people returned her to George who was in the office talking to a young woman about her portfolio for her Youth Achievement Award. The mother's comment was 'What an interesting hobby you have George but what's your real job?'

This is a revised version of the original text which appeared as Chapter 4 in *Delivering Good Youth Work* by Gina Ingram and Jean Harris. First published in 2001 by Russell House Publishing.

Obviously the joke has its origins in the fact that few people actually know what youth workers do and youth workers are bad at explaining this. If you asked people what youth workers do the general view is often that:

- A 'youth worker is a type of social worker who gets on well with young people.'
- 'They keep them out of trouble by doing things with them and often work with difficult young people whom no-one else wants to know.'
- 'Some do it voluntarily, like guides and scouts. A few are paid, but why that is, people are unsure. They do a bit of training to make sure they do things safely.'

In most groups of adults, there are those who have had experiences of youth clubs, projects or voluntary organisations. They tend to speak warmly of the youth workers and say how a youth worker helped them and was good to them, but they seldom specify what the youth worker actually did.

When asked to describe their job, youth workers often rely on words and phrases that mean little to the general public:

We work to empower young people; to help them take control of their lives.

Youth workers build relationships with young people…and help them to become effective adults.

We offer them learning opportunities through which they grow and develop.

We help young people do what they want to do.

Alternatively, youth workers offer a long explanation:

Well, it's hard to explain in a sentence, can I give you an example? We were working with Mike (that's not his real name, I can't tell you that because of confidentiality, you might recognise him from what I say). Mike had this problem…

No wonder workers can sometimes be seen as being woolly minded! There are a number of difficulties in describing youth work.

Identifying the skills

The first problem is that although the delivery of youth work is very highly skilled, youth workers are not always aware of the skills they are using. When they can describe their skills, they can accurately communicate what they are doing. Then, instead of saying things like:

> Well, I just do it: I don't really know why it works, it just does.

They would be able to say:

> I begin by making young people feel safe, no one can learn if they don't feel safe. I make opportunities for young people to talk to me about things that matter to them: for them to tell me their story. If a young person is a bit shy, I always try to…etc.

When people understand what youth workers do, and why they do it, they tend to be more sympathetic and supportive. It can also help people to be more aware of the difficulties that young people face.

The wide range of youth work

The second difficulty about offering an explanation is that youth work takes place in a very wide range of settings using a diverse set of activities. These include:

- Detached or outreach work and work in mobile centres.
- Clubs that may operate every night of the week in large urban centres, or once a week in rural areas.
- Specific project work, for example, the Duke of Edinburgh's Award, youth theatres, adventure clubs.
- Work in units based on the identity of the young people (young women's groups, groups of black young people, PHAB groups [Physically Handicapped and Able Bodied], groups for young people who are lesbian, gay or bisexual).
- In specialist projects based around such issues as health, prostitution.
- There are information services, one stop information shops and centres that offer counselling.

Youth workers may work in a wide range of other settings: colleges, schools, health centres, social service units as well as in multi-agency projects such as Connexions, Youth Offending Teams and social inclusion units.

This is a complex situation, difficult to explain to people quickly. It can be put like this:

> Youth workers work wherever young people are: in clubs, on the streets, in schools. The work is the same, it just takes place in a range of settings.

Competition between different settings for youth work

Some workers often see the work in their setting as being more relevant and appropriate than work in another setting. For example, workers say:

> Detached work is where its at. We work with young people on their terri-tory. This gives them power…they don't see us as an institution like building-based work.

> I work in a youth club, everyone says we are irrelevant and old-fashioned but where else is work so embedded in the community? The workers are off the estate: many were members themselves. Young people hear about the club from their parents, we're part of their scene…each generation makes the club their own.

> The Duke of Edinburgh's Award is fantastic. OK, so we do appeal to lots of kids who achieve more, they've got needs too, but we also run groups aimed at including disaffected young people. Our young people get a tremendous sense of achievement; a nationally recognised qualification…

There is a need for youth workers to celebrate that they work in a range of different ways. This level of differentiation means that a wide range of young people have their needs met. Additionally, they can move on to different things as their needs change. Youth workers offer a highly accessible and differenti-ated service. Working in different ways requires different skills. Youth workers are multi-talented.

Why working with the individual is important

We need to tell people that youth workers are not specialists, they are the last of the generalists and they should be proud of this. Educational establishments such as schools, colleges and universities offer a fixed curriculum and a system that takes the learners through it. Youth work is different, youth work starts where young people are, not from where we would like them to be. We identify their learning needs and design a learning pathway through which individuals and groups can have their needs met. It follows that because the learning pathway is based on the age, experience, needs and interests of individuals and groups of young people, the activities that make up the pathway are very wide-ranging.

In summary:

> Schools and colleges work on fixed programmes of learning. Youth workers are different: they base their work on the young people's needs and interests.
>
> We use this as a starting point to offer young people learning that is relevant to their lives and appropriate to their age, experience and interest.
>
> We offer a tailor made service of individual learning pathways.

Why making a relationship is paramount

Finally, youth workers are justifiably proud of offering learning through the caring, equal, relationships that they make with young people. People often do not understand how important this is. From their point of view:

> Why do you need a relationship to do what you do? Why don't you just get on with it and set things up for them?

When people say this, we need to explain that many young people do not have good experiences of adult relationships. It is important that they develop a good relationship with someone, to help them to become skilled parents, or good working colleagues, or friends. Youth workers act as role models so young people can learn and develop skills such as:

- caring and being cared for
- disagreeing and remaining friends
- negotiation and compromise
- building relationships that are open, honest and based in trust.

The skills of describing our work to others in ways that they can understand and sympathise with are vital. These descriptions, however, must not betray the work. This is the platform from which we can obtain wide support for the work.

2

Ethical conduct in youth work

Statement of values and principles from the National Youth Agency

Background

During Autumn 1999 the National Youth Agency circulated a discussion document, *Ethics in Youth Work*[1]. This contained a draft statement of principles of ethical conduct for youth work, and sought responses from the field via a questionnaire and two consultative seminars. The statement has now been revised and can be found in Section 5 [below]. It takes into account comments made in the questionnaire returns and the seminars. Whilst there was a variety of opinions about the exact wording of the statement, there was a general consensus of opinion that a statement should be developed and adopted, and that this should remain at the level of general principles, rather than giving detailed guidance on the conduct of practitioners (Banks, 2000)[2].

　　While there have been some calls for a longer, more detailed and rule-based code of conduct, this would be difficult to apply to all types of youth workers working in different settings and agencies. It might also be so prescriptive as to curtail the professional freedom and responsibility of the youth worker. Whilst the statement of principles presented here leaves some concepts unexplored (we may well ask, what do we mean by 'justice', when

---

This is a revised version of the original text which appeared in the statement of values and principles from The National Youth Agency.

is an interest 'legitimate'?), its aim is primarily to develop ethical awareness and to encourage reflection as the basis for ethical conduct rather than to tell youth workers exactly how to act in particular cases. More detailed documents on certain issues (such as what levels of risk are appropriate, how to handle conflicts of interest), and guidelines on particular aspects of professional practice (such as confidentiality, handling suspected cases of abuse) could be provided to supplement the statement of principles. These would come better from individual employers or organisations to fit particular local circumstances or age groups. And/or some bodies may wish to produce a shorter version of this text.

The statement of principles is in Section 5. Sections 1 to 4 offer some background comments on the nature and purpose of youth work, the importance of ethics in youth work, the purpose of the statement of principles and a short summary of the principles.

1. The nature and purpose of youth work

1.1.

The purpose of youth work is to facilitate and support young people's growth through dependence to interdependence, by encouraging their personal and social development and enabling them to have a voice, influence and place in their communities and society.

1.2.

Youth work is informed by a set of beliefs which include a commitment to equal opportunity, to young people as partners in learning and decision-making and to helping young people to develop their own sets of values. We recognise youth work by these qualities (based on Davies, 1996[3]):

- it offers its services in places where young people can choose to participate;
- it encourages young people to be critical in their responses to their own experience and to the world around them;
- it works with young people to help them make informed choices about their personal responsibilities within their communities;

- it works alongside school and college-based education to encourage young people to achieve and fulfil their potential; and
- it works with other agencies to encourage society to be responsive to young people's needs.

2. The importance of ethics in youth work

2.1.

Ethics is generally regarded as being about the norms of behaviour people follow regarding what is good or bad, right or wrong. Usually ethical issues are about matters of human (and animal) wellbeing or welfare.

2.2.

Ethics in the context of professional practice is about:

- developing the ability of practitioners to see the ethical dimensions of problems, to reflect on issues, to take difficult decisions and to be able to justify these decisions;
- acting with integrity according to one's responsibilities and duties (this may entail behaving in accordance with professional principles, guidelines or agency rules).

2.3.

The behaviour of everyone involved in youth work and youth services – political and managerial leaders, managers, trustees, employees, volunteers and participants – must be of a standard that makes it the basis of:

- the effective delivery of services;
- modelling appropriate behaviour to young people;
- trust between workers and young people;
- trust between organisations and services and parents and young people;
- a willingness of various parties to commit resources; and
- a belief in the capacity of youth work to help young people themselves learn to make moral decisions and take effective action.

2.4.

This requires all involved to be capable of appropriate thinking about ethics in practical situations.

3. Purpose of the statement of principles

3.1.

The statement in Section 5 outlines the basic principles underpinning the work with the aim of guiding the conduct of youth workers and managers and to serve as a focus for debate and discussion about ethical issues in practice. It is not a rulebook prescribing exactly what youth workers should do in every situation. This would be impossible to achieve, due to the variety of practice settings, age groups and types of work. Rather the statement is intended to be used as a starting point for outlining the broad principles of ethical conduct; raising awareness of the multiple responsibilities of youth workers (paid and voluntary) and their managers and the potential for conflict or at least tension between these responsibilities; and for encouraging and stimulating ethical reflection and debate.

3.2.

The first part of the statement covers 'ethical principles' which include the way that youth workers should treat the young people they work with (for example, with respect for their rights to make choices, without discrimination) and the kinds of values that youth workers are working towards (such as a just society). The second part of the statement covers 'professional principles' which relate more particularly to how the youth worker should act in the role of a practitioner with certain types of responsibility and accountability. The practice principles listed under each general principle are more specific, suggesting how youth workers would apply the broader ethical and professional principles. They are not exhaustive.

3.3.

Note: the term 'youth worker' in this statement is intended to include those who work in youth work directly with young people and people who manage those working directly with young people. The phrase 'professional' is to denote acceptance of a particular role within the 'profession' of youth work, not necessarily the employment status of the individual who may well, for example, be a volunteer.

4. Summary of the statement of principles of ethical conduct for youth work

Ethical principles
Youth workers have a commitment to:

1) **Treat young people with respect,** valuing each individual and avoiding negative discrimination.
2) **Respect and promote young people's rights to make their own decisions and choices,** unless the welfare or legitimate interests of themselves or others are seriously threatened.
3) **Promote and ensure the welfare and safety of young people,** while permitting them to learn through undertaking challenging educational activities.
4) **Contribute towards the promotion of social justice** for young people and in society generally, through encouraging respect for difference and diversity and challenging discrimination.

Professional principles
Youth workers have a commitment to:

5) **Recognise the boundaries between personal and professional life** and be aware of the need to balance a caring and supportive relationship with young people with appropriate professional distance.
6) **Recognise the need to be accountable** to young people, their parents or guardians, colleagues, funders, wider society and others with a relevant interest in the work, and that these accountabilities may be in conflict.
7) **Develop and maintain the required skills and competence** to do the job.
8) **Work for conditions in employing agencies where these principles are discussed, evaluated and upheld.**

5. Statement of principles of ethical conduct for youth work

5.1. Ethical principles

Youth workers have a commitment to:

5.1.1. Treat young people with respect

Practice principles would include:

- valuing each young person and acting in a way that does not exploit or negatively discriminate against certain young people on irrelevant grounds such as 'race', religion, gender, ability or sexual orientation; and
- explaining the nature and limits of confidentiality and recognising that confidential information clearly entrusted for one purpose should not be used for another purpose without the agreement of the young person – except where there is clear evidence of danger to the young person, worker, other persons or the community.

5.1.2. Respect and promote young people's rights to make their own decisions and choices

Practice principles would include:

- raising young people's awareness of the range of decisions and choices open to them and offering opportunities for discussion and debate on the implications of particular choices;
- offering learning opportunities for young people to develop their capacities and confidence in making decisions and choices through participation in decision-making bodies and working in partnership with youth workers in planning activities; and
- respecting young people's own choices and views, unless the welfare or legitimate interests of themselves or other people are seriously threatened.

5.1.3. Promote and ensure the welfare and safety of young people

Practice principles would include:

- taking responsibility for assessing risk and managing the safety of work and activities involving young people;
- ensuring their own competence, and that of employees and volunteers for whom they are responsible, to undertake areas of work and activities;
- warning the appropriate authority, and taking action, if there are thought to be risks or dangers attached to the work;
- drawing to the attention of their employer and, if this proves ineffective, bringing to the attention of those in power or, finally, the general public, ways in which activities or policies of employers may be seriously harmful to the interests and safety of young people; and
- being aware of the need to strike a balance between avoiding unnecessary risk and permitting and encouraging young people to partake in challenging educational activities.

5.1.4. Contribute towards the promotion of social justice for young people and in society generally

Practice principles would include:

- promoting just and fair behaviour, and challenging discriminatory actions and attitudes on the part of young people, colleagues and others;
- encouraging young people to respect and value difference and diversity, particularly in the context of a multi-cultural society;
- drawing attention to unjust policies and practices and actively seeking to change them;
- promoting the participation of all young people, and particularly those who have traditionally been discriminated against, in youth work, in public structures and in society generally; and
- encouraging young people and others to work together collectively on issues of common concern.

5.2. Professional principles

Youth workers have a commitment to:

5.2.1. Recognise the boundaries between personal and professional life

Practice principles would include:

- recognising the tensions between developing supportive and caring relationships with young people and the need to maintain an appropriate professional distance;
- taking care not to develop close personal, particularly sexual, relationships with the young people they are working with as this may be against the law, exploitative or result in preferential treatment. If such a relationship does develop, the youth worker concerned should report this to the line manager to decide on appropriate action;
- not engaging in work-related activities for personal gain, or accepting gifts or favours from young people or local people that may compromise the professional integrity of the work; and
- taking care that behaviour outside work does not undermine the confidence of young people and the public in youth work.

5.2.2. Recognise the need to be accountable to young people, their parents or guardians, employers, funders, wider society and other people with a relevant interest in the work

Practice principles would include:

- recognising that accountabilities to different groups may conflict and taking responsibility for seeking appropriate advice and making decisions in cases of conflict;
- being open and honest in all dealings with young people, enabling them to access information to make choices and decisions in their lives generally and in relation to participation in youth work activities;
- ensuring that actions as a youth worker are in accordance with the law;

- ensuring that resources under youth workers' control are distributed fairly, according to criteria for which youth workers are accountable, and that work undertaken is as effective as possible;
- reporting to the appropriate authority suspicions relating to a young person being at risk of serious harm or danger, particularly of sexual or physical abuse; and
- actively seeking opportunities to collaborate with colleagues and professionals from other agencies.

5.2.3. Develop and maintain the skills and competence required to do the job

Practice principles would include:

- only undertaking work or taking on responsibilities for which workers have the necessary skills, knowledge and support;
- seeking feedback from service users and colleagues on the quality of their work and constantly updating skills and knowledge; and
- recognising when new skills and knowledge are required and seeking relevant education and training.

5.2.4. Foster and engage in ethical debate in youth work

Practice principles would include:

- developing awareness of youth workers' own personal values and how these relate to the ethical principles of youth work as stated in section 5.1;
- re-examining these principles, engaging in reflection and discussion with colleagues and contributing to the learning of the organisation where they work;
- developing awareness of the potential for conflict between personal and professional values, as well as between the interests and rights of different individuals and between the ethical principles in this statement; and
- recognising the importance of continuing reflection and debate and seeing this statement of ethical principles as a working document which should be constantly under discussion.

5.2.5. Work for conditions in employing agencies where these principles are discussed, evaluated and upheld

Practice principles would include:

- ensuring that colleagues, employers and young people are aware of the statement of principles;
- being prepared to discuss difficult ethical issues in the light of these principles and contributing towards interpreting and elaborating on the practice principles; and
- being prepared to challenge colleagues or employing agencies whose actions or policies are contrary to the principles in this statement.

Notes

1 **National Youth Agency** (October 1999) *Ethics in Youth Work*, Leicester, NYA.
2 **Banks, S.** (2000) *Report to National Youth Agency on Ethics in Youth Work*, Durham, Community and Youth Work Studies Unit, University of Durham.
3 **Davies, B.** (1996) 'At your service?' *Young People Now*, August, pp. 26 to 27.

Common core of skills and knowledge for the children's workforce

Extract from DfES Common Core prospectus

Introduction

The consultation on the Green Paper, *Every child matters*, strongly supported the proposition that everyone working with children, young people and families should have a common set of skills and knowledge.

The DfES has worked with a partnership of service user, employer and worker interests to develop this Common Core of Skills and Knowledge.

The prospectus sets out required knowledge and skills to practise at a basic level in six areas of expertise:

- effective communication and engagement
- child and young person development
- safeguarding and promoting the welfare of the child
- supporting transitions
- multi-agency working
- sharing information.

This is a revised version of the original text which appeared in the DfES Common Core prospectus.

The Common Core reflects a set of common values for practitioners that promote equality, respect diversity and challenge stereotypes, helping to improve the life chances of all children and young people and to provide more effective and integrated services. It also acknowledges the rights of children and young people, and the role parents, carers and families play in helping children and young people achieve the outcomes identified in *Every child matters*.

The Government and partners who have endorsed the prospectus are looking to service managers to use the Common Core:

- in the design of induction and in-service and inter-agency training, building on existing practice. This will not only support strategies for enhancing front-line practice but will also help establish a greater shared language and understanding across different parts of the workforce;
- as a tool for training needs analyses that focus on supporting individual development;
- as a tool for workforce planning.

Looking ahead, as part of its strategy to build a world-class children's workforce, the Government is committed to the creation of a single qualifications framework to support career pathways. Over time, all qualifications for work with children, young people and families, and the occupational standards that underpin them, will include an appropriately differentiated Common Core.

1. Effective communication and engagement with children, young people, their families and carers

Good communication is central to working with children, young people, their families and carers. It is a fundamental part of the Common Core. It involves listening, questioning, understanding and responding to what is being communicated by children, young people and those caring for them. It is important to be able to communicate both on a one-on-one basis and in a group context. Communication is not just about the words you use, but also your manner of speaking, body language and, above all, the effectiveness with which you listen. To communicate effectively it is important to take account of culture and context, for example where English is an additional language.

Effective engagement requires the involvement of children, young people and those caring for them in the design and delivery of services and decisions that affect them. It is important to consult with them and consider their opinions and perspectives from the outset. A key part of effective communication and engagement is trust, both between the workforce, children, young people and their carers, and between and within different sectors of the workforce itself. To build a rapport with children, young people and those caring for them, it is important to demonstrate understanding, respect and honesty. Continuity in relationships promotes engagement and the improvement of lives.

The skills and knowledge highlighted here and throughout the prospectus are intended to provide a basic description of those areas you may need to develop through training, learning or experience in order to do your job well.

Skills

Listening and building empathy

- Establish rapport and respectful, trusting relationships with children, young people, their families and carers.
- Develop and use effective communication systems appropriate to the audience.
- Communicate effectively with all children, young people, families and carers.
- Be aware that some children and young people do not communicate verbally and that you need to adapt your style of communication to their needs and abilities.
- Understand the effects of non-verbal communication such as body language, and appreciate that different cultures use and interpret body language in different ways.
- Build rapport and develop relationships using the appropriate form of communication (for example, spoken language, play, body and sign language).
- Build open and honest relationships by respecting children, young people, parents and carers and making them feel valued as partners.
- Hold conversations at the appropriate time and place, understanding the value of day to day contact.
- Actively listen in a calm, open, non-threatening manner and use questions to check understanding and acknowledge that you have heard what is being said.
- Understand the role and value of families and carers as partners in supporting their children to achieve positive outcomes.

Summarising and explaining

- Summarise situations in the appropriate way for the individual (taking into account factors such as background, age and personality).
- Understand how to present genuine choices to young people and how to obtain consent to sharing information.
- Explain to the child, young person, parent or carer what kind of information you may have to share with others.
- Explain what has happened or will happen next and check their understanding and where appropriate, their consent to the process.

Consultation and negotiation

- Consult the child, young person, parent or carer from the beginning of the process.
- Inform, involve and help the child or young person to assess different courses of action, understand the consequences of each and, where appropriate, agree next steps.
- Understand the key role and value of parents and carers; know when to refer them to further sources of information, advice or support.
- Identify what each party hopes to achieve in order to reach the best possible and fair conclusion for the child or young person.
- Share reasons for action with the child or young person and those caring for them.
- Provide support and encouragement to children and young people.
- Know when and how to hand over control of a situation to others.

Knowledge

How communication works

- Know that communication is a two-way process.
- Know how to listen to people, make them feel valued and involved, and know when it is important to focus on the individual rather than the group.
- Be aware of different ways of communicating, including electronic channels, and understand barriers to communication.
- Be aware that the child, young person, parent or carer may not have understood what is being communicated.

- Know how to report and record information formally and informally in the appropriate way for the audience concerned, including how the use of the Common Assessment Framework for Children and Young People (CAF) helps communication between practitioners.

Confidentiality and ethics

- Remember and understand the procedures and legislation relating to confidentiality issues that apply to your job role.
- Understand the limits of confidentiality that apply to your job role and that sometimes it is necessary to go against a child or young person's expressed wishes in their best interests and, where this is the case, ensure that the child or young person understands what is happening and why.

Sources of support

- Know where education and support services for parents and carers are available locally.
- Know when and how to refer to sources of information, advice or support from different agencies or professionals.

Importance of respect

- Be self-aware: know how to demonstrate a commitment to treating all people fairly; be respectful by using active listening and avoiding assumptions.

2. Child and young person development

This core area covers the physical, intellectual, linguistic, social and emotional growth and development of babies, children and young people.

It is difficult to determine specific times when developmental changes occur, as these will differ from person to person. What is important is a basic understanding of those changes and how they can affect a baby, child or young person's behaviour. Parents and carers may be well placed to identify developmental and behavioural changes in their children but they may also find them difficult to cope with and seek reassurance, information, advice and support at various stages. It is therefore important that you have the ability to self-reflect and adjust your own behaviour appropriately.

Skills

Observation and judgement

- Observe a child or young person's behaviour, understand its context, and notice any unexpected changes.
- Listen actively and respond to concerns expressed about developmental or behavioural changes.
- Record observations in an appropriate manner.
- Understand that babies, children and young people see and experience the world in different ways.
- Evaluate the situation, taking into consideration the individual, their situation and development issues.
- Be able to recognise the signs of a possible developmental delay.
- Be able to support children and young people with a developmental difficulty or disability, and understand that their families, parents and carers will also need support and reassurance.
- Make considered decisions on whether concerns can be addressed by providing or signposting additional sources of information or advice.
- Where you feel that further support is needed, know when to take action yourself and when to refer to managers, supervisors or other relevant professionals.
- Be able to distinguish between fact and opinion.

Empathy and understanding

- Demonstrate your commitment to reaching a shared understanding with a child, young person, parent or carer by talking and listening effectively; make sensitive judgements about what is being said and what is meant by what is being said.
- Be able to support a child or young person to reach their own decisions (while taking into account health and safety and child protection issues).
- Encourage a child or young person to value their personal experiences and knowledge.
- Appreciate the impact of transitions on child development.

Knowledge

Understand context

- Know and recognise the child or young person's position in a family or caring network, as well as a wider social context, and appreciate the diversity of these networks.
- Understand and take account of the effects of different parenting approaches, backgrounds and routines.
- Know and recognise that for some children and young people, delayed or disordered development may stem from underlying, potentially undiagnosed disability and is not a reflection of parenting skills.

Understand how babies, children and young people develop

- Know that development includes emotional, physical, intellectual, social, moral and character growth, and know that they can all affect one another.
- Appreciate the different ways in which babies and children form attachments and how these might change.
- Recognise that play and recreation – directed by babies, children and young people, not adults – play a major role in helping them understand themselves and the world around them as well as helping them realise their potential.
- Know how to interact with children in ways that support the development of their ability to think and learn.

Be clear about your own job role

- Know who the experts are and when they are needed.
- Remember that parents and carers almost always know their children best.
- Know how to obtain support and report concerns.
- Have a broad knowledge of the laws and key policy areas related to children.
- Know about the Child Health Promotion Programme and Common Assessment Framework for Children and Young People (CAF) and, where appropriate, how to use them.

Know how to reflect and improve

- Know how to use theory and experience to reflect upon, think about and improve your practice.
- Highlight additional training and supervision needs to build on your skills and knowledge.
- Understand and behave appropriately for the baby, child or young person's stage of development.
- Be aware that working with children and young people may affect you emotionally and know some sources of help in dealing with the impact of this.
- Draw upon your experience and others' perspectives to enable you to challenge your thinking and assess the impact of your actions.
- Know your role in supporting and promoting development.
- Know how to motivate and encourage children and young people to achieve their full potential and how to empower and encourage parents and carers to do the same.

3. Safeguarding and promoting the welfare of the child

Those who work with children and young people have a responsibility to safeguard and promote their welfare. This is an important responsibility and requires vigilance. You will need to be able to recognise when a child or young person may not be achieving their developmental potential or their health may be impaired, and be able to identify appropriate sources of help for them and their families. It is important to identify concerns as early as possible so that children, young people, their families and carers can get the help they need. As well as ensuring that children and young people are free from harm, it is equally important to ensure their well-being and quality of life.

Skills

Relate, recognise and take considered action

- Establish rapport and respectful, trusting relationships with children, young people and those caring for them.
- Understand what is meant by safeguarding and the different ways in which children and young people can be harmed (including by other children and young people and through the internet).

- Make considered judgements about how to act to safeguard and promote a child or young person's welfare, where appropriate consulting with the child, young person, parent or carer to inform your thinking.
- Give the child or young person the opportunity to participate in decisions affecting them, as appropriate to their age and ability and taking their wishes and feelings into account.
- Understand the key role of parents and carers in safeguarding and promoting children and young people's welfare and involve them accordingly, while recognising factors that can affect parenting and increase the risk of abuse (for example, domestic violence).
- Understand that signs of abuse can be subtle and be expressed in play, artwork and in the way children and young people approach relationships with other children and/or adults.
- Make considered judgements about how to act to safeguard and promote a child or young person's welfare.
- Give the child or young person the opportunity to participate in decisions affecting them, as appropriate to their age and ability.

Communication, recording and reporting

- Use the appropriate IT and language skills to effectively observe, record and report – making a distinction between observation, facts, information gained from others and opinion.
- Undertake (formal or informal) assessments and be alert to concerns about a child or young person's safety or welfare, including unexplained changes in behaviour and signs of abuse or neglect.
- Be able to recognise when a child or young person is in danger or at risk of harm, and take action to protect them.

Personal skills

- Have self-awareness and the ability to analyse objectively.
- Have the confidence to represent actively the child or young person and his or her rights.
- Have the confidence to challenge your own and others' practice.
- Understand the different forms and extent of abuse and their impact on children's development.
- Develop appropriate professional relationships with children and young people.

Knowledge

Legal and procedural frameworks

- Have awareness and basic knowledge, where appropriate, of the most current legislation.
- Know about Government and local guidance, policies and procedure and how they apply in the wider working environment.
- Be aware of the Local Safeguarding Children Board and its remit.
- Be aware of national guidance and local procedures, and your own role and responsibilities within these for safeguarding and promoting children and young people's welfare.
- Know about data protection issues in the context of your role.

Wider context of services

- Know when and how to discuss concerns with parents and carers.
- Understand the roles of other agencies, local procedures on child protection and variations in use of terminology.
- Understand the necessity of information sharing within the context of children and young people's well-being and safety.
- Know about the Common Assessment Framework for Children and Young People (CAF) and, where appropriate, how to use it.
- Understand that different confidentiality procedures may apply in different contexts.

Self-knowledge

- Know the boundaries of personal competence and responsibility, know when to involve others, and know where to get advice and support.
- Appreciate the effect of witnessing upsetting situations and know how to get support.
- Have an understanding of issues related to aggression, anger and violence, and know the appropriate responses to conflict – whether the situation involves an adult, a peer, or the child or young person themselves.
- Know that assumptions, values and discrimination can influence practice and prevent some children and young people from having equality of opportunity and equal protection from harm.

4. Supporting transitions

Children and young people naturally pass through a number of stages as they grow and develop. Often, they will also be expected to cope with changes such as movement from primary to secondary school and for children with disabilities or chronic ill health, from children's to adult services. Such changes are commonly referred to as transitions. Some children may have to face very particular and personal transitions not necessarily shared or understood by all their peers. These include: family illness or the death of a close relative; divorce and family break-up; issues related to sexuality; adoption; the process of asylum; disability; parental mental health; and the consequences of crime.

As recognised in effective communication and child development, it is important to understand a child or young person in the context of their life, to recognise and understand the impact of any transitions they may be going through. It is also vital to recognise the role of parents and carers in supporting children at points of transition and to understand the need for reassurance, advice and support that parents and carers may express at these points.

Skills

Identify transitions

- Listen to concerns; recognise and take account of signs of change in attitudes and behaviour.
- Build open and honest relationships using language appropriate to the development of the child or young person and the family culture and background.
- Manage the process of transition in a timely way and help the child or young person reach a positive outcome.

Provide support

- Empathise by communicating simple, reassuring messages about key transitions.
- Reassure children, young people and those caring for them by explaining what is happening, and by exploring and examining possible actions to deal with new and challenging situations.
- Identify opportunities to discuss the effects and results of transition.

- Act to ensure that information transfers ahead of the child or young person, when appropriate, and respect other professionals when sharing information.
- Provide information relating to the facts surrounding the transition.
- Where appropriate, illustrate the benefits of transition.
- Make effective links with other practitioners should further support be necessary.
- Operate effective cross-agency referral processes.

Knowledge

How children and young people respond to change

- Consider issues of identity, delayed effects of change and be aware of possible signs that someone is going through a particular transition.
- Know about the likely impact of key transitions, such as divorce, bereavement, family break-up, puberty, move from primary to secondary school, unemployment, and leaving home or care.
- Understand patterns of transition from childhood to adulthood, and appreciate that it may be different from your own or past experiences.
- Understand that children and young people with disabilities or special educational needs may need additional support to manage transitions, and know when to seek specialist advice.
- Know that children and young people can be influenced by peer group behaviour and that this may vary according to culture.

When and how to intervene

- Know about organisational procedures and relevant legal frameworks, as well as appropriate referral routes within your own organisation and to other agencies.
- Know about local resources and how to access information including, where appropriate, a common assessment.
- Understand your own role and its limits, and the importance of providing care or support.

5. Multi-agency working

Multi-agency working is about different services, agencies and teams of professionals and other staff working together to provide the services that fully meet the needs of children, young people and their parents or carers. To work successfully on a multi-agency basis you need to be clear about your own role and aware of the roles of other professionals; you need to be confident about your own standards and targets and respectful of those that apply to other services, actively seeking and respecting the knowledge and input others can make to delivering best outcomes for children and young people. These behaviours should apply across the public, private and voluntary sectors.

Skills

Communication and teamwork

- Communicate effectively with other practitioners and professionals by listening and ensuring that you are being listened to.
- Appreciate that others may not have the same understanding of professional terms and may interpret abbreviations such as acronyms differently.
- Provide timely, appropriate, succinct information to enable other practitioners to deliver their support to the child or young person, parent or carer.
- Record, summarise, share and feed back information, using IT skills where necessary to do so.
- Work in a team context, forging and sustaining relationships across agencies and respecting the contribution of others working with children, young people and families.
- Share experience through formal and informal exchanges and work with adults who are parents/carers.

Assertiveness

- Be proactive, initiate necessary action and be able and prepared to put forward your own judgements.
- Have the confidence to challenge situations by looking beyond your immediate role and asking considered questions.
- Present facts and judgements objectively.
- Identify possible sources of support within your own working environment.
- Judge when you should provide the support yourself and when you should refer the situation to another practitioner or professional.

Knowledge

Your role and remit

- Know your main job and responsibilities within your working environment.
- Know the value and expertise you bring to a team and that brought by your colleagues.

Know how to make queries

- Know your role within different group situations and how you contribute to the overall group process, understanding the value of sharing how you approach your role with other professionals.
- Develop your skills and knowledge with training from experts, to minimise the need for referral to specialist services, enabling continuity for the family, child or young person while enhancing your own skills and knowledge.
- Have a general knowledge and understanding of the range of organisations and individuals working with children, young people and those caring for them, and be aware of the roles and responsibilities of other professionals.

Procedures and working methods

- Know what to do in given cases, e.g. for referrals or raising concerns.
- Know what the triggers are for reporting incidents or unexpected behaviour.
- Know how to work within your own and other organisational values, beliefs and cultures.
- Know what to do when there is an insufficient response from other organisations or agencies, while maintaining a focus on what is in the child or young person's best interests.
- Understand the way that partner services operate – their procedures, objectives, role and relationships – in order to be able to work effectively alongside them.
- Know about the Common Assessment Framework for Children and Young People (CAF) and, where appropriate, how to use it.

The law, policies and procedures

- Know about the existence of key laws relating to children and young people and where to obtain further information.
- Know about employers' safeguarding and health and safety policies and procedures, and how they apply in the wider working environment.

6. Sharing information

Sharing information in a timely and accurate way is an essential part of helping to deliver better services to children, young people, their families and carers. Indeed, sometimes it will help save lives. Practitioners in different agencies should work together and share information for the safety and well-being of children. It is also important to understand and respect issues and legislation surrounding the control and confidentiality of information.

It is important to build trust from the outset by clarifying issues and procedures surrounding confidentiality and information sharing. Practitioners must adopt the right approach to information sharing – by following the correct procedures and by ensuring that the child or young person, parent or carer understands the process.

Skills

Information handling

- Make good use of available information, for example whether a common assessment has been completed – appraise content and assess what else might be needed.
- Be able to bring together relevant information about clients either by completing paperwork or using IT skills.
- Be able to assess the relevance and status of information (for example, whether it is observation or opinion) and to pass it on when appropriate.
- Be able to identify gaps in information.

Clear communication

- Be able to use clear language to communicate information unambiguously to others including children, young people, their families and carers.
- Listen carefully to what is said and check understanding.

Engagement

- Create an environment of trust, by seeking consent where possible and appropriate, and in this way emphasising respect for the child or young person and their family or carer. Respect the skills and expertise of other professionals.
- Encourage children, young people and their families to share information where appropriate, ensuring that they understand why it is important to do so.
- Engage with children, young people and those caring for them and involve them in decision-making.

Knowledge

Importance of information sharing

- Understand the importance of sharing information, how it can help and the dangers of not doing so.
- Understand that consent is not always necessary to share information; even where information is confidential in nature, it may be shared without consent in certain circumstances (for example, where the child is at risk of harm or there is a legal obligation to disclose).
- Know that inference or interpretation can result in a difference between what is said and what is understood.
- Understand that it is not always necessary to collect information directly from children, young people and families as it may frustrate them if they are being asked to provide the same information repeatedly. Be aware that information can often be gathered from other sources.

Role and responsibilities

- Know who to share information with and when; understand the difference between information sharing on individual, organisational and professional levels.
- Know how to share information – in writing, by telephone, electronically or in person.
- Know what to record, how long to keep it, how to dispose of records correctly and when to feed back or follow up.

- Be aware of own (and others') professional boundaries.
- Know about the Common Assessment Framework for Children and Young People (CAF) and, where appropriate, how to use it.

Awareness of complexities

- Be aware that different types of information exist (for example, confidential information, personal data and sensitive personal data), and appreciate the implications of those differences.
- Appreciate the effect of cultural and religious beliefs; refrain from making assumptions about certain cultures or backgrounds.
- As far as possible, make clear to the child or young person, parent or carer how the information they provide will be used.

Awareness of laws and legislation

- Have awareness and basic knowledge of current legislation and the common law duty of confidentiality.
- Have awareness of any legislation which specifically restricts the disclosure of certain information.
- Know that the Data Protection Act can be a tool to enable and encourage information sharing.
- Understand legislation governing own profession; different policies and procedures surrounding confidentiality issues.
- Understand the principles governing when young people are considered sufficiently mature to give consent to their information (in particular, taking into account the Gillick test of competence).
- Understand the difference between permissive statutory gateways (where a provision permits the sharing of information) and mandatory statutory gateways (where a provision places a duty upon a person to share information) and their implications for sharing information.
- Know that the website www.everychildmatters.gov.uk provides further information about Children, Young People and Families services and practice.

Glossary

Abuse
A deliberate act of ill-treatment that can harm or is likely to cause harm to a child's safety, well-being and development.

Agency
An organisation in the statutory or voluntary sector where staff, paid and unpaid, work with or have access to children and/or families.

Child Health Promotion Programme
The Child Health Promotion Programme is delivered by multi-agency child, young person and family support services, and addresses the needs of children from pre-conception through to transition to adulthood. It offers a structure for the provision of essential activities to promote the health and development of children.

Child or young person
Someone up to the age of 19 (up to the day before their 19th birthday), care leavers up to the age of 21 (up to the day before their 21st birthday or beyond if they are continuing to be helped with education or training by their Local Authority) or up to 25 (up to the day before their 25th birthday) if they have learning difficulties or disabilities.

Child and young person development
How babies, children and young people grow and develop – physically, intellectually, linguistically, socially and emotionally.

Common Assessment Framework for Children and Young People (CAF)
The CAF is a nationally standardised approach to help practitioners in any agency assess and decide how to meet the unmet needs of a child. As part of a wider programme of work to provide more integrated services to families, the CAF will support earlier intervention, improve multi-agency working, and reduce bureaucracy for families, reducing the number of inappropriate inter-agency referrals, separate assessments and different agencies working with the child. Where the child has urgent or complex needs, requiring specialist assessment and intervention, the common assessment information will feed into the specialist assessment process.

Communication
The exchange of thoughts, messages or information – using spoken language, body language, tone of voice and gestures that demonstrate listening and understanding.

Concern
A suspicion or a belief that a child may be in need of help or protection.

Context
The circumstances that are relevant to a situation.

Developmental delay
Developmental delay refers to a lag in development rather than to a specific condition causing that lag. It represents a slower rate of development, in which a child exhibits a functional level below the norm for his or her age. A child may have an across-the-board developmental delay or a delay in specific areas.

Empathy
Being able to understand and identify with another person's feelings.

Engagement
Involving the customer (namely children, young people and their families) in the design and delivery of services and decisions that affect them.

Ethics
A code of behaviour agreed to be correct, especially that of a particular group, profession or individual.

Inclusion
Identifying, understanding and breaking down barriers to participation and involvement.

IT
Information Technology, for example the internet and email.

Information sharing
Passing on relevant information to other agencies, organisations and individuals that need it in order to deliver better services to children and young people.

Knowledge
Awareness or understanding gained through learning or experience.

Multi-agency working
Agencies, organisations and individuals working together.

Neglect
Failing to provide for, or secure for a child, the basic needs of physical safety and well-being.

Parents
Includes those who have parental rights as defined in law and those who have care of a child, for example foster carers and co-habitees.

Practitioners

Staff who work directly or indirectly with children, young people and/or families and can include (but is not exclusive to) police officers, doctors, nurses, teachers, nursery staff, social workers, therapists, dentists, youth leaders, leisure and recreational workers, housing staff, and staff who work in criminal justice, mental health or drug and alcohol services. It can also refer to volunteers who come into contact with children.

Safeguarding children

Safeguarding is taken to mean that all agencies working with children, young people and their families take all reasonable measures to ensure that the risks of harm to children's welfare are minimised; and where there are concerns about children and young people's welfare, all agencies and individuals take all appropriate actions to address those concerns.

Skill

The ability to do something, usually developed through training or experience.

Special Educational Needs (SEN)

A child has special educational needs if he or she has a learning difficulty which calls for special educational provision to be made for him or her. A child has a learning difficulty if he or she:

a) has a significantly greater difficulty in learning than the majority of children of the same age;

b) has a disability which either prevents or hinders the child from making use of educational facilities of a kind provided for children of the same age in schools within the area of the local education authority;

c) is under five and falls within the definition at (a) or (b) above or would do if special educational provision was not made for the child.

A child must not be regarded as having a learning difficulty solely because the language or form of language of the home is different from the language in which he or she is or will be taught.

Transition

A change of passage from one stage or state to another.

4

Concepts of youth

Jean Spence

In everyday life and language, the concept of 'youth' is associated in a common-sense manner with the state of being young, particularly with that phase of life between childhood and adulthood. Sometimes the word 'youth' is used inter-changeably with 'young person'. It appears to mean the same thing. Yet with the plural, 'youths', the meaning broadens. 'Youths' is a word carrying a great deal of baggage. That baggage includes ideas about unruly young people, often male, operating in groups, and at the very least, being a nuisance on the streets. The concept of youth is therefore not a neutral description of young people, though it is often used as though it were. When it is not used critically and carefully it brings with it mainly negative assumptions about the behaviour and character of young people both as individuals and in groups.

Being young relates to a natural biological phase in the life cycle associated with the growth from childhood to adulthood. The concept of youth is connected with this biological state, but it is also connected with society. It has *social* as well as *biological* meaning. People grow within a particular social context and young people occupy particular places within any given society. The experiences of being young and the meanings attached to 'youth' are derived directly from the social and economic positions occupied by young people as much as from their biological development. In this sense the meaning of youth, the 'baggage' which it carries, shifts and changes in time and place. Being young in the past was experienced and understood differently from being young today. By the same token, being young in one part of the world carries different implications from being young in another. Thus youth as a social concept has both *historical* and *spatial* dimensions.

Within time and place, any given society is structured in such a way that individuals and groups occupy different social positions and take different social roles. Usually social structures reflect the distribution of wealth and power and this distribution affects different groups unequally. In relation to youth, being a young prince brings with it an entirely different status and identity, different social behaviour and different expectations and opportunities from being a working class young man earning a minimum wage in a hotel kitchen. Therefore, even though it is possible to identify some common biological characteristics of being young, there is no one universal set of meanings into which all young people can fit. The concept of 'youth' is a generalisation which cannot be taken to represent the complex experiences of being young in any given situation.

Nevertheless the meanings attached to the concept of youth, and the way in which the term is commonly used, do say something about dominant attitudes towards young people. These, in turn affect the way in which young people in general are perceived and treated. Youth is itself a group affected by different access to wealth and resources. This is partly related to legal age barriers which define access to social opportunities such as voting, employment and welfare and housing benefits and partly related to the notion that youth is a period of 'learning', 'apprenticeship', 'training' to become adult.

The concept of youth is one which ultimately suggests similarity amongst people of a similar age and this concept is used as the basis for creating social rules and institutions which reinforce the similarities. This affects the way in which young people interpret and understand what it is to be young. 'Youth' is therefore a real social as well as biological experience. However, because at the same time, the reality of life for different individuals and different groups of young people is different according to questions of wealth or power defined by different categories such as class, gender or citizenship status, then there can be no universal experience of youth. Understanding something of the complex relationship between the idea or concept of youth and the different realities of young peoples' lives can inform our understanding of the world which different young people inhabit.

Contemporary ideas

In contemporary Britain, youth is often categorised as an unstable period of life between childhood and adulthood. Since the second world war, various social theorists (e.g. Eisenstadt, 1956) have described the period between childhood and adulthood as one of 'transition', but this description has not always been dominant. It came to be important as a means of understanding youth particularly during the 1980s and 1990s (e.g.Wallace and Cross, 1990;

Irwin, 1995) and has continued to influence government decision-making into the twenty first century (e.g. DfES, 2001).

'Transition' suggests a journey from one state to another. In relation to youth, it depends upon the idea that childhood and adulthood are distinct conditions, that there is something fundamentally different between the condition of childhood and the condition of adulthood. The personal aspects of transition are associated with biological maturity while the social aspects are associated with the movement from dependence to independence. The personal aspects involve the movement through puberty and adolescence towards sexual, emotional and intellectual maturity. The social aspects involve changing relationships with social institutions, in particular those concerned with family, education, work and leisure. These institutions must be successfully navigated by the individual in order to achieve the full and responsible adult maturity which is associated with citizenship in a democratic society.

In relation to the notion of transition, youth is perceived as an unusually intense and 'risky' period of life. When the transitions are not made successfully, there is trouble both for the individual and for society. For example, those who refuse schooling in early youth are less likely to access training and employment in later youth and therefore more likely to become poor as they fail to make a successful transition to the waged labour which would bring adult independence and responsibility. Because of this, policy makers stress the importance of education and training in the lives of young people (Hollands, 1990). As society becomes more complex, and the skills required of its citizens ever more sophisticated and diverse, so the age of social maturity expands upwards. Meanwhile improved nutrition and childhood health have been accompanied by a decline in the age of biological maturity, of puberty. Thus the period defined as 'youth', becomes ever longer and the journey fraught with ever more danger and risk.

Not only are the age related boundaries of youth expanding, but also youth is increasingly understood as a process of *becoming*, of apprenticeship and preparation for adulthood. The outcome of independent citizenship is stressed as the goal of youth and young people are directed by social opinion and policy to spend their youth working towards this goal. When they fail or refuse to do so, they are categorised as a social problem. Thus single motherhood, low-skilled employment, unemployment, anti-social behaviour and crime are perceived as particular problems associated with unsuccessful youth transitions, as problems of youth, even though it could be argued from a different perspective that such problems affect a wide range of ages and can be better explained with reference to the economy and to social structural inequalities such as class.

In contrast to the current situation, during the 1950s and 1960s for example, youth was thought of much more as a period of life to be celebrated and enjoyed for its own sake. Young people were able to use opportunities opened up to them by increased affluence and increased access to educational and employment opportunities to create meanings for themselves. In doing so, they began to develop their own ideas about the type of society they wanted and to experiment with new ways of living. They stressed the importance of young people being with other young people and they sought freedom from responsibility, freedom to seek new experiences and knowledge, and freedom to experiment with new ways of living. In this environment, *being* young in itself was understood as more important than *becoming* adult and at the same time, the young people themselves were trying to forge new ways of thinking about what it meant to be adult, which often questioned the values and beliefs of the older generation.

This new way of thinking about youth became possible partly as consequence of the large numbers of young people relative to other age groups during the 1960s, and partly a consequence of their newly won economic power. The development of ideas about youth as a time to be enjoyed for itself, was influenced by the fact that large numbers of young people were freed, for the first time in British history, from the cares of poverty and from the responsibility of contributing towards helping to keep their families. The children born in the years during and immediately after the second world war had benefited from an extended period of relative peace. They had enjoyed the redistribution of social resources brought by the Welfare State which meant that they were healthier and better educated than ever before. They were experiencing technical and scientific innovations which heralded mass communication, opportunities for travel and a sexual freedom hitherto undreamed of. They could afford to ask questions about society and their place within it identifying increasingly with each other as young people, rather than with their parents. In this situation, 'youth' became a powerful social group, with its own developing ideas and culture.

Sociologists of the 1960s and 70s were often themselves young people and they questioned the sociology they had inherited as much as the society which it came from. They became interested in understanding youth subcultural groups such as the mods and rockers and the hippies, and in the meaning of youth culture, identified with rock music, clothes and fashion, political activity, drug-taking and sexual liberation because young people seemed to be creating a new society. In this context, the notion of 'transitions' was almost meaningless.

This essentially hedonistic approach to the idea of youth started to become shaky as the British economy wobbled during the 1970s, and it had come to an end by the early 1980s as youth unemployment soared. The power of the majority of young people was undermined as their spending power collapsed and they became more dependent upon their families and the state. Those young people who did well in these conditions did so, not by questioning society, but by conforming and promoting conservative values. The 1980s were thus marked by a shift away from the idea of distinctive youth culture or cultures and 'sub-cultural' theories of youth towards renewed ideas about transition. Whereas subcultural theory presents young people centrally as creators and actors in their own destinies (CCCS, 1975; Willis, 1977), theories of transition emphasise the importance of processes and structures outside the control of young people in determining the conditions of their existence. In so doing, transitional theory is more directly relevant to policy decisions which shape the active choices of young people.

The tension between ideas of *being* and *becoming* is important for the development of policy and practice relating to young people and is a subject of continuing debate amongst commentators on youth issues (Jeffs and Smith, 1998/99; Davies, 2004). Yet these debates are only possible because there is a larger, overarching idea that youth is a social category which represents a particular group of people worthy of investigation. This idea is only possible as social forces create conditions in which young people occupy particular social spaces and status as youth.

Historical dimensions

Thinking about youth as a universal state of being with particular and common attributes emerged from the particular social and historical circumstances associated with the industrial revolution in Britain and other western societies. The development of industrial capitalism created a situation where social role and identity became increasingly dependent upon paid work. Previously, economic production was based upon agriculture and work was undertaken in the family with different members adopting different roles according to their age, gender and ability. In pre-industrial Europe, social relationships were defined by feudal rights and duties in which status and identity were fixed by relationships of birth and family. Young people expected to remain within the same social group as their parents and to learn the same work. Within this arrangement, which was one of interdependence rather than independence/dependence, age was not a significant indicator of social status.

In his classic text 'Centuries of Childhood', Philip Ariès (1965) describes and analyses the development of a conception of childhood as a state of being separate from, rather than continuous with adulthood. Ariès argued that in the middle ages in Europe, children were simply seen as small adults. This changed in the modern age when childhood began to be considered as a distinctive period of life with its own characteristics. To think of childhood as distinct from adulthood, begs the question of how children achieve adulthood and here the idea of 'youth' as a period of change, of rupture, disruption, discontinuity and transition is born. Whilst the work of Ariès is rather too simple in its historical approach, it nevertheless provides a broad brush-stroke view of the manner in which age relations and the representations of youth changed as industrialisation took hold in Western Europe.

The modern understanding of youth as a period which bridges childhood and adulthood ultimately derives from the manner in which children, young people and adults have been separated into distinct groups. This has taken place within industrial workplace and through the separation of family and work and of education, family and work. In the feudal, pre-industrial productive unit centred upon home, field, and craft production, education, training and work and the division of labour within work was centred within the family. Here it was closely related to physical and mental maturity and capacity.

In contrast, in the world of wage labour and mass production, the ability to work had to be fitted more formally with mechanised systems of mass production. These required a division of labour based not upon individual strength, knowledge and ability, but upon the various tasks involved in making an object. Some of the new productive processes required a capacity to work long and hard hours. Others required high levels of skill and knowledge.

In adapting to the new situation, family, work, and education became separated into distinct social processes and institutions, serving different and specialised functions, but ultimately shaped in response to the requirement for maximising productivity, profit and wealth. The development of separate institutions reinforced differences of class, gender and age in particular. Generally, the family came to be seen as the place for 'unproductive' women with young children, the school as the place for the older child who must learn the skills needed for employment and family responsibilities, and the workplace became the dominant arena for adult men. The workforce in turn was segmented by class divisions associated with levels of education and skill.

From this very rough sketch of the complicated processes of industrialisation, it can be understood how men, women and children were separated with reference to different institutions and in relation to dependent and independent status. By the same token, it begins to become clear how young people could be understood as 'in transition' – from school to family for young women and from school to adult employment for young men. In this, the experiences of young men and young women, of all classes, were similar in that they inhabited a low paid rung in the labour market. However, they were distinct in that their futures would differ. Thus boys received higher wages than girls and boys were more likely to be offered higher or vocational education and training. These distinctions, though no longer formalised, remained clear in the British social structure well into the late twentieth century and can still be traced in the decision making and choices as well as the opportunities offered to young people, despite equal opportunities policies and legislation.

With the development of the institutions associated with industrialisation and mass production, productive activity was no longer tied to the realities of the condition of any given individual. Instead it became standardised according to general criteria, particularly of gender and age. So, no matter that a strong healthy young woman could undertake work of equal or greater capacity than an ailing adult man, she was categorised into a narrow range of trades and lower wages because she was a woman and young. Standardised categories became increasingly written into law throughout the nineteenth and twentieth centuries in defining the parameters of childhood, youth and adulthood. For example, the restrictive and protective legislation enacted in a series of Factories and Mines Acts specified regulation in relation to gender and age categories. This was reinforced as the state increasingly took responsibility for the provision of educational, health and welfare services, for example in determining the school-leaving age. Meanwhile, specific systems for dealing with childhood and youth questions, such as Juvenile Courts, were introduced as principles of justice were brought into line with the emerging sympathy for childhood and youth as distinctive stages of life.

By the end of the nineteenth century, the lives of all young people in Britain were constrained and directed by the organisational relationships between family, work and school. Within this triangle, childhood dependency is located within the family; generational identity is fostered within the school; and the achievement of adult independence is achieved through work. They are supplemented and supported by an edifice of juvenile justice arrangements organised to deal with young people who are unwilling or unable to conform to the expected behaviour or who break the social rules set within these institutions.

Spatial dimensions

The particular historical circumstances of industrialising Britain created a distinctly *modern* understanding of youth which emphasises a series of institutionally based 'discontinuities' between childhood and adulthood. A certain degree of discontinuity is recognised in most societies in relation to the onset of puberty and traditionally, this has been marked by 'coming of age' ceremonies where the moment of becoming adult is marked and recognised (Mead, 1961). Whilst they continue to loom large in the lives of young people in some pre-industrial contexts, in modern complex societies, such ceremonies have lost much of their significance. The achievement of adulthood in the contemporary world is mainly dominated by social rather than biological development. In this social arena young people experience a wide range of different conditions and expectations.

In geographical and cultural space, the concept of youth and the experience of being young for the majority of young people in Britain today might be similar to the experiences of being young in other parts of the wealthy developed world. Young people who inhabit such a world have relatively easy access to the basic needs of life – to food and clothing, warmth and shelter. They can aspire to build upon their good fortune in this respect through education and training and hope in turn that this might provide access to a level of wealth and healthy adulthood undreamed of in other places. So even though 'youth' might be burdened with negative connotations associated with the risks of transition, if young people can navigate these risks successfully, they can hope for a positive future.

However, this bears very little relationship to being young in a poor, underdeveloped or conflict-torn environment. In an absolute sense, being young in Western Europe or North America must be a different experience from being young for example in Sudan, in the rain forests of South America or in Palestine. This is the case in any period of history but its significance is exacerbated by the extent of the inequalities of wealth and opportunity in the contemporary context of globalisation. Conditions of existence such as climate, war and peace, and environmental health facilitate or constrain access to resources and the type of resources available for everyone. This in turn impacts upon health, education and employment. In conditions of poverty or extreme social disruption, families do not have the luxury to accord special and distinct status to childhood. Children and young people are required to achieve independence, or to work to contribute to the processes of survival as soon as they are physically able. At the extremes, this might involve being sold into slavery, it might mean prostitution or abandonment on the streets, it might involve being kidnapped to join a military group, and at the very least can mean exploitative and disabling physical work. In such circumstances, ideas about the qualities or problems of 'youth' are virtually emptied of meaning. Young people are simply bodies and hands with particular physical capacities to be put to work.

The possibility of survival beyond mature adulthood and into a healthy 'third age' all favour the idea of youth as a period of preparation for a satisfying and fulfilled adulthood. In some parts of the world, this is not possible. Even surviving childhood and achieving young adulthood can be a remarkable achievement. For young people in societies where life expectancy is as low as forty, there can be no luxury of youth as a period of preparation. Youth must be used to the full in the here and now – whether that be in terms of working for a living or in terms of reproducing the next generation.

Circumstances in which the idea of youth as a separate and distinct stage of life loses meaning also afflict young people in the richer parts of the world.

Side by side with those undergoing recognised youthful 'transitions', exist those who are consigned to the margins, who in contemporary language are considered to be 'socially excluded'. Young people who live in pockets of poverty in the rich world often endure similar conditions to those in poorer places. For example Anuradha Vittachi (1989) describes conditions for 13 and 14 year old girls employed in a small workshop making shoes in Italy, where in a tiny enclosed space filled with the stench of glue, infested with rats and cockroaches, the girls are made chronically ill and left unfit for further work.

Poverty is a key determinant of the experience of youth all over the world. It is related to other structures of inequality such as 'race' or 'caste' which consign different groups to lesser social positions than others and in so doing force them into constrained and restricted spaces. In the circumstances of poverty, young people are more likely not only to become victims of exploitation which make youth almost meaningless, but also to participate in destructive activities or problematic behaviour which has connections with the dominant ideas about what it means to be young. So, for example, if youth is supposed to signify the achievement of independence and a young person sees no prospect of achieving such independence legitimately within their own environment, they turn to illegitimate means and move into spaces where they do not belong, where they are experienced by others as a threat. Crime might seem like an option towards the achievement of adulthood. This becomes particularly relevant in circumstances where young men are denied access to the paid employment which promises the achievement of adult status. In this way, particular groups of young people come to be defined as a particular problem for society. The emphasis is upon their youth because of ideas about the 'riskiness' of being young, but other factors are equally, if not more important.

The legal framework and the policy decisions associated with the concept of youth and which set the conditions under which youth is experienced, derive primarily from those who have greatest wealth and power in any given society. The further such definitions are from the realities of the lives of any given individual or any particular group of young people, the more likely that there will be a gap or conflict between expectations and achievement in relation to such young people. Differences in the experience and meanings attaching to youth therefore have consequences for the psychological and social development of young people. For example, if there is a gap between social expectation and achievement, the consequence might be low self esteem or disaffection amongst individuals and certain groups of young people. This need not necessarily be the result, but it is perhaps more likely if young people accept the given or inherited meanings.

Conclusion

Although the concept of youth seems to describe in a very straightforward way the period between childhood and adulthood, it is actually a highly complex notion. There is no necessary reason why 'youth' should be experienced as an 'in between' moment in life, or as a stage towards something else. In different times and places it becomes more or less irrelevant and is merely part of the seamlessness of growing older.

To understand youth as a period of transition, or a series of transitions, does help to understand the reality of the lives of some young people. However ideas about youth associated with transition or even with youth as a special period of freedom, refer to a distinctly modern experience which derived from industrialisation in the west. They do not adequately deal with the different conditions in different types of society. Nor do they distinguish between the different social worlds of young people living in the same geographical and historical space but experiencing very different circumstances. The here and now in which young people live is not just about being young, but about a whole range of personal and social circumstances and issues which can be equally, if not more important than age.

Insofar as law, policy and institutional arrangements situate young people in particular social locations, as young people, then there will be particular issues and experiences consequent upon being young. These create an awareness of generational differences and they frame the realities of life for everyone, not only the young people involved. Parents' lives are regulated by the school year and by the expectation that they might have to pay fees for university. The behaviour of young people who are involved in crime impacts upon their victims and has consequences for the overall idea of how youth are today. Thus youth is an important concept for understanding social relationships and for focusing upon particular groups. However, it is a concept which must be used critically and carefully if it is to be of value in understanding the lives of particular individuals and groups of young people.

References

Ariès, P. (1965) *Centuries of Childhood: A Social History of Family Life*, New York: Vintage Books.

CCCS (1975) 'Resistance Through Rituals', *Cultural Studies*, 7/8, University of Birmingham, Centre for Contemporary Cultural Studies.

Davies, B. (2004) 'Curriculum in Youth Work: an old debate in new clothes?' *Youth and Policy*, 85, pp. 87–98.

DfEE (2001) *Transforming Youth Work: Developing youth work for young people,* Nottingham: DfEE Publications.

Eisenstadt, S. N. (1956) *From Generation to Generation: Age Groups and Social Structure,* New York: The Free Press.

Hollands, R. (1990) *The Long Transition: Class, Culture and Youth Training,* London: Macmillan.

Irwin, S. (1995) *Social Change and the Transition from Youth to Adulthood,* London: UCL Press.

Jeffs, T. and Smith, M. (1998/99) 'The Problem of "Youth" for Youth Work', *Youth and Policy,* 62, pp. 45–66.

Mead, M. (1961) *Coming of Age in Samoa,* London: Penguin (First pubd. 1928).

Vittachi, A. (1989) *Stolen Childhood: In search of the rights of the child,* Cambridge: Polity Press.

Wallace, C. and Cross, M. (eds) (1990) *Youth in Transition: The Sociology of Youth and Youth Policy,* London: Falmer Press.

Willis, P. E. (1977) *Learning to labour: how working class kids get working class jobs,* Farnborough: Saxon House.

5

Modernising youth work: from the universal to the particular and back again

Simon Bradford

Introduction

Like other public sector services, professional youth work operates in a social and institutional climate that has radically altered during the last few years. The background to this has been well rehearsed elsewhere, but includes growing inequality in general and amongst young people in particular (Ridge, 2002; Sen, 1997), fundamental changes to the fabric of the welfare state (Pillinger, 2000), the wholesale 'managerialisation' of public services (Clarke, Gewirtz and McLaughlin, 2000) and moves to new service configurations, principally those emphasising 'partnership' or 'multi-agency' approaches (Powell et al., 2001; Banks et al., 2003). Youth work has faced difficult tasks on this new landscape and increased demands on diminishing or reconfigured resources have meant that it has had to represent itself carefully to survive.

In this chapter we offer a brief historical exploration of recent youth work and conclude by identifying tensions between the principle of 'universal' youth work provision (i.e. that it should be accessible, in principle, to *all* young people), and the increasing managerialist demand that youth work should demonstrate its value and outcomes in relation to specific groups of young people. We suggest that, ironically, youth work has become subject to a 'new universalism' constituted in part at least by the growth of managerialist practices.

A rationale for youth work

Youth work's roots lay in nineteenth century attempts to render the working class 'governable by reason' (Donald, 1992, p. 23) and the bourgeois desire to mould the character and conduct of working class youth. Victorian fear and fascination with the 'perishing and dangerous classes' have their contemporary expression in popular concerns about the so-called 'underclass' (MacDonald, 1997; IEA, 1996).

Despite having achieved some recognition as one of the 'caring' professions (Malin, 2000), youth work has remained an ambiguous set of practices, pushed in different directions at different times by different interests. It appears infinitely fluid, flexible, and mobile. It has a capacity to work in diverse settings and to shift its identity in response to varying conceptions of 'youth need', either self-defined or specified by others. In one guise for example, youth work appears to be aimed at the careful management of young people's leisure time, with youth workers organising a range of activities with young people: sports, arts, and drama in youth clubs, centres, and projects. Elsewhere, youth workers touch on therapeutic concerns through their work in counselling, advice, and information services. In yet another form, youth workers take an explicitly 'educational' role, helping young people to understand matters connected with health, sexuality and citizenship. Underlying all of these activities is a professional commitment to *voluntary* and *participatory* relationships between youth workers and young people. Youth workers argue that it is the intimacy of these relationships, freely chosen by young people, which leads to their potency. Importantly for some youth workers, it is precisely this voluntary aspect of relationships that is threatened by current policy developments in the UK.

As well as its strength, youth work's flexible nature is also a potential weakness. It has never been able to colonise a distinct territory of its own, and youth workers have been forced to occupy the spaces left by other institutions: social work, schooling, or leisure for example. Over the last decade or so, youth work has become increasingly deployed in work with young people variously considered to be 'at risk' and whose public visibility has animated a series of moral panics. For some youth workers this raises the dilemma of whether they are 'agents of social control' or 'informal educators' seeking to engage collaboratively with young people 'on their terms' (Banks, 1999, p. 10). The main problem in this apparently inexhaustible debate is that the concept of social control inadequately discriminates between the multiple interventions and initiatives which attempt to enact the administration of human conduct in modern societies (Rose and Miller, 1988, p. 172). Youth work *is* part of a network of institutions and practices whose task has been to ensure the stability, harmony, growth, and care of population: to contribute to the 'government' of modern societies (Foucault, 1991, p. 102). The concept of government in this sense denotes a characteristically modern and liberal form of political authority which is neither necessarily repressive, nor prohibitive. Rather, governmental power is intended to operate quietly and efficiently in managing and regulating populations, often through the 'technical' expertise of professionals: social workers, health visitors, and youth workers for example. Their particular contemporary role is to encourage individuals to exercise their own responsibility and freedom, in effect to 'govern' themselves. As one recent analysis suggested

> We want to help each young person to be somebody who not only enjoys life but is in good health, studying to the best of their ability, is challenged and stretched mentally and physically, is an active member of their local community and capable of understanding the consequences of their own actions. We want to develop young people who add value to their social surroundings rather than subtracting through anti-social behaviour (DEE, 2001, p. 13).

Responsible participation, self-reflection and striving to 'become somebody' are the essential principles upon which contemporary liberal democratic states rest, by which the social body is managed, and through which 'good citizenship' is realised. These are ideas that have a long history in youth work.

Social education discourses and youth work

The Thompson Committee's 1982 report on the future of the youth service confirmed that its specific task was '... to provide social education ...' as a *universal* service to all young people who might benefit from it (DES, 1982, p. 122). The concept of 'social education' has provided youth work with a relatively consistent, though shifting, centre of gravity since the late 1960s. Different nuances of social education can be discerned that are broadly associated with specific historical points.

Liberal-democratic accounts of social education – associated particularly with the 1970s – emphasise the (abstract) individual, and his or her relationships with others. Essentially humanist and 'person-centred', this account of social education sought to enable the individual young person to become more conscious of and better understand 'self'. One analysis suggested that social education could lead to an

> ... individual's increased consciousness of himself – of his values, aptitudes, and untapped resources...(Davies and Gibson, 1967, p. 12).

By fostering an 'ethics of the self' (a way of being or living 'correctly' in daily life), liberal social education aims in part at least to develop an introspective, 'reflexive' and active self, able to appraise, evaluate, and work on its constitutive feelings, attitudes, and opinions. For Davies and Gibson, social education in youth work should be initiated in the context of the personal relationships which young people form with others, enabling them to '… know first hand and feel personally how common interests and shared activities bring and keep people together and what causes them to drift apart' (Davies and Gibson, 1967, p. 13). Thus *experiential* and *participative* dimensions to social education emerge as its defining features. Typically, youth work activities are designed to maximise young people's participation in personal relationships, and to encourage them to reflect on and learn from these experiences.

An accommodation between individual desires and wider social responsibilities is one of social education's intended outcomes. As Davies and Gibson put it, 'truly helpful social education' must create a proper equilibrium between 'self-expression' and conformity, taking account of the demand to be '… "loyal", "responsible", "respectful", and especially "law-abiding"' (Davies and Gibson, 1967, p. 17). The concern here is with the production of a particular kind of self, sensitive to social values and responsibilities, yet simultaneously active in developing its own self-defined potential. This is of prime importance in a liberal democracy (perhaps specifically so in contemporary *capitalist* democracy where the values of individual enterprise and endeavour are cherished). Thus, social education aims to ensure that individual young people learn to 'govern' themselves, to '… effect by their own means, various operations on their own bodies, souls, thoughts, and conduct… (and) transform themselves, modify themselves' (Miller, 1987, p. 206–207). This is a practice compatible with and derivative of the principles of liberal democracy in which the self-regulating, rational and autonomous individual exercises choice, responsibility and freedom in the pursuit of 'good citizenship'.

Davies and Gibson's account of social education is definitive and has retained its persuasive capacity. Its dissemination in different forms over the years has given identity and meaning to youth work, although its individualistic stance and liberal outlook were subject to critique (Butters and Newell, 1978). During the 1980s this mode of social education was 'radicalised'. As elsewhere in the UK (and more widely), newly emerging 'liberationist' discourses drawing on the politics of gender, race, and disability became imprinted on youth work. The abstract subjects of earlier social education were transformed into 'young women', 'young Black people', 'disabled', or 'gay' young people. Youth workers (as social educators) came to see themselves as responding to a range of *'issues'* that mapped out material and symbolic aspects of young people's lives (their life-chances and identities, for example), thus structuring the terrain of youth work. Young people, it seemed, could receive an appropriate youth work response only if they were understood as being shaped by extant social forces: racism, sexism, disability, unemployment, poverty, and so on. Youth workers became concerned with 'empowering' young people, helping them to develop the skills, knowledge, and dispositions necessary to become active participants in society, rather than its passive victims. Youth workers took on a more self-consciously 'rights-based' trajectory, emphasising '… a belief in justice: all people have the same rights' (Karsh, c1984), retaining an individual focus but admitting the political and social background against which young people were illuminated.

In practice, different elements from the two modes of social education – the 'liberal democratic' and the 'liberationist' – have meshed. Youth work has become a complex of ambiguous aims, techniques and initiatives drawing on both modes. Social education, now frequently dubbed 'informal education' or 'informal social education' as this, allegedly, offers clearer definition (Banks, 1999, p. 7), remains a consistent theme, and has marked continuities: a focus on the problematic nature of young people's transitions to adulthood, experi- ence as the well-spring of learning, a concern with the relationship between the individual and the 'social', and perhaps above all the aim of cultivating the autonomous and self-regulating individual.

From universal to particular: work with 'at risk' young people…

As part of the deepening processes of 'modernisation' that have shaped educa- tion services in the UK over the last decade (Ferguson, 2000) youth work and youth services have come under managerial scrutiny. This has entailed a grow- ing political demand to identify *specific* young people to be targeted. However, and reflecting an underlying tension between universalism and targeting, it was *universalism* that seemed to be embodied in the following utopian 'state- ment of purpose' that was disseminated by the National Youth Agency in the early 1990s. Youth work aimed

> '… to redress all forms of inequality and to ensure equality of opportunity for all young people to fulfil their potential as empowered individuals and members of groups and communities and to support young people in their transition to adult- hood' (NYA, 1992, p. 21).

Drawing on earlier social education discourse, the statement went on to argue that youth work should be educational, participative, empowering, informal, responsive, based on secure relationships, and should provide information, advice and counselling to young people between the ages of 11 and 25, with those in the 13 to 19 age group being the priority (NYA, 1992). Despite this commitment increasing managerialism meant a greater emphasis on *outcomes* rather than on statements of professional values and belief. In the context of moral panic in the 1990s about the 'condition of youth' the idea that youth workers should target so-called 'at risk' young people became increasingly persuasive. Youth work with 'at risk' youth accorded with political priorities of the time. Great symbolic significance was attached to various 'risk' populations in the UK that had fallen under the popular and political gaze: the so-called 'underclass', young single mothers, drug abusers, truants, young homeless, and of course young offenders. Youth workers and youth services were drawn into a substantial role with such groups, exacerbating the tension between the principle of universal youth work and 'targeted' work. For some commentators, targeted work was part of a Faustian pact in which short-term funding would be paid for by youth work's long-term marginalisation (Gutfreund, 1993, p. 15). For others, perhaps more pragmatically, targeted and outcome-based work embodied the contemporary zeitgeist (France and Wiles, 1996, p. 49).

The concept of 'risk' has become influential for policy makers and practitioners. It offers infinite scope for constituting an expansive repertoire of conduct and circumstance as part of its special territory. Like other 'welfare' and educational practices, some youth work takes an approach (particularly toward 'difficult' young people) informed by the rationale that some young people are 'at risk' *rather than* simply 'dangerous'. This reworks the idea (implicit in many early accounts of youth work) that *vulnerable* young people can, without the right intervention, all too easily become dangerous. By identifying their 'at risk' status (that is, their vulnerability), early *diversionary* or *preventive* intervention becomes a rational strategy. Rather than privileging characteristics that are thought to be part of an individual's *make-up*, the concept of 'risk' concentrates attention on concrete and abstract factors (background, domicile, contacts with professionals, reputation, life-expectations, behaviour, feelings, etc.) that constitute an individual's identity as 'at risk'. Constructing such an individual (or, indeed, group or community) is part of what Hacking refers to as the process of 'making up people' (Hacking, 1986, p. 222). Almost anything can be plausibly incorporated as a so-called 'risk factor'. The notion of risk offers limitless possibilities for identifying new sites for expert intervention in the social and material worlds (Castel, 1991, p. 289), powerfully justifying professional activity, particularly 'multi-agency' approaches. The concept's utility lies in its capacity to render aspects of the domain in which the young person is situated potentially amenable to the calculus of professional evaluation and intervention. As such it greatly facilitates the expansion of governmental (professional) activity.

Work defined under the rubrics of targeting and risk is, most significantly, open to the audit and managerialist practices already flourishing in public services in the UK and elsewhere (Power, 1999; Flynn, 2000). Targeted, rather than universal, provision provides opportunities for the identification of clear 'outcomes', as well as for the deployment of apparently unambiguous 'performance indicators' in measuring these.

Transforming youth work: agendas of inclusion

New Labour's commitment to youth work as a component in the regulation of youth transitions in the UK is embodied in 'Transforming Youth Work' (DEE, 2001; DES, 2002), the policy narrative that now defines central government requirements of youth work and youth services. Transforming Youth Work (TYW) is a radical departure from the accepted, and hitherto, dominant *educational* tradition of youth work. In this, there are three main factors that determine the relevance and effectiveness of youth work (Bradford, 1999).

First, youth work is characterised by young people's *voluntary* participation in a broad range of informal leisure and educational opportunities: arts and sports, health promotion or various forms of community involvement, for example. The desire for 'something to do' is an important factor in many young people's lives and activity programmes offered by youth workers can counter corrosive boredom. They may also lead to opportunities for creative learning. Participation and inclusion (in the sense that anyone – not just those defined as 'at risk' – can be involved) have been central values in youth work. Although young people, like adults, inevitably regard these in different ways it seems that when they experience participative and inclusive approaches in youth work they become significant factors in their involvement (Williamson et al., 1997).

Second, one of youth work's principal aims is to enhance young people's ability to make *informed* decisions about their lives. This means that youth workers are often involved in the provision of relevant information (about health, educational opportunities or housing, for example) and support to young people in working out how to use it effectively. Youth workers become involved in this as a routine element of their work, particularly with older young people who may be negotiating labour market, housing or domestic transitions. When offered in a sympathetic and confidential way, such informal support may enable young people to make wise decisions about their lives.

Third, youth workers offer safe spaces in which young people can meet. This is especially important at a time when, perhaps for economic reasons, substantial numbers of young people have limited access to space in which they can meet with friends in an informal and sympathetic context. Such spaces are often established in youth centres or projects, youth information and counselling services or activity centres. Detached youth workers operating on the streets create 'virtually' enclosed spaces in which relationships between young people themselves and between young people and youth workers mark out geographical and social boundaries to create settings which young people recognise as their own. By offering accessible and responsive meeting places, youth workers can develop close relationships with young people and respond to them in ways that *young people themselves* define as important. They also support young people in their friendships and personal relationships, seeing these as enhancing and developing trust and respect amongst young people and adults. The acknowledgement of young people as *active agents* in the process of youth work is vital in achieving this.

TYW departs from this account of youth work. One way of thinking about this is to see it as a fundamental shift from *expressive* to *instrumental* functions (Parsons, 1951). Traditional youth work has seen itself as having largely expressive purposes (emphasising the possibility of emotional engagement, seeing personal relationships as a 'good' in themselves and offering spaces in which young people can convey and work with their own and others' emotions). So-called 'modernisation' in UK public services has entailed a much more instrumental view and the attempt to achieve a 'functional authority' for youth work emphasising its capacity to achieve *particular* goals, a focus on task performance and a pre-occupation with effectiveness and efficiency. We identify three ways in which this has become particularly evident on the TYW agenda.

First, the assumption is made that young people are an essentially problematic social category requiring careful management and regulation. This relies on the notion of youth as 'transitional status', a perspective developed by British sociologists in which youth's trajectories into adulthood and their associated shifting statuses from dependency to autonomy are, allegedly, the defining features of youth in late modern societies (Jones and Wallace, 1992; Coles, 1995; Furlong and Cartmel, 1997). In this perspective, young people are significant only insofar as they are thought of as problematic: incomplete 'proto-adults', suffering 'cultural deficit' and subject to the exigencies of an uncertain, risky and dangerous world. Such a view makes intervention designed to render the transition to adulthood successful (in terms of young people acquiring the 'right' cultural competencies and dispositions) in young people's lives appear entirely necessary. The discourse of transition is itself contestable despite it so often being presented as taken for granted (Webster et al., 2004, p. 2). There is little that can be isolated to define an *exclusive* transitory status to youth: not their location in education (this is shared with children and mature students), neither their dependency on family (this is shared with many others), nor their non-participation in the labour market. As Mizen suggests '... age criteria alone still provide the principal means through which [young people's] lives are organised into something approaching a coherent and meaningful category'

(2004, p. 8). However, in *instrumental* (and governmental) terms, the discourse of transition offers a firm rationale for the 'management of growing up'.

Second, New Labour's preoccupation with 'social exclusion' (and its other: social *inclusion*) has led to youth work being incorporated into an increasingly baroque *technology* designed to secure inclusion by countering the marginalising tendencies of contemporary society. Charles Clarke emphasised the significance of processes of exclusion for young people, knowing

> ... only too well the consequences of young people becoming disaffected from their communities – the sense of worthlessness and the drift into anti-social behaviour and crime which can result (DfES, 2002, p. 3).

However, social exclusion as a concept is amorphous, contested and highly ideological; its utility lies in its capacity for deployment in diverse ways and to support diverse positions. Ruth Levitas (1998) identifies three discourses of social exclusion currently at work in New Labour thinking:

- A 'redistributionist' discourse: poverty and economic disadvantage as the cause of exclusion;
- A 'moral underclass' discourse: exclusion is the consequence of individual (and community) inadequacy;
- A 'social integrationist' discourse in which employability and labour market participation are the principal routes out of excluded status.

It is the latter 'social integrationist discourse' (SID) that dominates current policy and practice and in which youth work has come to play a significant part. TYW has determined that youth work should be closely integrated in the Connexions strategy of managing young people's transitions into the labour market, although recent research into the organisation of Connexions may give cause for reflection on the wisdom of this (Coles et al., 2004). The defining feature of the Connexions Service is its largely individualised (casework, 'key-work' or work by 'personal advisers') with 'NEETS' (those young people 'not in education, employment or training'), a group defined as particularly at risk of exclusion and requiring intervention to ensure their 'social inclusion'. Inclusion in this context is defined by the social integrationist discourse outlined by Levitas and is constituted by developing young people's employability (through education and training), emphasising opportunity and securing their labour market participation.

Third, and consistent with audit culture (Power, 1999; Strathern, 2000), youth work has become fundamentally managerialised in order to secure the accountability of youth work and youth workers. Rather than engaging with young people in ways that young people themselves partially determine, youth workers now operate in a range of pre-set targets, standards and performance indicators. For example, a new curriculum (including 'content', 'pedagogy' and 'assessment') for youth work sets a national framework against which local authorities' performance can be judged. A 'pledge' to young people further formalises what can be expected from service providers. A set of 'standards of youth work provision' goes even further in defining a shared and agreed national minimum service level (DfES, 2002). These practices signal a marked shift towards a range of second order activities associated with audit practices (for example, completing arcane audit returns and making statements of performance achieved). The outcomes and indicators that are defined by these will determine the way in which services and professionals undertake their work. Unless their activities are consistent with these definitions of provision (determined through an apparatus of inspection), there are, of course, serious risks to funding. Inevitably in such performative cultures it is those who are most able to frame achievement in convincing narratives (in whatever form demanded: numbers, measurements, personal accounts and so on) who will be most able to attract funding.

The TYW agenda offers a *technical* or *formal* representation of what youth work's professional culture has hitherto identified as an *informal* (and indeterminate) *process*. It embodies a practical and procedural rationality intended to contribute to the effective (and, undoubtedly, efficient) management of youth work (at either practitioner or manager level), determined by the objectives that it specifies and achieved by carefully regulated youth worker intervention. Particular outcomes *may* coincide with interpretations of youth need defined either by young people themselves or in conjunction with youth workers. However, spaces for intervention opened up by the 'curriculum' or the 'pledge' are intended to facilitate the management of a repertoire of largely pre-determined outcomes. Thus, TYW is designed to guide the production or transformation of particular kinds of young people whose self-formation is consistent with wider political aspirations to 'responsibility', 'active citizenship' and 'social inclusion'.

Conclusions: emerging 'new universals'

In this chapter we have discussed youth work's development as part of a range of initiatives designed to manage and regulate the exigencies of 'growing up'. The significance of 'social education', its role in encouraging young people to govern their own conduct and experiences and its deployment in dealing with contemporary concerns about young people have been discussed. Some difficulties associated with the 'universal' provision of social and informal education and the political and practical utility of the concept of risk have also been highlighted.

In the context of the managerialisation and modernisation of UK public services, youth work has been drawn into a range of new settings, altered institutional and organisational arrangements and, sometimes, novel practices of audit and accountability. The historic commitment to *universal* practices (a commitment to work with 'all' young people, for example) seems to have diminished and youth work has moved into initiatives explicitly designed to manage specific groups of young people, particularly those thought to be 'at risk' in some way. Youth work's close relationship with the Connexions service, for example, has embodied these changes.

However, Transforming Youth Work should be seen as part of another *universalising* process. Its commitment to a pragmatic and technical approach, resonant of the current vogue for 'what works' and 'evidence-based practice' constitutes a move to *universal* standards and in so doing greatly increases the capacity for centralised accountability and control practices within youth work. For example, the 'Standards of Youth Work Provision' contained in Transforming Youth Work: Resourcing Excellent Youth Services (DfES, 2002, p. 23–26) offer a codified and formal specification that can be used to secure accountability through measurement and comparisons between different services. With an inventory of performance indicators contained in the same document, these universal definitions eschew the tacit and local knowledges that have, until recent times, characterised professionalism. The development of a 'common assessment framework', an 'outcomes framework' and the incorporation of youth services into the proposed Children's Trusts, all as part of the 'Every Child Matters' agenda will further embed these tendencies. Interesting questions are raised about the specific role and status of 'youth work knowledge' that has developed in its very particular work setting, based on specific values and incorporating distinctive approaches. It is difficult to know at this point how such knowledge will figure in the contested and shifting grounds of professional work with young people. As Newman and Nutley (2003) argue, such developments in the 'public professions' generally have already begun to disrupt existing relations and structures of professional life and have effectively re-defined what counts as professional knowledge. As such, they suggest, these new forms of knowledge (contained in standard assessment outcomes or 'identification, referral and tracking' procedures, for example) come to represent new forms of cultural capital that professionals – like youth workers – will deploy in their quest for legitimacy in the developing context of multi-agency and partnership work (Newman and Nutley, 2003, p. 560). How this will turn out for youth work is unknown.

Undoubtedly, young people's identity as a source of political and social concern in late modernity continues to develop in different directions, and no doubt new aspects of their lives await revelation or construction. Youth work in one form or another will continue to offer a flexible, yet changing, means of contributing to the governance of young people.

References

Banks, S. (ed.) (1999) *Ethical Issues in youth Work*, London, Routledge.

Banks, S., Butcher, H., Henderson, P. and Robertson, J. (eds) (2003) *Managing Community Practice. Principles, policies and programmes*, Bristol, Policy Press.

Bradford, S. (1999) 'Youth Work: Young People and Transitions to Adulthood', in Hill, M., (ed.), *Effective Ways of Working with Children and their Families*, (London, Jessica Kingsley).

Butters, S. and Newell, S. (1978) *Realities of Training, a review of the training of adults who volunteer to work with young people in the youth and community service*, Leicester, National Youth Bureau.

Castel, R. 'From Dangerousness to Risk', in Burchell, G., Gordon, C. and Miller, P. (eds) (1991) *The Foucault Effect, Studies in Governmentality*, London, Harvester Wheatsheaf.

Clarke, J., Gewirtz, S. and McLaughlin, E. (eds) (2000) *New Managerialism New Welfare?*, London, Sage Publications.

Coles, B. (1995) *Youth and Social Policy. Youth citizenship and young careers*, London, University of London Press.

Coles, B., Britton, L. and Hicks, L. (2004) *Building better connections. Interagency work and the Connexions Service*, Bristol, Policy Press.

Davies, B. and Gibson, A. (1967) *The Social Education of the Adolescent*, London, University of London Press.

Department for Education and Employment (2001) *Transforming Youth Work*, London, Department for Education and Employment.

Department for Education and Skills (2002) *Transforming Youth Work, Resourcing Excellent Youth Services*, Nottingham, DfES Publications.

Department of Education and Science (1982) *Experience and Participation, Report of the Review Group on the Youth Service in England and Wales*, Cmnd 8686, London, HMSO.

Donald, J. (1992) *Sentimental Education, Schooling, Popular Culture and the Regulation of Liberty*, London, Verso.

Ferguson, R. (2000) 'Modernizing Managerialism in Education', in Clarke, J., Gewirtz, S., and McLaughlin, E. (eds), *New Managerialism New Welfare?* London, Sage Publications.

Flynn, N. (2000) 'Managerialism and Public Services: some International Trends', in Clarke, J., Gewirtz, S. and McLaughlin, E. (eds), *New Managerialism New Welfare?* London, Sage Publications.

Foucault, M. 'Governmentality', in Burchell, G., Gordon, C. and Miller, P. (eds) (1991) *The Foucault Effect, Studies in Governmentality*, London, Harvester Wheatsheaf.

France, A. and Wiles, P. (1996) *The Youth Action Scheme. A Report of the National Evaluation*, London, Department for Education and Employment.

Furlong, A. and Cartmel, F. (1997) *Young People and Social Change. Individualization and risk in late modernity*, Buckingham, Open University Press.

Gutfreund, R. (1993) 'Towards 2000: Which Direction for the Youth Service?', *Youth and Policy*, 41, 13–19.

Hacking, I. 'Making Up People', in Heller, T. (ed.) (1986) *Reconstructing Individualism: autonomy, individuality, and the self in Western thought*, Stanford, Stanford University Press.

Howarth, A. (1989) *A Core Curriculum for the Youth Service?*, Ministerial Address to the First Ministerial Conference with the Youth Service, 13/14 December 1989.

Institute of Economic Affairs (1996) *Charles Murray and the Underclass: The Developing Debate'*, London, IEA Health and Welfare Unit.

Jones, G. and Wallace, C. (1992) *Youth, Family and Citizenship*, Buckingham, Open University Press.

Karsh, H. (c1984) *Social Education Defined?*, an editorial from an ILEA newsletter.

Levitas, R. (1998) *The inclusive society? Social Exclusion and New Labour*, London, Macmillan.

MacDonald, R. (ed.) (1997) *Youth, the 'Underclass' and Social Exclusion*, London, Routledge.

Malin, N. (ed.) (2000) *Professionalism, Boundaries and the Workplace*, London, Routledge.

Miller, P. (1987) *Domination and Power*, London, Routledge and Kegan Paul.

Mizen, P. (2004) *The Changing State of Youth*, London, Palgrave Macmillan

Murray, C. (1990) *The Emerging British Underclass*, London, IEA.

Newman, J. and Nutley, S. (2003) 'Transforming the probation service: 'what works', organisational change and professional identity', in *Policy and Politics*, Vol. 31, No. 4.

National Youth Agency, (1992) *'Background papers to the third ministerial conference for the youth service*, Leicester, NYA.

Parsons, T. (1951) *Towards a General Theory of Action*, Cambridge, Harvard University Press.

Pillinger, J. (2000) 'Redefining Work and Welfare in Europe: New Perspectives on Work, Welfare and Time', in Lewis, G., Gewirtz, S., and Clarke, J. (eds), *Rethinking Social Policy*, London, Sage Publications.

Powell, M., Exworthy, M. and Berney, L. (2001) 'Playing the Game of Partnership', in Sykes, R., Bochel, C. and Ellison, N., *Social Policy Review 13, Developments and Debates, 2000–2001*, Bristol, Policy Press.

Power, M. (1999) *The Audit Society. Rituals of Verification*, Oxford, Oxford University Press.

Ridge, T. (2002) *Childhood, Poverty and Social Exclusion*, Bristol, Policy Press.

Rose, N. and Miller, P. (1988) 'The Tavistock Programme: the Government of Subjectivity and Social Life', *Sociology*, Vol. 22, No. 2.

Sen, A. (1997) 'Inequality, Unemployment and Contemporary Europe', in *International Labour Review*, Vol. 136, No. 2.

Strathern, M. (ed.) (2000) *Audit cultures: anthropological studies in accountability, ethics and the academy*, London, Routledge.

Webster, C., Simpson, M., MacDonald, R., Abbas, A., Cieslik, M., Shildruck, T. and Simpson, M. (2004) *Poor Transitions. Social exclusion and young adults*, Bristol, Policy Press.

Williamson, H., Afzal, S., Eason, C. and Williams, N. (1997) *The Needs of Young People aged 15–19 and the Youth Work Response*, (Cardiff, Wales Youth Agency and University of Wales Research Partnership).

6

Challenging practice:
a personal view on 'youth work'
in times of changed expectations

Howard Williamson

Introduction

Recurrently described as the Cinderella of professional services for young people, 'youth work' encapsulates a broad church of both practice and contexts. Some practice is highly focused and targeted, other practice remains 'open door' and generic. It is delivered *through* local authority youth services, an array of voluntary youth organisations, and specialist agencies. It is delivered *by* a relatively small cadre of 'nationally recognised' professionals trained to diploma and degree level, a much larger number trained at the local level, and battalions of volunteers. Surrounding this body of practice are *public perception* of youth work still largely locked into ideas about youth *clubs* and 'table tennis and pool', and *political expectations* that it must make a clearly defined contribution to wider 'youth policy' agendas on issues such as crime, health and vocational preparation. This chapter offers a personal account of how and why 'youth work' often gets trapped within these competing images, and some ways in which it might free itself from them, while retaining its essential principles and distinctive place in the lives of young people.

An autobiographical note

Early days

My own involvement in the 'youth service' started when I was a teenager myself in the 1960s. With friends we established our own youth 'club'. It was a place to go, a place to meet, and we worked on things to do. We had no desire to be 'informally educated' or to engage in a 'programme'; indeed, we had no 'leader' – we did it for ourselves. Later, I became a volunteer in a number of different youth clubs, providing activities for young people (yes, table tennis and pool!), talking with them ('casual conversations'?) and responding to their aspirations and 'needs'. Though I did not know it, this was bedrock youth work practice – building relationships and trust, meeting requests and demands, working at the level of individuals and of the group. Never did I think I was guiding young people on a process of self-discovery (Young, 1999), though I did realise I was providing young people with new opportunities, new experiences and the chance to consider things in different ways. I became aware that the *way* I engaged with young people and provided those opportunities was of critical importance: it was based on relationships grounded in mutual respect, not on authority, power or control. Young people who did not like my 'style' simply walked away. I recognised they would stay involved only if my style had relevance and meaning for them.

'Professionalising' practice

I continued as a volunteer in a range of youth work settings throughout the 1970s. In 1979 I became involved, initially as a volunteer, in a voluntary youth and community centre, grant-aided by the local authority. It was then that I had my first experience of residential weekends, as well as specific projects and city-wide activities. Twenty-five years later I still work occasionally at the centre, having been its (part-time) senior youth worker between 1985 and 2002. Throughout that time, the core of my work was to run 'open access' youth *clubs*, for different age groups on different nights of the week. This was, however, the foundation for different, and diverse forms of practice – mainly activity-based for the youngest (10–13) age group, more issue-based for the intermediate group (14–19) and very individually responsive youth work for the oldest group (20–25). The 'youth work' involved exposing young people to a range of different experiences (such as photography, horse-riding and sports-based competitions), reacting to individuals' needs and concerns (in relation to home life, school and the peer group) and addressing key 'issues' affecting different groups at different times (such as skateboarding, graffiti and drug misuse). I always used to say I could not predict what kinds of issues would come to the surface, but that I should be judged on what I had *done* over the previous year or so.

The skills required?

Priorities shifted, according to the young people concerned and the situations they encountered. I engaged them in youth training schemes, attended court, negotiated with teachers, liaised with the local police, oiled relationships with residents and shopkeepers, advocated for them in family disputes. I even (successfully) defended one individual – at his request – at an industrial tribunal. On one residential weekend, one young man, who had been a constant thorn in my side over many years, asked me what it took to be a youth worker. Though my mind raced to the official matrix of youth work skills, my answer was rather different. First and foremost, I told him, you needed acutely sensitive *listening skills*, both to 'tune in' to the language of young people and to be alert to their anxieties and concerns. Secondly, you needed a good *sense of humour*, and thirdly, you needed *eternal patience*. He recognised these characteristics immediately! More profoundly, however, youth work is about sensitisation and appropriate response: keeping promises, delivering to time, remembering detail (starting with people's names) – however much the young people concerned may let you down. This earns respect for commitment and reliability: young people come to realise they are not 'just another case' and that what the worker is doing is not 'just a job'. The commitment youth work calls for, when it is needed or requested, a rapid response; the most important thing for young people is what I came to refer to, years later, as 'critical people at critical moments' (Social Exclusion Unit, 2000).

Staying realistic

Some years ago I was having a particularly difficult time with a group of dope-smoking skateboarders and discussed the situation with a former youth club member. He made an apposite observation when I mentioned my desire to *change* the attitude and behaviour of this group: 'come on, How, you never stopped us doing anything... but you slowed us down and made us think'. I was quite comforted by this depiction. I realised that some of my practice was about no more than 'holding the line', helping to prevent some young people from slipping further to the edge. With others, it was about consolidating and encouraging their existing pathways and aspirations. With some, it was more clearly about supporting their development and fostering new directions – 'turning lives around'. I recall a teenage heroin user whom I encouraged to return to college, and a young woman with learning difficulties whose father was convinced that my 'youth work' had produced a level of 'social inclusion' for her that otherwise would never have been achieved. Thus the work operates at a myriad of levels in relation to different individuals. Some young people who engage with youth work are little more than 'leisure users', somewhat disinterested in active interventions. Others are just 'passing through'; their engagement so fleeting that any impact on their lives is unlikely. There are others, however, whose involvement is both sustained and committed – and one can and should expect, though not necessarily require, some 'deliverables' from those relationships.

Getting a result

I can think of many individuals with whom I had such long-term contact and for whom I made a difference at critical points in their lives. Those moments could not be predicted, but my response when they arose was trusted and effective. They covered many 'issues': substance misuse, the criminal justice system, school exclusion, family conflict, peer group relationships – indeed, the repertoire of issues of concern to the political establishment. Long before the Connexions Service commandeered it as their mantra, my youth work was a 'universal service differentiated according to need'. The door to the youth club was open for anyone, but my practice was tailored to issues that emerged. Group work and group activities gave way to intensive personal support when that was needed. And it is important to add that it was not always successful; there were still 'failures', despite the very best of intention and effort even within the most promising of relationships with young people. Yet, even when all hope appeared to be lost, it was still sometimes possible to 'get a result'. I have often talked about one deeply alienated young man who hated all professionals, but hated me slightly less than others. He was the classic focus of political attention and concern – from a 'broken home', excluded from school, using hard drugs, serving time in custody – yet had been largely untouched by (constructive) professional intervention. I 'stood by' him for at least six years, making little difference and constantly rebuffed by him. Eventually, however, while he was serving his fifth period in youth custody, he sought my support – and, along with his girlfriend, we helped him to turn his life around. This is a salutary lesson for those preoccupied with 'quick wins' and evidence of fairly immediate impact; politicians and funders also have to learn the art of patience (Williamson, 2001).

The latest political agenda for children and young people

Pinning it down!

It is actually rather difficult to be certain about the 'latest political agenda' for young people. On the one hand, there is intensification of the demonisation of the young and calls for greater control, surveillance and punishment. On the other hand, there is celebration of young people as emergent citizens, and corresponding calls for greater participative practice and their involvement in public decision-making. What is not contested (at least rhetorically), on both sides of this divide, is that something called 'youth work' has some kind of contribution to make – both in regulating the negative behaviour of the young (through occupying them more purposefully) and in fomenting their civic and community contribution. Behind that rhetoric, however, remains relatively limited political and financial commitment to the youth service. The 1998 youth service Audit in England noted that infrastructure questions were rendering even the very best of youth work practice precarious and vulnerable (DfEE, 1998). Subsequent developments designed to 'transform' youth work (Department for Education and Skills, 2001, 2002) have made some progress in the funding, management and operation of youth services, but they still remain 'precarious'.

Positive aspirations

In England, though initially an agenda for children, the government has expressed five aspirations for children and young people: to stay safe, be healthy, make a positive contribution, enjoy and achieve, and to secure an economic future. One might have thought that youth work would have a part to play in some, if not all, of these. From *Agenda for a Generation* (United Kingdom Youth Work Alliance, 1996) to the De Montfort University evaluation of youth work (Merton et al., 2004), there has been repeated advocacy for a blend of 'open' and more 'targeted' youth work provision, as one contribution to supporting young people's positive transitions to adulthood. Young people cry out for places to go; local people said that young people need something (constructive) to do; professionals acknowledge the need for young people to have someone to talk to. But the political establishment still harbours doubts. The remainder of this chapter therefore examines why the jury is still out and why, on the balance of probabilities let alone beyond reasonable doubt, the judgement may still not swing in youth work's favour.

The poor reputation of youth work

The case for life-wide learning

With the contemporary emphasis on 'soft' skills, citizenship and personal development, one might have thought youth work's time had come – as a full partner, alongside formal education, in learning pathways for young people. Indeed, at the European Union level, within the 'Lisbon Strategy' of 2000 which aspires to produce a European 'knowledge-based economy' by 2010, there is a serious commitment to the place of non-formal education within a process of 'life-wide' learning. There is clearly less commitment in the United Kingdom. The reasons, I would suggest, are fivefold.

So what's the problem?

First, despite a proliferation in the ways in which maintained and voluntary sector youth services deliver their services, such practice has been poorly explained and promoted. Secondly, this weak self-advocacy by 'traditional' youth services has been overshadowed (and arguably overtaken) by the slick marketing of new competitors in the field, which make (almost certainly false) claims that they can transform the lives of even the most challenging young people almost overnight. Thirdly, however, partly as a result of an absence of effective promotion, there remains a lack of understanding of conventional (statutory and traditional voluntary sector) 'youth work'. Fourthly, youth workers have become notoriously reluctant to engage in the unfolding policy agenda for young people, however much it may relate closely to youth work practice and aspiration. And, lastly, there is considerable poor practice, routinely described in OFSTED reports as 'low-level recreation' and more caustically by others as 'adolescent child-minding'.

Youth work training and delivery

All youth workers, surely, should have some grasp of theories of youth and adolescence, good knowledge of the wider policy context in which young people are growing up, and a toolbox of competencies for collective and individual intervention and support. The focus of training, however, or at least the balance of emphasis, often lies elsewhere. Furthermore, the fact that service delivery is undertaken largely by voluntary and part-time workers compounds these problems. This is not to criticise the part-timers who are recurrently proclaimed as the backbone of the youth service, but to argue that if effective professional delivery of an educational service is to be achieved, it must become more significantly the responsibility of full-time and professionally-trained workers. No self-respecting health minister would see the future of clinical practice within the NHS lying in the hands of health service auxiliaries. Yet as practice with young people becomes more complex, it is part-timers with limited training who are expected to carry the burden.

The paradox for youth work

Here, therefore, lies a paradox. Decision-makers somehow carry two competing and contrasting images in their head: on the one hand, that youth work is too often low-level recreational activity and, on the other hand, that youth work *should* be able to effect significant change in young people's attitudes and behaviour. Both images misrepresent what youth work is, and can be about, yet both, for quite different reasons, guarantee little in the way of a future for the youth service, for they cement an inherently critical and negative view of youth work. If it is simply recreation, then it is unworthy of public support; if it cannot deliver on behaviour change, it is also unworthy of public support. A different rationale for youth work needs to be advanced, and evidence of a different practice promulgated.

Improving practice

Learning environments?

Youth workers proclaim to be in the business of developing the knowledge, attitudes and skills of young people through non-formal education, in which case they need to demonstrate how they assist the learning of young people. I am often saddened by the unwillingness or inability of many youth work practitioners to maximise their own potential as 'educators' and to describe why apparently modest practice still provides environments in which young people can – and do – learn.

Reactive or proactive?

Attention needs to be given to more creative and imaginative developmental work within routine provision, not just to adopt a *laissez-faire* position. The much-maligned pool table provides a stark example. It is, too often, a safe way of occupying the 'lads', playing to time-honoured, culturally dominant, 'winner stays on' rules. This should not be why pool tables are in youth clubs. There they are learning tools, to be 'exploited' in a variety of ways (such as 'loser stays on', mixed doubles, separate lists for young men and young women, playing 'killer'), ensuring wider participation and enabling young people to recognise that there are *always* alternative ways of doing things. This inevitably invites controversy and sometimes conflict, but that is the very stuff to promote dialogue and learning. It demands planned and responsive *intervention*. Youth workers sometimes fail to bite this bullet and opt instead for a quiet life.

Casual conversations?

Youth work should be about a capability to engage young people (as individuals and in groups) in *serious* conversation and discussion on key issues affecting their lives. Sensitised and sensitive reactions to experiences, incidents and comments always provide a learning opportunity. Cursory and fleeting banter is clearly not enough (though it may be a launching cornerstone of positive relationships). Yet it may be all that is achieved in some youth work settings or all that youth workers give in others. But real conversations which probe motives, outline options, accommodate different perspectives and explore the consequences of various forms of behaviour offer an invaluable learning context, which – potentially – enables young people to reflect upon and perhaps reconsider the course their lives are taking.

Participative practice?

'Participation' may be a buzz-word at the heart of youth work practice but it often remains rhetorical, significantly because of the pressures on youth workers to be *seen* to get things done. More genuine participative approaches carry far greater risks of apparent failure. There is often little more than lip service to the celebrated message about young people as 'creators not consumers' (Smith, 1980). Youth work should be about facilitating young people to pursue their own activities and aspirations through adherence to a principle that youth workers only *do* those things that young people cannot do by virtue of their age. The trouble is that many plans and ideas supported in this way will fall by the wayside; on the other hand, providing on a plate clearly does not assist the learning and development of young people, even if it may look rather more impressive to external audiences. As I once told a group of young people on a residential weekend, when we were all at loggerheads about what to do next, I was an 'educator' not a tourist guide!

A proactive and reactive flexible 'curriculum'

Youth work is a dynamic process which combines in a variety of ways four discrete, though overlapping, components: contexts of practice, target groups, priority issues, and working methods. All youth work can be located within this framework, but the relation between the components will change over time. Yet every intervention should be recountable (and thereby accountable) through attention to these four planks of practice. Some will have been 'one-offs' – in one place, with one group or individual, on one issue, in one way. Most will have been *evolving* practice, involving shifting locations (centre-based, residential, an off-site visit), a focusing in and out on different target groups (by gender, ethnicity, perspective or experience), a coverage of a number of issues (family, education, health, crime) and the use of different tools of inter-vention (personal advice, educational resources, group work, opportunistic discussion, policy information).

The challenge for practice is not only to define, but also to describe, the territory on which it operates and what it seeks to achieve. A more convincing hand on this front would permit a more persuasive rebuttal of both the deflated assumptions and the inflated expectations attached to youth work and a re-positioning of its role and function within the context of wider govern-ment policies for young people.

Expectations and possibilities

A leisure-time (but not a leisure) option?

Youth work must try to establish a more realistic position about its contribu-tion both to the lives of young people and to the aspirations of public policy. We must always remember that, for the most part, it is a leisure-time *option* for young people and, as Cohen (1986) once reminded us, leisure is the weak link in the chain of socialisation. It is that space which allows for youthful experimentation and identity formation. Youth work may guide those who opt to participate in its provision, but it cannot compel them to move in particular directions. It has neither the authority nor the formal bargaining power of other institutional influences on young people's lives. So it does not, can not, coerce compliance; instead, it seeks to win their consent (Davies, 1986). Learning possibilities are delivered in a context of mutual commitment.

Not just for the 'disengaged'

There has been an increasing political focus on youth work's contribution to making a difference in the lives of more 'marginal' or 'disengaged' young people. But youth work is not just about more excluded young people, although these often consume a significant proportion of youth work time. For other young people, it represents a safe haven and a space for association and activity, which otherwise is only available on the streets. Targeted intervention anyway appears to work best within a context of more 'universal' provision, serving a variety of young people's needs (see France and Wiles, 1996).

A platform for learning and development?

Youth work provides 'foundation' work for the wider policy objectives of active citizenship, lifelong learning, social inclusion and community safety. It encourages involvement and self-determination, enables young people to consider alternative perspectives and arguments, values the contribution of all, and encourages respect for the feelings and position of others. This is 'first base' activity, assisting young people to take steps on a wide path; more specialist support and intervention are required on the narrower tracks which run parallel with and subsequent to youth work experiences. Therefore youth work needs to be connected to more specific policies in the wider policy arena – in schooling, training, employment, youth justice, health promotion and volunteering.

Youth work has tended to resist engaging with these connections, reluctant to become 'contaminated' by wider public policy objectives on the grounds that it is a 'person-centred' practice. Yet young people's lives are integrally connected to the structures of opportunity around them. If youth work is to support those aspirations, it does so best from a position of maintaining (both in the sense of asserting and sustaining) the *complementary* nature of its practice in relation to wider policy effort.

Working within the triangle

There is a triangle which should inform everyday youth work practice, within which an accommodation needs to be reached between the expressed needs of young people, the policy priorities which affect their transitions, and the values and principles underpinning the delivery of youth services. These three arenas are not always compatible and in harmony. However, when youth work is sucked into any one of these corners, its practice becomes paralysed. It is important to remember, and assert, that youth work operates from a privileged position at the interface between the private worlds of young people and the imperatives of public policy. Its greatest strength, perhaps, is the capacity to mediate between the two. Youth workers should certainly *not* be the unquestioning lapdogs of political agendas for young people, but equally they should not be the unconditional advocates for young people. And it is here that the capacity to *explain* the role of youth work (both to those who control the purse-strings and to young people) is critical (see Williamson, 1983).

Attitude and language

Not about changing the world

Youth work is, too often, perceived not only as isolationist but as *oppositional*. The first sentence of the original National Statement of Purpose for England (produced in 1990; National Youth Bureau, 1990) suggested that youth work was about redressing all forms of inequality, which was quite frankly absurd. Youth work is, however, about *addressing* inequality; that is quite a different matter.

Re-appraising attitudes

Youth workers appear to derive a perverse pleasure in framing their activity in direct opposition to the practice of other agencies seeking to intervene in young people's lives. No wonder youth service ministers have seen youth work as out of touch with the current political mood and the new agendas of youth policy. Informed choices by young people to pursue negative or anti-social lifestyles are, later if not sooner, cul-de-sac choices. Connecting young people to mainstream transition routes is both in their interests and, ultimately, in ours. There may be 'political' battles to fight (about the ideology and quality of wider policy and provision for young people), but they should not be at the expense of the 'best in the circumstances' for the young people with whom we work (see Williamson, 1988).

Getting the language right

Ironically, what youth work actually does, if it is done well, contributes significantly to the very centre of the new policy agenda for young people. It enables young people to *learn* (through the appreciation of different perspectives and difference, through becoming confident to express their views, and so on). It assists young people in acquiring *skills* for employability and citizenship, both 'soft' transversal skills proclaimed by employers as central to their needs and sometimes 'harder', more practical skills. And it encourages young people to *participate* actively in their own development and in their own environment. How often do we describe our work in this way – that youth work is about 'learning, competence and citizenship' (which just happen to be the main planks of the EU youth policy agenda; see also United Kingdom Youth Work Alliance, 1999)? Framing the language of the practice of youth work in such terms immediately strikes a chord and secures a more favourable response. Many of the new specialist youth work organisations have adopted this approach and are recipients of levels of public sector finance which are the envy of more traditional youth services. The challenge is therefore concerned with establishing a more conciliatory attitude towards the prevailing policy agendas for young people (at European, UK and devolved levels of government) and offering a positive view about the contribution to be made by youth work.

Conclusion

Much of the very best of youth work remains rather invisible in its delivery. This is not very helpful in these days of planning, performance monitoring and measurement of outcomes. But we must not substitute glitzy, flagship activity for its own sake. Instead, it is important that youth workers learn to articulate the rhyme and reason of more substantive, if apparently more pedestrian and routine, practice.

Non-formal education and policy engagement

The challenge for everyday youth work practice is twofold. The first is to be confident that we engage with young people in ways that are authentically *educative* (leading them out and forward), and to be able to explain, in contemporary language, how and why this is done. The second is to become more proficient in engaging with the broader policy context – demonstrating the ways youth work practice 'fits' between the aspirations *of* young people and those of public policy *for* young people.

The right to criticise is earned by the willingness to engage

Closer engagement with other local services directed at young people (schools, police, health, leisure, careers) is not about selling young people down the river. It is an opportunity for youth workers to become more informed about the practice and priorities of other agencies affecting young people's lives. It is also an opportunity to inform those agencies of factors which may be impeding their effectiveness. Only through such closer dialogue can the credibility of youth work be enhanced in professional and political circles. And only through such dialogue can the interests of young people be more effectively promoted.

Connecting young people to their wider world

Young people participate in youth work provision largely for social and recreational reasons. That is a home truth we are often reluctant to acknowledge. They do not turn up to be 'educated' or subjected to a curriculum. But the social learning that takes place is indisputably educational if interventions are professionally and reflectively managed. Thinking through my own practice over the years, a raft of issues quickly surface: racism, democratic participation, disability, numeracy (doing the coffee bar), confidence (through helping plan a playscheme), alcohol and drug misuse, family relationships, schooling, criminal justice, practical skills such as using telephones and lighting stoves on residentials. These represent the specific memories of individual young people, the key moments of learning from their youth work experience. Other memories are more distant and less precise, but good youth work should always be attuned to ensuring the provision of experiences which, through challenging values, views and decisions, equip young people to be better prepared for navigating and managing the increasingly complex pathways to adulthood. Unless youth work can articulate this contribution to the wider world, the void will be filled – to its detriment and downfall – by misplaced assumptions or absurd expectations about its role and purpose. And young people themselves will be the poorer as a result.

References

Cohen, P. (1986) *Rethinking the Youth Question*, University of London: Institute of Education/ Post-16 Education Centre.

Davies, B. (1986) *Threatening Youth: towards a national youth policy*, Milton Keynes: Open University Press.

Department for Education and Skills (2001) *Transforming Youth Work*, London: The Stationery Office.

Department for Education and Skills (2002) *Resourcing Excellent Youth Services*, London: The Stationery Office.

DfEE (1998) *England's Youth Service – the 1998 Audit*, Leicester: Youth Work Press.

France, A. and Wiles, P. (1996) *The Youth Action Scheme: an evaluation*, London: Department for Education and Employment.

Merton, B. et al. (2004) *An Evaluation of the Impact of Youth Work in England*, London: Department for Education and Skills.

National Youth Bureau (1990) *Danger or Opportunity? Towards a Core Curriculum for the Youth Service?*, Leicester: National Youth Bureau.

Smith, M. (1980) *Creators Not Consumers: Rediscovering Social Education*, Nuneaton: National Association of Youth Clubs.

Social Exclusion Unit (2000) *National Strategy for Neighbourhood Renewal: Report of Policy Action Team 12 – young people*, London: The Stationery Office.

United Kingdom Youth Work Alliance (1996) *Agenda for a Generation*, Edinburgh: Scottish Community Education Council.

United Kingdom Youth Work Alliance (1999) *Learning, Competence and Citizenship – the role of youth work*, Leicester: National Youth Agency.

Williamson, H. (1983) 'A duty to explain', *Youth in Society*.

Williamson, H. (1988) 'Youth Workers, the MSC and the Youth Training Scheme', in T. Jeffs and M. Smith (eds), *Welfare and Youth Work Practice*, London: Macmillan.

Williamson, H. (2001) *Learning the Art of Patience: Dealing with the Disengaged*, British Youth Council Youth Agenda No 17, London: British Youth Council.

Young, K. (1999) *The Art of Youth Work*, Lyme Regis: Russell House.

PART 2

Issues in practice

7

Identifying and meeting young people's needs

Gina Ingram and Jean Harris

This is a systematic process underpinned by several theories. Here are three examples of work that is:

- needs led
- systematically planned
- evaluated.

All are based on the NAOMIE framework explained below.

Identifying and meeting the needs

Once the needs are known, the worker has to decide how to work systematically to meet the needs. One approach is to use the **NAOMIE** model:

N   Identifies the **Needs**.
A   Set the **Aim**: whatever it is that you are working towards.
O   Set the **Objectives**: those smaller steps that will get you to your aim.

This is a revised version of the original text which appeared as Chapter 5 in *Delivering Good Youth Work* by Gina Ingram and Jean Harris. First published in 2001 by Russell House Publishing.

M   Decide what **Method** you are going to use.

I   Decide what **Indicators** you will use to show you are on course, then go ahead and **Implement** it.

E   Decide how you are going to **Evaluate** the outcomes and review the process.

Each of these Case Study examples occurred in a different context.

El's involved a neighbourhood worker on an estate and took place over ten weeks. Niek's occurred in an information shop and was completed in two hours. Peta's concerned the development of one person over three years using the Duke of Edinburgh's Award. What these cases have in common is that they:

- Began with needs identification.
- Involved systematic planning to meet the needs of young people, to evaluate, review and feedback to them.

Such work is at the heart of good practice when working with young people.

Case study: El

Needs

El is a 16-year-old young woman who lives with her mother and two younger brothers on a run down nearby estate. She is intelligent and doing well at school. She is a confident and able athlete but the school has no capacity to develop this. She hangs out with three friends in her class: Chevella, Kay and Leanne, they have been friends since year five at junior school. El is the leader of the group, the ideas person, she takes the lead in finding fun things to do. She tells you that she is bored as there is nothing to do on the estate and she has no money to get off it. She wants to go to college if she can and has a cousin who is a lawyer: she likes the sound of that. She and her friends are beginning to get into difficulties. They steal from the local shop and smoke cannabis. Her mother came to see the worker, she is very concerned about what is happening. El spends a lot of her time looking after her two younger brothers (aged 8 and 6) during the school holidays as her mum works until 5.30 p.m. The mum seems tired, stressed and in need of support.

Identification of needs

The Neighbourhood worker felt that:

1) El is lacking stimulation and challenge. She wants and needs achievement.
2) In some ways she is a young adult too soon because of her 'parenting' role in relationship to her brothers. Her growth is stunted socially, emotionally, spiritually and politically because of the lack of opportunities locally.

This is resulting in her finding challenge, stimulation and fun in ways that are not positive and are illegal. This is discussed with El and she spontaneously agrees that this is the case.

Aim

To provide El with learning opportunities to help her reach her potential.

Objectives

To offer El new experiences with which she can continue away from the estate.

To keep her and her friendship group together in the process.

To support El in the leadership role that she has begun to develop.

To support her mother in her parenting of El and her two brothers.

Method

The worker has a link with social services and they have a small amount of money to be used for taking young people on holiday who would not otherwise have had that opportunity. Simply providing a holiday would only meet the first two objectives. Instead the worker decided to run a short programme:

Stage 1. Ask the four young women if they would like to help run a holiday for ten young people who would otherwise not have had a holiday. This would involve some fund raising off the estate.

Stage 2. Fund raise: letters, phone calls and visits.

Stage 3. Plan the holiday. This will include visiting the holiday venue and trying out the activities. The idea is that the young women will enjoy themselves and learn about the organisation and safety.

Stage 4. Run a planning weekend.

Stage 5. Run the holiday with the young people: these will include El's two brothers. This will give the mother a break and it may be possible to get the brothers involved in an after-school club and a play scheme in the future.

The periods between each stage are used to look at the young women's:

- achievements
- roles, including leadership
- support mechanisms
- and to offer positive feedback and constructive criticism.

Stage 6. After the programme: the group was asked if they would like to join the town's volunteer programme, which has Millennium Volunteers funding and can pay expenses. Volunteers go away from the area most weekends.

Indicators

Do the young women want to join in?
Do they turn up for the slog of fund-raising?
Do they remain involved?
How do they respond to leaving the estate and meeting new people?
What roles do they take up?
How is El working as a leader in all of this?
Is the young people's participation real or are they just hanging in there for the sake of the holiday?
Can they identify their learning?
Do they turn up for the planning weekend: are they active participants?
Do they turn up for the holiday, do they stay in role as helpers or do they behave like big children?

Evaluation

Formative evaluation   After each session, and the planning weekend, the following questions need exploring to discover how each young person is developing:

- What has happened that is of significance to the young people's learning?
- What needs to be done to progress their learning?
- The programme's successes?
- Its not so successful parts?
- What role did you take?
- What have we all learned?

Summary evaluation (at the end)

- What did the children get from the holiday?
- Did it go to plan?
- Good bits, bad bits, points to look out for if done again?
- What has each of us achieved and learned?

For the record, the project ran to the end. All the children had a holiday that they would not forget for a long time. El became totally absorbed in the project and grew in confidence and skills through the whole process. Her friends were not so enthusiastic: they enjoyed the weekend and the holiday, but found the fund-raising and planning 'a bit boring'.

Each gained and developed in a number of ways. Only El went on to join the volunteers groups and goes away with them most weekends. She still spends weekdays and evenings with her friends. Just recently, she came to see the youth worker. She asked why they did not fight to get more resources on the estate, instead of working to expand people's worlds by leaving it.

Case study: Niek

The planning and delivery may only take one or two hours.

Needs

Niek is 19, a quiet, tall young man. He lives with his family (mother, father, grandmother, and two older siblings) on the estate. He has a long-standing girlfriend and they intend to get a flat together when they can afford it. Niek plays the drums in a group formed from friends he met doing his A-levels at the local sixth form college. He seldom goes off the estate. He has applied for a course at University to do computer studies and is due to go for the interview next week. The University is far enough away from home for him to have to live there in term time.

He has sought out the local information service explaining that he is not going for the interview. He cannot explain why, except to say, 'it isn't here: all my life is here'. He is obviously distressed.

Aim

To help Niek to make a considered decision about his future.

Objectives

To help Niek to:

- Identify what his reasons are for not wanting to go to the interview.
- Identify the range of possibilities that exist, for example:
  - dealing with the issues of going to the interview
  - doing a computer course elsewhere
  - considering other possibilities for his future
  - making decisions about the interview and perhaps about his future.

Method

Niek is an analytical thinker: that is why he is so good with computers. He is not so good at talking about feelings. He finds eye contact quite difficult.

The method chosen was to stick four pieces of flip chart paper on the wall, provide coloured pens and to support and encourage Niek to work through the process of analysing his situation. Niek was asked to list all the things that were going through his mind about his future. He was then able to group these factors and make links between the groups. Niek used this analysis to answer the questions that he was posing himself.

Indicators

- Can Niek get into this method?
- Does it engage him?

It was necessary to have alternative methods in mind as time was short and this method does not suit everyone. Alternatives included:

1) Working with Niek and his girlfriend.
2) Directing him to the careers service.
3) Making contact with the access section of the University to see if they can help.

Evaluation

Niek took to the methodology like a duck to water. He remarked, 'I never thought it would be so easy to sort things out like this'.

After about an hour he decided to:

- Go to the interview for practice.
- Take up the worker's offer of having a practice interview before going to the interview.
- Explore the possibility of getting a job locally and doing a degree with the Open University or by a distance learning package.

He recognised his difficulties in leaving the area and in talking about feelings, but did not feel like facing these at this time. He was offered a place at the University and was extremely proud of this but didn't take it up. He did a distance learning course that he completed satisfactorily and was supported in the process through a job.

It is not always practical or necessary to design a piece of work to meet a specific young person's or group's needs. The programme that the unit is running can be a vehicle for this.

Case study: Peta

This is a summary of some 50 cycles through the NAOMIE process over three years.

Peta was 16 and had had a very difficult life. She had been abused by one of her mother's boyfriends. At 14 she was a prostitute and using alcohol and drugs in dangerous quantities. She was very aggressive, had low self esteem and self harmed on a regular basis. She had few skills in making relationships and was very lonely.

After a referral, a Duke of Edinburgh's Award worker formed a relationship with her, as a means of working with her.

In the next two and a half years, Peta made two unsuccessful suicide attempts and spent six weeks in hospital, as her mother had rejected her and she refused to go anywhere else. She also spent nine weeks in an adolescent unit. She walked out, despite the fact that she was doing well. She assaulted two young people and an Award worker, and returned to prostitution and drugs, on various occasions.

The Award scheme worker did not give up on Peta, and little by little she completed sections of the Award. These were tangible measures of her personal growth and development. She became less aggressive and more consistent. Each completed section raised her self esteem and confidence, although Peta herself would not admit this.

The major difficulty was the expedition section that required Peta to work with three others for two days in the countryside. No other young people wanted to work with her as she was disruptive. Peta sensed this and did not want to be with them. At the third attempt, she managed to complete the practice and final expedition with the same group. She recognised this as the massive move forward that it was. The mixture of systematic working through cycles of NAOMIE together with:

- befriending
- modelling
- instructing
- and never giving up
- counselling
- coaching
- doing things together

…began to move her on. She still has a long way to go but is thinking about her Silver Award.

8

Working with people as an informal educator

Mary Crosby

Informal educators* work in many different kinds of settings with individuals and groups who choose to engage with them. Their purpose is to work in ways which encourage people to use their experiences of everyday living as opportunities for learning about themselves and others (YMCA George Williams College *Handbook*, 1998: 4).

But what precisely do we mean when we talk about 'working with' people? In this chapter I want to look at what I believe to be the nature of 'working with', the kind of relationships within which it can flourish, and what capacities informal educators need to develop within themselves in order to work with others effectively.

Often when we think about working with someone we focus on the external actions which the worker performs. Of course this is important. However, it is impossible to separate the actions of a worker from the thinking, attitudes and values which generate those actions (Carter, Jeffs and Smith, 1995: 4). They are part of the same whole. It is the values, attitudes and thinking involved in 'working with' which I want to focus on; the processes in which workers need to engage within themselves, which we might call their 'internal work' (Whitaker, 1989: 193).

*(Note: the terms 'worker' and 'informal educator' are used interchangeably in this chapter) This is a revised version of the original text which appeared as Chapter 4 in *Principles & Practice of Informal Education* edited by Linda Deer Richardson and Mary Wolfe. First published in 2001 by RoutledgeFalmer.

Working with people means extending ourselves

Dewey regarded education as a way of 'emancipating and enlarging experience' (1933: 240). But how can experience be emancipated or 'set free'? How can it be enlarged? Surely experiences are something which simply happen *to* us? However, they can be thought about and understood. We can act *upon* our experiences rather than simply 'have them'. It is this process of drawing out meaning from experience, often through reflection and discussion with others, which extends and deepens that experience, freeing us to learn from it: 'meanings arise in the process of interaction between people ...' (Bullough, Knowles and Crow, 1991: 3).

If informal educators aim to encourage this process through their interactions, then clearly they must spend time learning about the experiences of those they work with and seeking to understand the meaning these have for them. Informal educators will be unable to do this unless they can 'make room', as it were, in their minds to think about the world as it appears to those they work with. Making room for this kind of thinking entails workers recognising and managing their own opinions and feelings so that they do not get in the way.

Each person with whom they work has a unique set of perceptions and experiences but, too often, informal educators do not take the time to learn about these. It is important that they do so because: 'while ... others may attempt to impose their meanings on us, we ultimately define our own experience ...' (Boud, Cohen and Walker, 1993: 10).

Of course, we can never view other people in ways which are value free, objective or neutral because our perceptions will always be filtered through the many layers of our own experience. So a vital part of informal educators' 'internal work' is in seeking to recognise and reduce the effects of distortions in their perceptions of the other person. This entails submitting their perceptions to a continuous process of reflection, checking and analysis:

P was an outreach youth worker on a large, inner city local authority housing estate. He had identified some young men who tended to hang around a row of shops on the estate and was attracted to working with them, feeling he could understand them because of his own experience of growing up on a similar housing estate. In thinking further about this, P reminded himself that he was in danger of making assumptions about the young men because of his own experiences. 'I had to be aware of this – that even if my experiences might be similar to those of the young men, they were not the same. I needed to spend time finding out from them how they thought and felt about their lives rather than assuming I already knew.'

Peck (1990) has called this process of working to appreciate the experiences of others 'extending ourselves' because it entails pushing out the limits of our thinking and feeling, assumptions and prejudices so that we can take in the perceptions and experiences of the other person. It involves deliberately setting out to do so out of a commitment to those we work with.

This means that working with others also means working with *ourselves* in this process of self-extension. Without this we will not be 'big enough' to work with others in any meaningful way because our own desires, beliefs, prejudices, assumptions and needs will cloud our view of them and limit our capacity to appreciate their world.

Implicit in this approach to working with people is an attitude of respect which does not depend upon how the worker feels about them or whether she or he agrees with the way they see things. Developing this attitude of respect requires workers to become increasingly self-aware, open to change, willing to question and challenge themselves: in other words to engage in 'a constant process of self-education' (Schön, 1983: 299).

J was working with S, a young woman who attended the 'drop in' project with a group of her friends. S and some of her friends were involved in prostitution and the workers at the project had tried to persuade them to join in various programmes aimed at changing their lifestyle. The behaviour of S and her friends was at odds with J's own beliefs and values. However J realised that she had little understanding or appreciation of how they saw and felt about themselves and their situation and that it was important for her to learn about this from S and her friends. So instead of approaching the work with a pre-set agenda for the young women, as other staff had done, J spent time with them: 'I engaged in their conversations about their views and concerns.' This enabled J both to build a working relationship with the young women and begin to understand how they saw themselves and their lives. 'I found that my personal values were challenged and I had to work really hard to keep my mind open and to prevent my feelings from taking over. But, despite this, I continued to work with them on the issues they raised and the feelings they expressed.' Through these conversations J began to appreciate how the young women's common experiences enabled them to understand and accept each other. The friendship group functioned as a kind of extended family through which they supported, advised and set their own moral guidelines for each other. This was valued by the young women who did not receive this kind of acceptance and support elsewhere. A change of lifestyle for any of them carried with it the risk of isolation from this important resource. 'The young women were aware that I was concerned for their health, safety and well-being; we discussed this at length in the group. I may not like what they do, but I have grown to respect them, and I can now understand their situation and what is important to them. Hopefully, my continuing work with them can grow out of this.'

We can see from this example how J's commitment to 'extending herself' made it possible for her to work *with* these young women as opposed to working *on* them as some of her colleagues had done. J's internal work of managing her own values and feelings meant that she was not so much looking *at* the young women 'but looking *with* them at what they are seeking to communicate' (Jeffs and Smith, 1996: 19).

The work of attention

Fundamental to this process of extending ourselves in order to work with others is what Peck calls 'the work of attention'. He regards attention as work because it is an act of will, of 'work against the inertia of our own minds' (1990: 128). It may be much easier and more comfortable for us not to really attend to those we work with; to stay with our own preconceptions and agendas; to imagine that we already know what they need.

The work of attention demands self–discipline and constant practice but it underpins all other aspects of working with people. It includes, as demonstrated in the example of J, observing, thinking, listening, exploring, in an effort to appreciate the other person's perceptions and experiences: what Erikson has called 'their universe of one' (Erikson, in Lerner, 1958: 72).

All this is hard work so it is not surprising that many of us tend to avoid it. We may, for example, regard ourselves as good listeners, but in reality we often listen selectively with a pre-set agenda in mind, wondering as we listen how we can re-direct the conversation in ways more satisfactory to us.

This is not to say that workers should never express a view of their own, disagree or challenge the other person's perceptions or behaviour. But it does mean that, when they do so, it grows out of an appreciation of the other person's world.

Of course, informal educators engage in all kinds of activities with people and this may not always involve sitting down having long conversations with them. Often their contact with people may be quite fragmented. Nevertheless it is always important that they engage in the work of attention; noticing what people say about themselves and how they say it; how they interact with the worker and with others; how others (including the worker) respond to them. At the same time workers need also to be paying attention to themselves, working 'internally' to recognise the impact of their own feelings, attitudes and agendas.

M was in contact with a group of young men who attended the youth project in which she worked. She was trying to get them interested in some activities at the project which she felt would be useful to them. She was frustrated that the group did not take up her suggestions and she felt 'they are just not interested in anything'. Their main interest was in playing football together but M had not thought about this in her efforts to work with them. Thinking this through in supervision, M realised how little she knew about the young men or appreciated what their experiences, interests and priorities were. 'I realised that I was always coming up with my own agenda for them and not actually taking time to find our theirs. I need to spend more time doing their normal activities with them, trying to understand them better.'

In order to reach this conclusion and begin to act differently toward the young men, M first had to understand something about herself. She understood that she had been acting as though she already knew what the young men needed. She realised that perhaps this was more about what *she* needed in order to feel that she was achieving something. Instead of seeking to accompany (Green and Christian, 1998) the young men on their 'road' she had been making working with them conditional upon their joining hers.

So the basis of attending to someone is spending time with or around them, and using this time to engage in the work of learning about them and about your own response to them. It involves staying in touch with your own feelings and attitudes and how these may be influencing the work. As I said earlier, workers are not neutral, and your feeling response to someone may be telling you something about them, about yourself, and about the relationship. As a worker your task is to discern whether these feelings are connected to your own issues (as seen in the example of M) rather than those of the other person.

Often, however, this task is far from easy, especially when workers identify closely with the feelings and experiences of the people they are working with. Workers will only be able to disentangle the emotions if they are constantly working to 'know themselves' and are able to acknowledge their own issues and feelings. If not, then they will remain unaware of how they may be affecting the quality of their work with people. They may even attribute any difficulties in the work to the other person, as M did in our example when she saw the young men as 'just not interested in anything'. Here is another example of this process:

H was working in a youth project which was coming to the end of its funding. She had worked particularly closely with a group of young women throughout the life of the project and she felt very concerned about what would happen to them when it ended, because they had become so used to being a part of the project. As the time for the closure drew near she felt that the young women were not willing to face up to it and avoided talking about it.

> On reflection H began to consider her own feelings about the closure and realised that she had been avoiding these by focusing on what she imagined the young women were feeling. She realised then that she was part of the problem, that she had been placing her own feelings on to the group instead of owning them. Because she could not face up to the ending she was unable to work with whatever the young women felt about it.
>
> As H faced up to her own concerns, talking them through with her line manager, she found she could open up conversations with the young women and pay attention to their experience instead of only to her own.

Delivery or discovery?

Compare the examples of work done by M, J, P and H with the approach of those who work to an externally–set curriculum or agenda. This often involves them in 'delivering' programmes to people where the desired 'learning outcomes' are already set.

Many informal educators, perhaps due to the demands of funders, appear to be increasingly pre-occupied with this kind of approach rather than working with people's experiences and concerns, with what is important to *them*, in order to 'foster learning in life as it is lived' (YMCA George Williams College, 1998: 4). An emphasis on delivery of programmes can imply a ready-packaged approach to education where the workers assume they already know what people need to learn.

Any programmes or techniques used need to be thought about carefully. An over–reliance on techniques can be a way of workers avoiding their anxiety about dealing with new and uncertain situations, by trying to somehow standardise them or make them 'the same' as those already encountered. Schön (1983) sees this as workers trying to '… preserve the constancy of their knowledge', turning practice into an application of techniques rather than an evolving process of discovery.

Informal educators often have to work in practice situations which are complex, uncertain and full of conflicting values and demands. They therefore need to avoid what Mills called 'the fetishism of method and technique …' (1959: 245) and instead engage creatively with the people and situations before them.

But workers may find it difficult to give up their sense of knowing what to do; it can be difficult to remain in uncertainty and to think things through without reaching prematurely for an answer. Knowing can give a feeling of control and security, however illusory. But to work with what people bring, with their experiences and perceptions, requires workers to develop an ability to tolerate uncertainty, their 'negative capability' as the poet Keats described it, because this is a pre-requisite for learning and discovery:

> If we … do not allow ourselves … to experience newness we also shut ourselves off from the perception of something different, discovering new things … producing something fresh … however, if we do not thus rigidify our thinking we pay the price of the agony of helplessness, confusion, dread of the unknown, of being in a state of beginning once more.
>
> (Salzberger-Wittenberg, Henry and Osborne, 1983: 9)

Small wonder that many workers prefer the less painful, well-trodden pathway of 'delivery' and techniques! But unless workers can bear the anxiety of uncertainty, how will they take time to learn about their clients and work with *their* experiences and concerns, so that they may become 'creators' of their own learning rather than simply 'consumers' of programmes (Smith, 1980)?

Of course, the traditional view of professional workers is that they *do* have answers and know what is best for their clients. But the approach to working with people discussed in this chapter demands that workers develop a different kind of relationship where the client is 'an active participant in a process of shared inquiry' with the worker (Schön, 1983: 302), and where the worker's chief concern is to discover and work with the client's meanings. In this kind of working relationship, worker and client are engaged together in a process of discovery.

Bruno Bettelheim (1990) gives a lovely illustration of this kind of working relationship when he describes his first meeting with his psychoanalyst. Bettelheim was feeling anxious about entering analysis so he asked the analyst, 'Do you think this will help me?' The analyst replied that he did not know, but that they could do some work together and Bettelheim would probably know the answer to this question before he did. At first Bettelheim felt disconcerted and rather alarmed at this unexpected reply. Surely this professional must *know*! But then he realised that the analyst's reply had placed their working relationship in a more realistic and humane context:

> [analysis] was not something he would unilaterally do *to* or *for* me, but rather a joint undertaking in which the participation of both of us was critical … we were equal in our efforts to learn significant things about me.

The development of this kind of working relationship depends upon the worker being willing to let go of their certainties and extend their capacity to:

> reveal [their] uncertainties … make [themselves] confrontable … give up the comfort of relative invulnerability, the gratifications of deference. The new satisfactions open to [them] are largely those of discovery …
>
> (Schön, 1983: 299)

Conclusion

Working with people is often a confusing, complex and demanding experience, both mentally and emotionally. I have tried to show how workers may retreat from these demands in a variety of ways, though perhaps not deliberately or consciously. Their retreat may be concealed, even from themselves, by all kinds of activities which may look like 'working with' people but are, perhaps, more a means of managing their own anxieties.

I have argued for an approach to practice which respects the uniqueness of people and the validity of their experiences; which is committed to working with people rather than on them; and which requires workers to engage in the constant discipline of their 'internal work'.

References

Bettelheim, B. (1990) *Recollections and Reflections*. London: Thames and Hudson.

Boud, D., Cohen, R. and Walker, D. (eds) (1993) *Using Experience for Learning*. Buckingham: SRHE and Open University Press.

Bullough, R. V. Jr., Knowles, J. G. and Crow, N. A. (1991) *Emerging as a Teacher*. London and New York: Routledge.

Carter, P., Jeffs, T. and Smith, M. K. (eds) (1995) *Social Working*. Basingstoke and London: Macmillan.

Dewey, J. (1933) *How we Think*. Lexington, MA: D.C. Heath & Co.

Green, M. and Christian, C. (1998) *Accompanying young people on their spiritual quest*. London: The National Society/Church House Publishing.

Jeffs, T. and Smith, M. K. (1996) *Informal Education – conversation, democracy and learning*. Derby: Education Now Publishing Co-operative Ltd.

Lerner, D. (ed.) (1958) *Evidence and Inference*. Glencoe, IL: The Free Press of Glencoe.

Mills, C. Wright (1959) *The Sociological Imagination*. Harmondsworth: Penguin.

Peck, M. Scott (1990) *The Road Less Travelled*. London: Arrow Books Ltd.

Salzberger-Wittenberg, I., Henry, G. and Osborne, E. (1983) *The Emotional Experience of Learning and Teaching*. London: RKP.

Schön, D. A. (1983) *The Reflective Practitioner: how professionals think in action*. New York: Basic Books.

Smith, M. (1980) *Creators not Consumers: rediscovering social education*. Nuneaton: N.A.Y.C.

Whitaker, D. S. (1989) *Using Groups to Help People*. London: Routledge.

YMCA George Williams College, London (1998) *Programme Handbook*. 1998–2000.

9

Counselling and the youth support worker role – are these connected?

Jane Westergaard

Introduction

With the emergence of an increasing number of youth support workers employed in a range of contexts (for example, the Personal Adviser within the Connexions Service, the Government's Youth Support Service for all 13–19 year olds), the time is right to clarify the role and responsibilities of this relatively new profession. Greater understanding of the youth support worker role will ensure that practitioners, who are working alongside a range of existing professional services within schools and the community, are recruited, selected, and trained according to clear and well thought out job specifications. In my position as an educator of youth support workers and a counsellor for young people at risk, I have a keen interest in ensuring that appropriate approaches to practice are adopted by those engaged in work with young people.

I have recently undertaken research with twelve Personal Advisers employed by the Connexions service in a range of contexts across a broad geographical area, in an attempt to ascertain their perceptions of their role and responsibilities in relation to work with young people. In this chapter I will consider the questions that I posed to them; questions about their role (which can equally be applied to most practitioners working in a youth support context), and I will identify some key professional practice issues pertinent to those who work in this field. In addition, I will establish the relevance of the activity of 'counselling' and the use of counselling skills in work with young people.

Three areas will be considered:

1) What do practitioners who work with young people with complex needs do?
2) What are the key professional practice issues for youth support workers in their one to one work with clients?
3) How is counselling relevant to the youth support worker role?

1. What do practitioners who work with young people with complex needs do?

A good starting point to answer this question is the wealth of documentation issued by the DfEE about the Connexions youth support service. Anyone who has had even a passing interest in the evolution of Connexions, will be aware of the different (and sometimes conflicting) emphases placed on the development of this service. However, what has remained consistent, is the overarching aim of the service to 'work with young people to identify and overcome barriers to learning and progression' (DfEE, 2001a).

Publicity leaflets produced by DfEE explain that 'teenagers will be able to get the help and support they need to reach their full potential' (DfEE, 2001b), and it is these notions of 'help' and 'support' about which those who manage youth support services, educators of practitioners and youth support workers themselves require clarity. How far, for example do the activities of 'help' and 'support' reflect current professional definitions of advice, guidance, and counselling? Is the nature of 'support' purely practical, involving youth support workers in accompanying clients to appropriate agencies, for example, or does it, in addition, involve the practitioner in offering emotional support, enabling clients to deal with internal as well as external issues? I would argue that in many cases the two are inextricably linked. If, on a practical level a youth support worker is accompanying a young homeless person to a hostel, then on an emotional level, they are likely to engage with the detail of why this situation has arisen and how the client is feeling. Often, this detail will be difficult and painful and clients will need help in dealing with the emotional impact of their situation in addition to meeting their practical needs.

Although the DfEE leaflet provides examples of youth support workers engaging with clients who are presenting with diverse needs, it does not specifically detail the types of intervention tools being used by practitioners, nor does it seek to clarify the boundaries of the role.

Youth support organisations seem unable to translate the very broad definitions of the responsibilities of their workers. For example, one Connexions service Personal Adviser job specification identified the following tasks:

- providing individual support
- providing intensive sustained support
- providing in-depth guidance
- empowering and enabling young people.

To carry out these complex and challenging tasks, the specified knowledge, skills and attitudes are also stated in generic terms:

- communicating and relating to young people
- maturity and a positive outlook
- showing patience and composure
- knowledge of education, training and employment provision.

No specific qualifications are required and no definition of what is meant by 'support' and 'intensive and sustained support' is provided.

What about the youth support workers themselves? What do those individuals who have been working as Personal Advisers, for example, in the Connexions service, understand their role and responsibilities to be?

Having spoken at length with twelve Personal Advisers working in Connexions services in a range of contexts (school, FE, community based, outreach), the lack of shared understanding about the role is striking. The kind of activities in which PAs are engaged appears to depend more on their own training, background and experience than on any clear guidelines or recommendations about what they should be doing and how they should be doing it. For example, a Personal Adviser with a youth service background had developed a peer education project, bringing young people together in a group context to share their issues and concerns and to seek solutions. A PA with a counselling background had undertaken in depth one to one work with clients, to enable them to identify, understand and face their problems and consider strategies for overcoming them. Both were addressing the aims of Connexions, but each had employed different methods according to their own previous professional training.

Some PAs in my research expressed uncertainty and a lack of confidence about how they could set out to achieve the outcomes of the Connexions service. 'I'm not sure exactly what I'm supposed to be doing, so I just get on with what I think I can do' was one reflection by a PA working in an FE college. Several felt that the role had proved to be very different to that which they were expecting and described experiences that had taken them out of their 'comfort zones' in terms of their own professional expertise and backgrounds. 'I'm fine with establishing relationships with young people – that's what my previous training as a careers adviser prepared me to do. This job seems to require so much more and I'm not always sure about my ability to do whatever it is that's needed. Actually, I'm not even sure what's needed.'

In brief then, the answer to the question 'what do youth support workers do?' appears to be 'it depends who you speak to'. The youth support workers I interviewed chose to focus their work with young people on methods and approaches with which they were familiar from their previous experience and training. However for quality services to young people to be developed and maintained, the time is right to draw together models of good practice and to provide a clearer definition of the function, role and responsibilities of youth support workers, thus ensuring effective delivery methods, training and support for the future.

2. What are the key professional practice issues for youth support workers in their one to one work with clients?

a) Definition of 'support'

In spite of the lack of clarity about the role of the youth support worker, it is true to say that one to one work with clients will form a significant part of the work and it is therefore imperative that practitioners have the knowledge and skills necessary to form effective, supportive and purposeful relationships with clients. Before the specific and detailed knowledge and skills required for the work can be identified, the nature of the one to one relationship with clients – its purpose, aims and outcomes must be defined.

It appears that there has been a deliberate attempt made to avoid placing a professional label on the one to one interaction.

Recognised professions, drawing from academic disciplines, with their own training and qualification routes, overseen by professional bodies such as:

- advice
- guidance
- counselling

have been replaced by generic 'activities' which can be applied across a number of professions, with no recognised theoretical base, training or qualification routes:

- support
- in-depth support
- help.

This may, in part, be because the terms advice, guidance and counselling (particularly counselling) have certain connotations which may distance and alienate the group of young people that youth support services are seeking to serve. In a survey of young people on this subject, the conclusions reached were that 'the term support is preferable to advice and even more so than counselling' (Carnegie Young People Initiative, 2000). Some academics demonstrate a similar scepticism for use of the term 'counselling' in relation to youth support work. 'If too much emphasis is placed on the role of counselling, there is an inherent risk that undue emphasis to psychological analysis will cast individuals as the problem' (Irving and Marris, 2002). However, counsellors will know that most counselling approaches seek to achieve quite the reverse, i.e. the externalisation rather than internalisation of 'the problem'.

Clearly, the views of young people are important. However, we should not be tempted to dismiss the academic disciplines that provide the theory underpinning one to one work with clients. If we do, we are in danger of operating without a foundation for good practice and without an understanding of what we are doing and why we are doing it. This will not benefit those we are setting out to help.

We need to seek clarity about the following:

When young people identify *support* as a preferred descriptor, what does it mean?

What does *support* look like in terms of the one to one interaction?

Are young people only concerned with practical help or are they also looking for *support* in dealing with their emotional lives?

The answers I have received to these questions, from youth support workers, are not conclusive. However, without exception they acknowledge the client centred nature of their one to one relationships with young people. Put simply, the client and the client's needs are at the heart of the relationship, and these needs can be either practical or emotional, or, as is most often the case, both. Practitioners stress the importance of engaging young people, building relationships over time, of trust and understanding, and developing strategies to work towards positive change. These relationships are open, genuine and non-judgemental. In short, youth support workers are describing, and adhering to, the three core Rogerian conditions of:

- empathy (working to understand the client's situation and frame of reference)
- congruence (being genuine and transparent in the relationship)
- unconditional positive regard (seeking to ensure that pre-conceptions and judgements are not acted upon).

(Rogers, 1951)

These core humanistic conditions form the basis of person centred counselling relationships. The activity of counselling *does* underpin the work – but very few youth support workers are willing to admit it, feeling that they are ill-equipped to use counselling approaches in their work. Hence the confusion, lack of confidence, deskilling and absence of professional focus that some youth support workers describe.

b) Boundaries

For many young people, this kind of relationship with an adult will be a new and powerful experience. It is likely that clients will not have felt 'listened to' or understood in quite this way before in their lives. Here is an adult who is wanting to understand them, who is treating them with respect, who is not judging them, who has time for them – a potent mix, and clients will respond accordingly, in many cases feeling safe enough to share very difficult and some-times traumatic aspects of their lives with their youth support worker. This may present the practitioner with difficulties of their own. For example, there may be issues with the youth support worker's own personal boundaries – 'how do my client's problems, issues and emotions impact on me?'

One of the Personal Advisers I interviewed described the traumatic effect that working with a particular client had on her. 'I was struggling with my own feelings of despair for this young girl. I could not get her out of my head. This raised issues from my own past and had an immediate impact on my relationship with my own family'.

There may also be professional/ethical boundaries issues – 'how does my organisation expect me to respond to what my client is telling me?' and prac-tical boundaries – 'how much support can I offer, and what form will this support take?'

In promising 'intensive support' to their clients, youth support services will need to be mindful of their own legal, ethical and moral boundary issues. Establishing clear boundaries should be a priority, thus enabling practitioners to be transparent with their clients about the nature and scope of the support which they can provide.

c) Legal context of working with young people – rights of young person, child protection, confidentiality

In addition to the key professional practice issue of establishing clear boundaries in one to one work with clients, practitioners will also need to clarify their legal responsibilities to clients within the framework of their organisation. The Human Rights Act, 1998, states that a young person has the right to privacy and protection of reputation. Clearly this has significant implications for the work that youth support workers undertake with young people. The Gillick case establishes the duty to keep information confidential where there is a 'special relationship' of trust, for example doctor/patient or counsellor/client (House of Lords, 1985). I would argue that in many cases, the relationship between the practitioner and the young person could be included in this category – 'special relationship', and this will have implications for youth support workers in working with issues of child protection and confidentiality.

Counsellors frequently face these challenging issues in their practice. It is because of the complexity of the moral and ethical dilemmas encountered by counsellors in their work with young people, that regulatory and professional bodies such as the British Association for Counselling and Psychotherapy provide clear and detailed guidelines on best practice, to which counsellors are able to refer when in doubt. My concern about the lack of a readily identifiable professional framework in which many youth support workers operate, is that they may, in some cases, be left to 'find their own way' with clients. Practitioners may discover themselves using their own judgement, instincts and most worryingly, 'common sense' in cases of child protection and confidentiality. There is a danger in continuing to insist that practitioners working with young clients are not 'counselling' but are simply 'supporting' young people. Organisations are taking a risk that the legal, ethical and moral aspects of this in-depth and challenging work, will not be appropriately addressed in practice.

d) Support and supervision

The three key professional practice issues that I have identified so far are central to the fourth area of concern for professional practice – the need for support and supervision for practitioners working with young people. Without exception, the personal advisers with whom I spoke stated a very real need for the kind of support and supervision currently experienced by counsellors. It appears that the Connexions service was slow to address this need. This should not come as a surprise. The Careers Service (at the core of Connexions) had little experience of offering contracted, formal support and supervision to staff, although the case for doing so had been argued for some years by Jenny Bimrose and Sally Wilden at the University of East London (Bimrose and Wilden, 1994). However, there is an increasing recognition of the need to adequately support those who are often working in challenging circumstances with young people and to provide supervision which fulfils three key functions:

- **Normative** – management of case loads, of legal and ethical issues
- **Formative** – reflection on the theories and concepts underpinning practice, to develop skills and knowledge, to focus on continuous professional development
- **Restorative** – focusing on the emotional and psychological well-being of the supervisee.

(Inskipp and Proctor, 1993).

There are various approaches to, and models for, effective supervision including managerial supervision, group supervision, peer group supervision and external supervision. I do not intend to explore these in this chapter. However, the argument for implementing a policy and guidelines for supervision of PAs within Connexions and youth support workers in other contexts is clear. Again, it appears that it is the lack of definition concerning the role of the youth support worker and the academic and professional disciplines from which this role is derived, that is inhibiting the policy makers. If youth support services can accept that the work undertaken by practitioners is underpinned by related areas of practice including counselling, then they will be able to put in place the necessary conditions and support to enable their employees to do their job with confidence and in safety.

3. How is counselling relevant to the youth support worker role?

I have made clear throughout this chapter my own thoughts about the relationship between 'intensive support' and the activity of counselling. If part of the support refers to the emotional support of young people, then isn't this what counselling is all about? It appears that the DfEE agrees:

'Counselling is an integral aspect of guidance. It refers to purposeful relationships, which help individuals to understand and cope more effectively with themselves and their circumstances' (Ofsted/DfEE National Survey of Careers Education and Guidance, Secondary Schools 1998).

This seems to be an accurate description of at least part of the function and responsibility of any youth support worker. However, the PAs I've spoken to have, without exception, been quick to deny that they have a counselling role. When invited to develop this argument they explain that they do not have counselling training, neither do they feel that they develop a counselling relationship with their clients. However, they each identified the need for far more in depth counselling skills as a key element of their training.

The PAs who helped with my research gave numerous examples of these 'purposeful relationships' as defined by Ofsted/DfEE. At times, however, they commented on the tension between a truly client centred relationship and the need to work towards targets set externally by Connexions, based on the principles underpinning the service (e.g. to raise attainment). 'I know that I'm supposed to be working towards reducing teenage pregnancy in this area. But when I work with a 15 year old who sees pregnancy as a real option, I feel confused about where my loyalties and priorities lie'.

Perhaps some of the difficulty in inviting PAs to accept that part of their role involves counselling, lies in a perceived misunderstanding about what counselling is and who does it. Additionally, the emphasis on the achievement of *service* targets may, in some instances, conflict with the personal targets set by *clients*, therefore placing practitioners in a dilemma about whom they are ultimately responsible to.

Clearly youth support workers are *not counsellors* (i.e. they do not solely carry out a counselling function). However, I would argue that they do, when appropriate, use *counselling approaches* with clients according to the Ofsted definitions. Indeed the stated need from all the PAs I spoke to for counselling skills as a key aspect of their training would suggest that in some part they do recognise the need to use counselling in their work – if not, why do they need the skills? Paula Pope (2002) argues the case for training in counselling skills for youth workers 'Given that they (youth workers) are already involved in either formal or voluntary relationships with young people, they are likely to be an early point of contact' (Pope, 2002). Youth support workers may, in many cases, be in a similar 'front line' position.

There is, of course, a danger in developing skills without at the same time having an understanding of what you are doing – and why. The use of counselling skills without knowledge of the theories and concepts underpinning counselling practice could cause problems for both client and counsellor and is, in itself, unethical. It is for this reason that I believe that it is imperative for practitioners to receive counselling skills training and, in addition, gain an insight into counselling theory and approaches to ensure that they are able to operate as informed and confident practitioners. The concepts and skills introduced in training to most youth support workers offer a useful starting point, but will require detailed development if they are going to provide practitioners with the knowledge and expertise to carry out their role effectively.

The challenge now is for youth support agencies, practitioners, policy makers and academics to accept that counselling does have a part to play in service delivery and to establish the most relevant counselling approaches to youth support work. Of course, the theories underpinning counselling practice are many and varied, but it is possible to draw from those which most closely reflect the aims of the youth support services. Already practitioners are identifying client centred approaches as being helpful. Other models such as solution focused and cognitive behavioural approaches could perhaps be drawn upon, developed and incorporated further in the training of practitioners to offer a framework for practice.

Conclusion

If it is acknowledged that counselling is an activity undertaken by youth support workers, then the professional practice issues identified in this chapter could be more effectively addressed. Counsellors are clear about their role and the purpose and nature of their work. They are trained to understand boundary issues and use supervision to ensure that boundaries are being appropriately maintained. Counsellors have guidelines issued by professional bodies concerning the legal implications of working in confidential relationships with young people. Counsellors are actively encouraged to receive professional, contracted supervision.

Far from daunting youth support workers by recognising that counselling has a part to play in their work, the acceptance of counselling as an integral and necessary element of their role by all those with responsibility for youth support services (policy makers, managers, trainers, academics and practitioners), will surely prove positive. It will provide a clearer definition of the support worker's function and will ensure that appropriate training in skills and theory is provided. In addition, the support necessary for practitioners to be able to establish effective, purposeful, safe relationships with their clients will be put in place. Without recognising the contribution that established areas of professional practice, like counselling, can make, there is a strong possibility that the role of youth support worker will be reduced to a 'common sense' job that is neither understood, valued nor recognised within a professional framework. More importantly, there is the potential for damage to both clients and practitioners if these issues are not recognised and addressed.

References

Bimrose, J. and Wilden, S. (1994) Supervision in Careers Guidance: Empowerment or Control? *British Journal of Guidance and Counselling,* 22(3) 373–383.

Carnegie Young People Initiative (2000) *Young People Now.* March 2001.

Department for Education and Employment (2001a) *Connexions Pilot Notes.* London: DfEE.

Department for Education and Employment (2001b) *Get Involved to Make a Difference.* London: DfEE.

House of Lords (1985) Gillick v. West Norfolk and Wisbech Area Health Authority.

Inskipp, F. and Proctor, B. (1993) *The Art, Craft and Tasks of Supervision, Part 1. Making the Most of Supervisors,* Twickenham, Cascade Publications.

Irving, B. and Marris, L. (2002) A Context for Connexions. Towards an Inclusive Framework. *Careers Guidance: Constructing the Future.* Stourbridge. ICG.

OFSTED/Department for Education and Employment (1998) *National Survey of Careers Education and Guidance, Secondary Schools.* London: DfEE.

Pope, Paula (2002) Youth-Friendly Counselling. *Counselling and Psychotherapy Journal,* Vol. 13 (pp. 18–19).

Rogers, C. R. (1951) *Client-Centred Therapy.* London: Constable.

10

Handling feelings

Neil Thompson

Introduction

People work can be understood in terms of three dimensions: thoughts, feelings and actions – 'Think–Feel–Do'. This chapter focuses specifically on the second of these – the ways in which feelings affect practice.

There are two main sets of issues to be addressed: dealing with other people's feelings, and dealing with our own. The emotional dimension is often one that may be neglected and, where it is considered, it may well be that only the first aspect is addressed – the feelings of others. In a sense, this is not surprising, as it can be quite unsettling to delve into our own emotional responses. It can make us feel very uncomfortable, and therefore reluctant to consider them at anything beyond a superficial level. However, as I shall argue below, it is important that our own feelings are taken into account, as a failure to do so can lead to a number of problems, both for ourselves and for the people we work with.

Feelings can often have a subtle effect on our practice without our realizing. They can colour our perceptions and shape our actions. In this respect, actions and attitudes can often be 'feelings in disguise'. That is, they can stem from an emotional response to a particular situation. This can apply in one of

This is a revised version of the original text which appeared as Chapter 15 in *People Skills, second edition* by Neil Thompson. First published in 2002 by Palgrave Macmillan. Reproduced with permission of Palgrave Macmillan.

two ways. First, feelings can act as an 'accelerator'. They can push us forward into doing certain things. That is, feelings act as motivators, although they can sometimes motivate us too much in the sense that they can make us act rashly.

Second, feelings can act as a 'brake'. That is, they can demotivate us and stand in the way of achieving our goals. For example, feelings of loss and sadness can rob us of our energy and commitment, and leave us struggling to cope with the demands made upon us.

Clearly, then, the emotional dimension of human experience raises a number of important issues for people workers. A better understanding of the role of feelings can therefore help to equip us for the demands of the job. I shall first of all address some of the important questions that arise in attempting to deal appropriately and constructively with the feelings of others, before moving on to consider the complexities of handling our own feelings.

Other people's feelings

Perhaps the first point that should be emphasized is the importance of being able to recognize feelings, to be able to detect their sometimes subtle influences. Sensitivity to feelings is an essential part of good practice but this can often be blunted, particularly at times when people are busy or under pressure (or, as I shall argue below, when we are preoccupied with our own feelings). It is therefore important that we do not allow pressures of work or other concerns to reduce 'Think–Feel–Do' to a simple matter of 'Think–Do'.

However, it is often the case that feelings are expressed openly and explicitly, and so there is no question of not recognizing them. When this occurs, there is a very strong temptation to acknowledge this by saying something along the lines of: 'I know how you feel'. However, as many practitioners have found to their great cost, comments such as this can be disastrous when feelings are running high. It can provoke a very strong reaction. This is because it fails to recognize that a bland response to intense feelings is likely to be experienced by the service user as an intrusion that alienates the individual and serves to invalidate his or her feelings.

A more helpful or appropriate comment would be something like: 'I can see that this is upsetting ...' or 'I realize you must be angry about this'. Such comments acknowledge that there are strong feelings but do not give the impression that we 'know' what is inside the other person's head or heart.

This raises a key distinction that we should bear in mind, namely that between sympathy and empathy. Sympathy entails sharing the same feelings as the other person at a particular time or in particular circumstances. Empathy, by contrast, refers to recognizing the other person's feelings (and responding accordingly) without actually feeling them ourselves.

Of course, empathy rarely occurs in a pure form. It is perhaps inevitable at times that we feel at least a hint of the feelings the other person is displaying. However, if we were to take on board all of the feelings that we encounter in undertaking people work, we would very quickly become swamped and overwhelmed. The essential task, then, is to remain sensitive to people's feelings so that we do not become callous or unfeeling, but without being so sensitive that we become disabled by the welter of emotions that we come face to face with. That is, we need to nurture the skills of empathy, rather than run the risk of allowing sympathy to disempower us, thereby rendering us of little use or value to people at the very point when they may need us most.

Other people's feelings can make us feel very uncomfortable, and this can sometimes lead some workers to gloss over the feelings dimension and give it as little attention as possible. One of the ways in which this can manifest itself is through a 'macho' attitude in which feelings come to be seen as an encumbrance, a barrier to 'getting on with the job' – as if feelings were not part of 'the job'. This 'be tough' approach can be a misguided attempt to deal with the pressures of the work (Pottage and Evans, 1992). As such, it is very destructive, as it reduces effectiveness, increases the likelihood of mistakes being made and creates an unsupportive atmosphere by excluding or marginalizing the emotional dimension.

A 'macho' approach, although more closely associated with men, can none the less apply to women. A 'be tough' attitude is not an exclusively male phenomenon but can be equally problematic wherever it is adopted. Similarly, we should avoid the stereotype that men are not capable of sensitivity and emotional responsiveness. The idea that emotional issues are 'best left to the women' is a very unhelpful one, as it places an unnecessary burden on women and devalues the part that men can play in high-quality people work.

At the opposite extreme from the macho approach is what I would describe as a self-indulgent voyeurism. This is where a worker may become preoccupied with the feelings issues involved in a particular situation at the expense of other important aspects. This can extend to the point where the worker seems to get some sort of psychological benefit from working closely with other people's feelings. It becomes a type of 'voyeurism' in which close exposure to someone's intimate personal feelings provides a form of gratification. This is not to say that dealing with feelings should not be enjoyable and bring job satisfaction, but there are dangers involved when the process becomes one characterized by a degree of self-indulgence.

Where this occurs, it may indicate that the worker has unmet emotional needs of his or her own. Its results are potentially very serious as the service user may experience the situation as intrusive and oppressive, and therefore be very distressed by it, in what is already likely to be a distressing situation. The situation may also prove to be damaging for the worker, especially if the service user rejects him or her, or makes a complaint.

Responding appropriately to other people's feelings is a complex and demanding task. Furthermore, particular emotions may require a particular response, rather than a blanket approach. Some examples of this would be:

- *Loss*   When a person experiences a significant loss, his or her emotional needs will be different at different stages in the process of adjusting to the loss. For example, in the early stages of a loss reaction, there is little point in trying to advise people or give them information, as they are likely to be in a state of shock in which they are unable to take very much in. All that may be possible initially is simply 'to be there' and thereby provide what may be a very important source of moral support (Thompson, 1991).
- *Anger*   When someone is feeling very angry, there is a danger that saying the wrong thing may inflame the situation even further. Words therefore have to be chosen very carefully in such situations.
- *Guilt* Feelings of guilt can arise when someone genuinely has something to feel guilty about. However, they can also arise in response to a loss, even where the person concerned has nothing to feel guilty about. For example, when someone dies, a common response from a person grieving is to keep saying things like: 'If only I'd…', as if he or she were in some way responsible for the death. It is important to remember, then, that guilt is often an irrational response to a painful situation. Providing reassurance can be helpful, but it is unlikely to be enough in itself, as a person in this situation is likely to need time to work through their feelings.
- *Joy*   We also need to consider responses to positive emotions such as joy. At certain times, we may have to help keep such feelings in perspective without being seen as a 'killjoy'. For example, in a situation where someone is 'counting their chickens before they're hatched', and the worker may need to help him or her adopt a more realistic perspective in order to avoid the pain of disappointment. In this respect, even responding to positive emotions needs to be a skilled activity.
- *Anxiety*   Anxiety is a state of generalized emotional discomfort. It is similar to fear, but also different in so far as fear tends to be more specific – we tend to know what it is that we are afraid of. Anxiety is less specific, a less focused sense of unease. It is this that makes anxiety more difficult to deal with. But this also gives us a means of dealing with anxiety – by 'translating' it into fear. That is, we can help service users develop a better understanding of what is causing their anxiety and, by identifying specific fears, outline a way forward for tackling them.

One very important concept in relation to dealing with feelings is that of 'catharsis'. This refers to the process of setting people free when they have encountered an emotional 'blockage', for example as a result of bereavement. Sometimes, people's lives can be highly problematic because they have reached an emotional impasse. This can be very disabling, leaving people very ill-equipped for the day-to-day demands that they face.

There can therefore be a very significant role for the worker in unpicking the lock of this impasse in order to allow people to regain control of their lives and come to terms with the emotional pain and difficulties they have encountered. Helping someone to achieve catharsis can therefore be a task of major importance, a significant form of empowerment.

Our own feelings

Although people workers should aim for some degree of objectivity and detachment, it is of course inevitable that our own feelings will have at least a small part to play in influencing the complex interactions that characterize people work. Indeed, in many cases our own feelings can be very much to the fore and can play a major part in influencing the outcome of the intervention. It is therefore important that we address the question of the impact of our feelings on practice (and, of course, the impact of practice on our feelings).

People work involves a set of processes in which workers engage with, and respond to, a range of other people – service users, colleagues, staff from other organizations and so on. When people come together in this way, a variety of emotional responses will be generated, including jealousy, hope, anger, frustration, disappointment, joy and anguish; we could not possibly predict what emotion will arise in what situation, but there are some guidelines or general principles that can help us to appreciate the significance of the emotional dimension.

One such principle is the need to avoid adopting a 'stoic' response. This is the equivalent of adopting a macho approach to other people's feelings. Once again, it entails a 'be tough' attitude that seeks to play down or marginalize the role of feelings in human interactions. The stoic approach attempts to bypass or repress one's own feelings, rather than deal with them openly or constructively.

There are three main problems associated with a stoic approach. These are:

1) Often the energy it takes to repress the feelings leaves less energy for tackling the problems that gave rise to the feelings in the first place. That is, it is counterproductive in so far as it distracts attention from the main task at hand.
2) Our own feelings can be a source of positive and constructive energy, a tool to be used to promote change and enhance problem-solving in

people work. That is, the process of repressing feelings not only wastes personal resources in itself, but also stifles what can be an important contribution to effective practice.

3) If feelings are repressed over a long period of time, the result can be that 'burnout' is experienced. This is an important point to which I shall return below.

An important issue in relation to the stoic response is the extent to which the organization in which one works encourages or discourages it. The key concept here is 'organizational culture', the shared values and practices that character-ize an organization (Thompson et al., 1996). If the atmosphere in which we work is a 'stoic' one, then the expression of feelings may prove difficult. If, however, the atmosphere is a positive one that accepts and acknowledges the emotional demands of people work, then the expression of feelings will be much easier, and may even be positively valued.

Each of us can play a positive role in creating or maintaining an 'ethos of permission', a work environment that permits or even encourages expression and discussion of feelings. We can do this by:

- Not being afraid to express our own feelings;
- Not disapproving of other people expressing or discussing their feelings;
- Recognizing when someone is distressed and offering support; and
- Including the emotional dimension in discussions of work.

An ethos of permission can be very supportive, whereas an ethos of sto-icism can produce an oppressive atmosphere that can be experienced as stress-ful. This is particularly important for people workers due to the tendency to regard such workers as 'special people' who are good copers and resilient to life's pressures with little need for support.

A concept closely linked to stress, and very relevant in this context, is that of burnout. This refers to a condition in which the worker becomes numb to the emotional aspects of his or her work, and practises in a routine, unfeeling way. This tends to arise as a response to prolonged exposure to the stresses associated with a job in which the emotional demands are high.

Burnout represents a highly problematic situation in a number of ways, including the following:

- *For the worker* Burnout minimizes or destroys job satisfaction and can, in extreme cases, lead to mental health problems such as depression.
- *For service users* Effectiveness is reduced by burnout and many serv-ice users will recognize that there is little or no sense of commitment on the part of the worker.

- *For colleagues*   A person experiencing burnout can be quite a damper for colleagues, undermining positive attitudes and team spirit. This can have a detrimental effect on a whole group of staff.
- *For the organization*   A burnt out worker can destroy an organization's reputation for high-quality work through poor quality, insensitive practice.

The key issue with regard to burnout is that, if our own emotional needs are not met, then we shall be ill-equipped to deal with the feelings of others in a responsive and constructive way. It is therefore vitally important to ensure that we pay heed to our own emotional needs in order to minimize the risk of falling victim of burnout.

The concept of 'counter-transference' is also relevant to the question of dealing with our own feelings 'Transference' refers to the process whereby the service user imports feelings about a previous relationship into his or her relationship with the worker. 'Counter-transference' is where this operates in reverse. That is, it describes a process whereby a previous relationship influences the worker's attitude and response to the service user.

This usually happens because there is something about the service user that reminds the worker of someone who is well known to him or her. For example, if the service user looks or acts like a person the worker dislikes, then the worker may have to guard against transferring the negative feelings on to the service user. Similarly, if the service user reminds the worker of positive associations, then he or she may well have to guard against being uncritically positive. Counter-transference can therefore lead us into adopting an unbalanced attitude towards particular service users. In this respect, we need to be very conscious of our feelings towards the people we work with in order to ensure that our practice is not coloured by prejudices caused by counter-transference.

One principle that can help us to guard against such difficulties is that of 'unconditional positive regard'. As noted earlier, this is an idea to be found in the work of Carl Rogers (1961) which is used to describe an attitude of mind that ensures that we are positive towards the people we work with, regardless of our personal feelings towards them. That is, good practice is premised on doing our best for all service users, not only the ones that we like.

This is particularly important in certain types of people work. For example, in working with perpetrators of child abuse, what they have done may fill us with revulsion. However, if we allow this to colour the extent to which we help them deal with their problems, we are, in effect, reducing our own effectiveness. In this way, a failure to adopt unconditional positive regard is likely to result in less effective child protection practice. Unconditional positive regard is therefore not only a moral ideal, but also a fundamental principle of good practice.

This does not mean that we have to like everyone we work with, or that we are 'not allowed' to have negative feelings, but it does mean that we need to be as effective as possible with all the people we work with, regardless of our feelings towards them or what they may have done. Difficult though it may be to be positive towards people we do not like, good practice requires us to overcome these difficulties.

Conclusion

The feelings dimension of people work is perhaps one of the most difficult aspects to deal with. This is, as we have seen, partly because the feelings of others can be so intense and powerful, and partly because our own feelings can be intertwined with our practice in complex and subtle ways. Consequently, it is not surprising that many workers seek to ignore or minimize the role of feelings in people work.

However, the dangers associated with the failure to grasp the nettle of feelings should, by now, be quite clear. If we try to turn our back on the emotional issues involved in people work, we not only reduce our chances of being effective, we also run the risk of doing more harm than good, to ourselves and to the people we are trying to help.

References

Pottage, D. and Evans, M. (1992) *Workbased Stress: Prescription is Not the Cure*, London, NISW.

Rogers, C. (1961) *On Becoming a Person*, London, Constable.

Thompson, N. (1991) *Crisis Intervention Revisited*, Birmingham, Pepar.

Thompson, N., Stradling, S., Murphy, M. and O'Neill, P. (1996) 'Stress and Organizational Culture', *British Journal of Social Work*, 26(5).

11

Working with groups

Malcolm Payne

Starting points

Working with groups as educators is a complex task. It demands of us that we bring together in our practice three areas of experience, skill and knowledge: understanding groups; working to promote learning; and project management.

First, we need to understand about groups themselves and how they work. We need to recognise and understand patterns which are common to groups in general (theory) and to transfer our understanding to working with particular groups (practice). Choosing to work with a group (rather than with individuals) involves a number of decisions; choosing how to work with a particular group involves yet more. Practice also involves me – the practitioner. So I need to understand how I work with and behave in groups, so that I can understand how I am working with this particular group. For however much we know about groups, we are likely to be faced at some time with something new in every group with whom we work. And at that point, we need to be able to choose how to move on, based upon some clear principles about who we are as workers.

Next, there is the question of learning. In group settings we have the chance to enable people to learn from one another and from the task or activity in

This is a revised version of the original text which appeared as Chapter 15 in *Principles & Practice of Informal Education* edited by Linda Deer Richardson and Mary Wolfe. First published in 2001 by RoutledgeFalmer.

which the group is engaged. In order to do this we need to know how to use the group setting to promote learning. Education is a conscious process: it implies that the educator, acting with intent, has some purpose in mind. Purpose is closely connected with values – what we believe in. In groups, people are 'acting out' their beliefs and values in how they treat one another and how they express themselves. Every group is a micro-version of our world. It can be a more or less democratic place, a more or less fair place, a more or less creative, satisfying place for those who are part of it. It may confirm 'who they are' in helpful or unhelpful ways, or it may offer opportunities for change. How we work with groups also reflects our own values as educators – the way we see the world and how we wish it to be.

Finally, educators pursue different activities and projects when working with groups which demand a wide range of skills and knowledge to do with defining goals and managing tasks. These management skills need to be integrated with educational purposes and values, and with group processes.

Projects are usually time-limited: they have a beginning, a middle and an end. They may be short-term, lasting only a few hours or days, or be sustained over weeks or months. Taking on a project means that we have chosen to use our resources in a particular way. It implies that a decision has been made to try to meet certain educational goals by, for example:

- running a residential;
- offering a training course;
- helping people to mount a campaign;
- forming a new community group;
- working with a group of excluded students; or
- raising awareness about local environmental concerns.

These are just examples; you can probably think of many other aims which might lead you to decide to work with groups on a project. The list is endless, reflecting the very wide variety of contexts, agencies and tasks within informal education. Often, a project arises from everyday contact – from 'being around' people in the places where we work (Jeffs and Smith, 1996: 67). Listening to their concerns and ideas may lead to the decision to develop a project.

To sum up, then, three broad questions form the basis for this chapter:

- What do we need to know about groups and working with them?
- What do we need to know about learning in groups?
- How can we design and manage projects with groups so that their members can achieve and learn?

Case study 1: The dance group

The idea to form a dance group had emerged from two or three of a larger group of teenage friends in a conversation about being bored, not having anything to do. For a while, it had just been a 'bright idea' but no more than that. They were unsure about what they could achieve. They met often as a group and there was a shared interest in dance – but could they really become a dance group? Could they perform in front of others?

There would be a lot to think about if they were to become a dance group. No longer could they just turn up at the youth centre and chat. They would need to get organised. Everyone needed to play a part – it could not be left to chance. Decisions needed to be taken – how often they would practise, what music they would dance to, who would take the leading roles and who would be less prominent. And, when they reached a crisis point – and groups often do – where some key members threatened to leave, they had to find a way to talk about what was going wrong and how they would begin to mend some of the relationships which had become damaged. This meant going back over the group's life: did they all want to be there, or was the goal less important to some than others? Some members felt left out – that their views were not being heard. They began to resent the more vocal members who, in turn, felt that the quieter ones were not fully committed.

What was to be done? In the simplest terms, the group needed to learn how to *sustain* itself. That meant giving themselves a regular opportunity to talk about what was going on in the group – their relationships, how they were communicating, how decisions were being made – so that members could learn and practise all of the skills that are required for group life. Before, they had simply focused upon the *task*: putting on a dance performance. Now, they had learned that the *process* – how that task was tackled – was just as important if they were to succeed. The *primary goal* for the group was to dance and to put on a performance. But in order to achieve this, the group had taken on a secondary goal: group *maintenance*.

Working with groups

In many ways human nature is co-operative. We are more like ants and wolves than like cats. We readily join groups and form attachments, and receive powerful biological and emotional rewards for doing so.

(Argyle, 1991: 247)

Case Study 1 illustrates some familiar features of group life that we are likely to encounter when we work with formal groups. To begin with, however, we need to understand what we mean by a group.

Whenever three or more people come together we can call them a group. Three people standing at the coffee bar together, having a chance conversation as they wait to be served, constitute a group in this simple sense of the word.

But to work with groups we need a better definition than that. For the purposes of this chapter we will ignore these sorts of groups – except perhaps to say that such informal groups may be the start of something more. That conversation might lead to an idea, to them meeting again, to the group beginning to have some sort of life of its own, as we saw in Case Study 1. In the day-to-day work of many informal educators, such beginnings can be very important – but they are not our primary focus in this chapter.

Defining these chance groupings as *informal* groups begins to throw some light onto what we mean when we speak about *formal* groups. By formal we do not mean that the group behaves in formal (or conventional) ways, but that the group begins to take on a *form* of its own: its own distinctive shape or identity. In a formal group, we might, for example, know who are its members (and therefore, who are not). And we might begin to see some particular patterns of behaviour – whether we feel these are good or bad. So, relationships in the group might be seen as close, supportive or co-operative; or they may be felt to be distant or competitive. Each of these features of a group's behaviour will affect what the group can achieve. The pattern within a particular group is unique to that group, but the study of human behaviour in groups suggests that most groups exhibit similar patterns.

Hare, writing in 1962, attempted to define the five features of groups which are likely to interest us as informal educators:

> The members of the group are *in interaction with* one another. They share a common *goal* and set of *norms* which give direction and limits to their activity. They also develop a set of *roles* and a network *of interpersonal attraction* which serve to differentiate them from other groups.
>
> (Hare, 1962: 5; my italics)

Taken together, these five features of a group represent its unique culture and identity and serve to distinguish it from other groups. They also suggest questions which we can use to think about the group:

- *Interaction:* how are people communicating in this group? What patterns can be seen for different group members? Is there more interaction between some than others? Are some members silent or marginalised?
- *Goal:* what is the group trying to achieve? Are all members equally interested? Does motivation change at times? Are some more confident than others? Is everyone satisfied with the group's progress? What does the group need to learn and do in order to achieve its goals?
- *Norms:* what norms and values have the group adopted, for example about how decisions are made, or who is listened to? How do those affect its members? Are they helping the group to achieve its goals? Might it wish to adopt different norms?

- *Roles:* what roles exist in the group? Are some members more powerful than others? How aware are members of their own and others' roles? Are they happy with them or do some want them to change?
- *Relationships:* what sorts of relationships are there? What patterns, e.g. of dominance, dependence, friendship or hostility (Argyle, 1972) can be seen? Are some members popular while others appear less valued? Are relationships helping or hindering the group?

For educators, formal groups present a range of opportunities for members' learning: about themselves; about themselves in relation to others; and about whatever it is the group is engaged in. This familiar triangle of *individual, group* and *task* can be said to define a fertile arena for learning, if an environment is created to enable that learning to take place.

In Case Study 1, the group is attempting to make a difficult transition: from simply being a group of friends (what is sometimes known as a natural group) to becoming something more formal. The group wants to take on a purpose or goal (the task). This will make all sorts of demands upon its members which did not exist before. Some examples of the challenges they face are offered in the case study: getting organised; paying attention to who is to do what; giving themselves time to reflect.

Learning in groups

We never educate directly, but indirectly by means of the environment. Whether we permit chance environments to do the work, or whether we design environments for the purpose, makes a great deal of difference.

(Dewey, 1916: 16)

As informal educators we are concerned with enabling people to learn. Research suggests that we learn a lot from being with others in groups. For some, working with groups is a – or even *the* – primary means of encouraging learning, because those with whom we work are able to learn from and with one another, rather than simply from us as the worker. Learning in groups can therefore promote what Mullender and Ward (1991: 11) call 'self-empowerment' – people's ability to make choices for themselves. However, we as educators are still important to this process. The choices we make about how to work with a group will make a difference to what is learned. These decisions represent our attempt to 'design the environment' as Dewey suggested – where the group itself is a central feature of that environment.

Promoting learning by working with groups rather than simply with individuals is probably as old as education itself. The history of what has come to be known in the helping professions as 'group work' is much more recent. Much of the literature which focuses upon such work – and there is a great deal – has been developed in the field of social work since the 1920s. Practitioners have tried, through careful study and reflection about its purposes and methods, to identify how group work can be used, and to what effect, in order to establish this form of work with people as a discipline.

Another origin of this sort of work comes from educational work with groups which 'developed from the need for mutual aid and support' (Kunstler, 1955: 40). This was a way of working which challenged traditional ideas about the 'giver' and 'receiver' of help, and instead recognised people's abilities to support one another and to achieve social change. These philosophical ideas remain important. Original forms of this work were found in informal education settings: self-help groups, playgrounds, summer camps, settlements and neighbourhood centres.

Informal education work with and through groups is not a universal method, however, to be applied in all circumstances. Its use in a disciplined way implies that we must decide when and how to apply the range of methods generally referred to as group work. A decision to pursue particular educational goals by such methods should mean that we think that they will be effective – that they will achieve certain purposes and fit with the ethics of our practice.

Why should educators work with and through groups?

There have been a number of attempts to identify the benefits of working with and through groups (see for example Brown, 1992: 12–27).

- Being part of a group is a normal and everyday experience for most people. Group experience matters for virtually everyone and therefore provides a potentially fertile learning environment.
- Being part of a group makes a number of demands upon people: negotiating what will or will not be done; performing tasks; taking on roles and responding to those of others; sharing thoughts and feelings. Each of these features of group life contains the potential for personal development and growth, if the group environment is conducive to it.
- Many people with whom we work experience a sense of isolation. This may arise from their home situation (living alone, bringing up small children, a family where they are the main carer, for example) or from

other aspects of their life – for instance if they are disabled, suffer from illness, or face discrimination. Being with others, especially if they share some of the same experiences, can reduce people's feelings of being alone in their world. New friendships and support networks can be built.

- People often want to create change for themselves – to find new ways to react or behave, to understand themselves better, or to learn new skills. Being part of a group with others who also wish to change can support learning.

- People seeking to bring about social and political change, particularly those facing oppression, have long seen the potential for groups to raise consciousness among members and confront oppressive social structures. Feminist groups, for example, have an important place in the history of modern social change (see Butler and Wintram, 1991).

- Doing things – whether taking up a leisure activity, pursuing some local political issue, or building a new community group – frequently depends on finding others who share a similar passion or interest. From an early age we learn that there are many things that can be achieved only by co-operating with others.

These ways in which group experience offers opportunities for learning also hint at the wide range of group tasks and projects which educators might pursue. If we were to attempt to mention them all, a very long list would result. Drawing upon Jeffs and Smith (1996) we can see, however, that what they all have in common is that the worker is using the medium of association (people being with others) to enable people to gain and provide mutual aid, a sense of belonging, identity and self-esteem; and to foster learning, change and development. As educators, we must attend to all of the features of groups which might serve to promote these ends. Conversely, since being in a group with others can also confirm feelings of isolation, reinforce oppressive structures or behaviour or damage self-esteem, we must also establish ways of working which avoid – or at least limit – these risks.

Contemporary group work practice, then, drawing upon the history of informal education and social work, attempts to establish a systematic *methodology* to guide our work with and through groups in order to promote learning and growth.

The educator's role in the group

People take on roles when they belong to or work with a group. It is helpful to think about two types: *functional* and *behavioural* roles. As educators, both aspects of our role are important. There is no one role which can always be applied in whatever group we are working; we need to be flexible and adaptable. In one group, we may need to be much more assertive than in another. Or we may need to be prepared to take the lead until the group's confidence has grown. These should, ideally, be conscious decisions. We must be aware of and be able to choose the roles we perform, based upon our judgements about what is appropriate, ethical and effective. What is constant is the functional role we perform as an educator. In order to perform this, we must adjust the ways we behave and the tasks we take on.

As workers we often hold a lot of authority, power and influence – based upon our knowledge and expertise, our position in the community, our age, gender, or race, or our ability to offer resources to the groups with whom we work. How we exercise such influence in groups is a key aspect of professional practice and goes to the heart of questions about learning and democracy. Gibson and Clarke (1995: 64), discussing the role of youth workers in groups, identify three styles of working:

- *authoritarian:* the worker makes the decisions and presents or sells them to the group;
- *consultative:* the worker offers tentative decisions, invites discussion but reserves the right to decide;
- *enabling*: the worker sets boundaries, shares information, initiates discussion and supports decision making by the group.

It is clear that it is the third style, that of the enabling worker, which is likely to be most empowering to those with whom we work. It most closely accords with the democratic ideals which have shaped group work practice and informal education, because it encourages participation by group members and a climate of support and co-operation. It also reminds us that, when we are able to, we will want to encourage groups to adopt a similar style of decision-making themselves. But not all groups will be ready or able to work in participative or co-operative ways. As Gibson and Clarke point out (1995: 47), good practice in informal education will sometimes mean that we have to exercise our power, to set the boundaries, to persuade or cajole. For example, if we perceive that a group might come to harm, or harm others if we allow it to continue to do something, we need to be prepared to step in, perhaps even to become authoritarian. We cannot avoid such responsibilities at times, although we would want the group to understand why we had to act in such a way.

Davies reminds us that workers may adopt non-directive techniques, trying to appear as self-effacing and uninfluential as possible, but can never succeed in eliminating their own impact. They will see themselves, and the group will see them, as 'the worker' (Davies, 1975: 107). The role itself inevitably brings with it some power and authority, whatever style of working is adopted.

In our first case study, young people were trying to develop a dance group. Below, the same case study is revisited in order to examine the role of the worker.

Case study 1: Revisited

The youth worker is employed by a local authority to develop work under Local Agenda 21. She sees that there might be an opportunity to support the group to achieve what they want and, at the same time, by working with them, to promote some of Agenda 21's objectives concerned with young people's involvement in their community. Her intentions as a worker, the aims of her agency and the young people's interests are, she judges, congruous. Offering the group her support involves exploring with the group what she is able to offer and what might be their needs and expectations. She is not an expert in dance, but she feels that dance provides a useful vehicle for informal education.

The worker begins by talking with the group about their intentions: what they want to achieve. They want to form a dance group; they want to perform in front of others. She asks why, thinking through with them what the project will involve. She explores some of the possible benefits: for example, that it might show young people in a positive light in the community, as well as lots of opportunities for learning new skills. Worker and group consider what will be needed if they are to be successful: the time that will be required, a place to practise, things to be organised.

The worker needs to take care at this point. It is *their* idea and she must not 'take it over'. She must support, but not lead. She must not push the pace faster than the group wishes to go, but at the same time, she wishes to encourage. She can offer help, but she must do so in ways which they will find acceptable, and which will allow them to retain control.

We need to ask ourselves some sharp questions about our role, and the power and influence we bring to our work. Notice how, in Case Study 1 Revisited, the worker's role is partly defined by the fact that she is employed to pursue the objectives of Local Agenda 21 for young people. That means that she is concerned with such things as citizenship, participation and democracy, and environmental issues. At the same time, she is working from informal education principles. This is a common enough scenario: the agency, job title or funding source provides the focus for the work; our profession (as youth workers or community educators) offers the framework of principles, values and methods. Similar situations may also occur in health education, 'community safety' or school exclusion projects.

It is not always easy to bring these two sets of expectations together. For example, we may be expected to work more quickly than we judge that a particular group is capable of, or we might be expected to take some decisions on behalf of the group which we would prefer the group to take.

It is clear that, as informal educators, our intentions to promote learning are never value-free. We believe certain human values to be important, and this gives rise to an agenda for the learning we want to promote. Indeed, some would argue that the informal education task *is* the promotion of learning about values (Young, 1999: 3). For youth workers, Young argues, this gives rise to a learning agenda which is intended to give young people opportunities to examine their own values, think about the principles on which they are based, and make informed decisions and choices.

The choices we make will strongly influence the group learning environment: what and how group members learn, and our relationship with them. Smith refers to this as a choice we make about our *disposition* (1994: 77): how we conceptualise and approach our task as educators. Will we choose to be an expert or teacher, ready to pass on our knowledge and expertise? Or a kind of 'group parent' who will set the boundaries and rules of behaviour? Or perhaps a manager: the person who ensures that the task gets accomplished effectively? The basic disposition we choose will be recognised by those with whom we work. And they are likely to react to us by adopting a reciprocal role, as pupil, child or subordinate.

Group work texts and manuals are not short on lists of roles which workers and members take in groups (see , for example, Harris, 1994). Perhaps the usefulness of these suggested roles lies in what they say about the practitioner's overall task – to work in such ways as to support the group to achieve the objectives of the project in which it is engaged. As with the choice of 'dispositions', this involves the worker making sensitive decisions about what is needed at a particular time. None of these roles is owned only by the worker however: any group member may take any of them on. Indeed, Davies (1975: 106) suggests that interventions by the worker are only justified when they are unlikely to be made by another group member. And the more the worker says and does, the fewer openings there are for others to do what is meaningful for them.

[…]

Case study 2: The anger management project

A youth work agency wishes to offer young people an opportunity to learn how to manage their anger better. Put simply, the experimental project is based upon the idea that, for some young people, becoming angry and aggressive leads to confrontations – at school with other students and with teachers, and outside school with peers, parents and authority figures. The agency's workers have done some analysis of this issue and want to pilot a project to tackle the problem. They work closely with schools, education welfare, youth justice and social services in order to develop the proposed scheme. Subsequently, they will undertake a careful evaluation of the pilot scheme to judge its effectiveness.

Six young men between thirteen and sixteen are invited to participate in the project, which will consist of an intensive course during school time. All are in contact with welfare agencies, where concern about their anger has been expressed by the young people themselves as well as those working with them. The group project is intended to supplement individual educational work being undertaken with each of the participants by the agencies involved.

Clear aims and objectives are set for the course by the agencies. A conversation is held with each of the young men before the course begins, so that they are fully informed of what it is about and able to decide for themselves whether to attend. The programme reflects what could be achieved by working with a group rather than with individual work. For example, participants are asked to work in two groups and helped to devise a script to be performed by the other group, based on an example of the sort of situation in which they become angry, and how they had dealt with this. The performance was followed by discussion of what had happened and whether there were alternative actions open to the characters.

[…]

Designing and managing projects for learning

In this section we will consider how we set about devising projects in ways which fulfil their potential for learning. The main focus is on two aspects: deciding whether and how to pursue a project, and agreeing project objectives. The section ends with a brief consideration of project management.

As informal educators, we are concerned with what Brookfield (1986: 233) refers to as mutuality: the idea that we are engaged with learners in collaborative activity. Young (1999: 69) uses a similar idea, that the youth work relationship is based upon reciprocity. This leads to two important observations. First, the more we take the lead role as educators in defining needs and designing learning, the less space we leave for those with whom we work to do it for themselves. Second, that in designing learning, the more closely we specify objectives, content and methods, the less emphasis is likely to be given to all of the learning which might arise informally and in response to people's own identified needs and reflection.

Why a project?

When as educators we become involved with people in designing, supporting or running group projects, we will already have made a number of decisions about how we will work. As suggested at the beginning of the chapter, projects are by definition time-limited. Doing a project suggests that the intentions we started out with will be met by the time it is complete. This might suggest that project work is straightforward and predictable. In my experience, however, projects rarely follow a purely logical and text-book process. In theory, the steps might look something like this:

1) Identify a need and examine whether or how this need can or should be met.
2) Decide whether meeting the need identified fits the purposes of your agency.
3) Decide whether meeting this need is a priority when compared with other work.
4) Draw up a draft project plan including the objectives to be met, the time-scale and, ideally, the success criteria.
5) Identify the resources which will be required to implement the plan.
6) Gain agreement for the project plan from those who will be involved or affected.
7) Carry out the planned project.
8) Evaluate the process and its effects and decide what (if anything) to do next.

The trouble is that what appears as a relatively straightforward process is much more complex when applied to real life. We cannot always see clearly what a 'need' is, and others may have a different view. Agency purposes are not always so clearly defined that, when a new situation arises, we can make a decision about whether we should pursue a course of action. Priorities change: what seemed important yesterday may be overtaken by something more urgent. People may become enthusiastic and we will want to avoid disappointing them; or they may lose interest.

Because of the ways in which we work, projects will come about in a variety of ways, for example:

- someone has a 'bright idea' about which they are enthusiastic and we latch on to their idea;
- in conversation with those with whom we work, we begin to see a way in which a project might create an opportunity or meet a particular need;

- in developing a programme for our centre or club, we try out some ideas for a project which we hope will catch members' imagination;
- a source of money becomes available and we try to think about a useful way of using it;
- we attempt to extend the work of our agency by undertaking some research and developing a project;
- we work with other agencies who have identified an issue or problem they wish to tackle.

Doing projects has to be a mixture of science and art: we must be both rational and creative, logical and reflective, analytical yet opportunistic, prepared to lead and able to 'go with the flow'. So we need some adaptable tools and techniques for thinking our way through the complexities. Perhaps we should return to the two projects we considered earlier in order to illustrate the process.

Case Study 1 involves a group of young people following a dance project that they have thought up themselves. The youth worker responds to the idea. What then, is the 'need' to which she is responding? […].

A number of points arise here that we can apply to other projects. First, our practice is guided by the way in which we, and our agencies, view our purpose. In this case, as we saw earlier (Case Study 1 Revisited), the worker's intentions arise partly from policy (Local Agenda 21 and its intentions for democracy and participation), and partly from her own professional knowledge, skills and values.

Second, we have to think ahead in order to see what will be needed for the project to work: the resources (skills, money, time, equipment); the motivation of those who will be involved. Can we do it? Will their interest be sustained? Have we helped them to think about the consequences?

Third, we need to be clear about the role we will take in the project. What will the group need from us if the project is to succeed? What is our judgement about the group's readiness – its internal resources of skills, knowledge and ideas, its ability to maintain itself? How can our involvement enable the group's resources to grow?

These initial questions guide our decision to develop (or support) a project:

- What is the need as we perceive it?
- What purposes and policies will be fulfilled?
- What are the intended benefits, including learning?
- What opportunities are available (or can be developed)?

- What resources will be required (and can be obtained)?
- What will be my (and my agency's) role, and who needs to agree?

Case Study 2 is an interesting example. Here, the youth agency concerned did not simply have to ask itself critical questions about the need identified, the intended benefits and impact, but also to think hard about the approach it would adopt and the resources required. This led the agency to pilot the programme in one or two schools before proceeding. From its evaluation, it learned that its first idea was not sufficiently developed: if it was to make a difference to young people's lives, the programme needed to be longer and there had to be opportunities built in for the young people to be supported after the initial course.

The agency also needed to ask questions about its role: what does a youth work agency bring to this issue which means that it is best placed to intervene? Its decision to go ahead was based on the conviction that it could promote learning for these young men that might not otherwise be available to them. This raised questions about how schools would use the programme: for example, did the young people come to the programme under pressure from teachers? This had implications for how the project was designed, as well as raising fundamental questions about whether it should be offered at all.

We need to think critically about the nature of need: what are its causes, whose perceptions are at work? And if we have doubts about a project but still wish to proceed, can we do so in a way that allows us to adjust plans or change tack once we know more? For example, we might agree that there will be a review point after a few weeks, or that we will only commit limited resources in the first instance. The bigger the project, the more important it is to get things right. This is one aspect of what is often referred to as 'cost–benefit analysis'.

Planning the project and setting objectives

Let us assume that you have now made a decision to go ahead with your project. This means that you have:

- a clear analysis of a need;
- a clear purpose and aim;
- an idea for pursuing the project.

How good our idea is will be central to the success of our project. This is the creative side of our work. It doesn't matter how careful is our analysis of need, or how clear our aim. If people are not attracted to the idea, if it does not win their enthusiasm, it is unlikely to work. Sometimes, we will be able to hitch our plans to their enthusiasm (as in Case Study 1); at other times, we might need to stimulate them to come up with a good idea, or enthuse them with our own. Whichever way we do it, though, a 'trigger' for the project will be needed.

At the same time, we have to recognise that the idea is not in itself the purpose, only the *medium* through which the need identified is to be met, and the aim to be fulfilled. It is the *how*, not the *what* or *why* of our plan.

Before we go much further, we will want to try out our idea to see whether it is likely to get support: from the people we are working with, from our colleagues, and perhaps others too. We will want to encourage as much talking about the idea as we can. There is little point in devising a detailed project plan if the idea turns out to be a dud, so a little 'market-testing' may save a lot of wasted time and energy. In testing the idea, it will usually get better as others' ideas begin to be included.

By now we can assume that there is a viable project idea: we believe it will work. So we are ready to undertake some detailed planning. That will mean devising the objectives which the project will meet: the specific things the project will achieve. Who is going to do this and how will it be done? These are important questions because they demand that we think both about the outcome of our work (in this case, the outcomes of the project), as well as the process by which it will be achieved. We can think back to Case Study 2 in order to illustrate this issue. The youth work agency involved devised the anger management programme with other agencies concerned with young people's welfare. A project group drawn from the agencies devised the objectives.

In this sort of project, there is a strong emphasis upon curriculum. The objectives define what participants will learn – and will reflect perceptions and values held by the agencies and their (adult) workers about young people. In this case, young people themselves are not closely involved in devising the project and setting its objectives. They may have been involved at an earlier stage, but the project is essentially adult-led (i.e. educator-led). This further illustrates my earlier point: the central idea of the project is only the means by which purposes are fulfilled. There may be many other ways that the same overall aim of helping young people to manage their anger could have been tackled, for example through a peer-led project. The agency's view is that the approach it has agreed is, in some way, the most likely to achieve its purpose.

In devising project objectives we are enacting the principles and values by which we work. In Case Study 2, young people are involved by ensuring that they have a clear idea about what the programme will offer, and by trying to ensure that their participation is voluntary. A contract or agreement with each young person is made before the programme begins. Once they are involved, the programme then gives the young people some control over its content: a broad and agreed framework is set for the learning, then participants choose its focus so that it best meets their particular needs. Dialogue and negotiation are built in to what are broadly pre-defined parameters.

Contrast this with Case Study 1. There, the worker might help the group to identify the objectives to be met. Some may be identified only once the project is under way, for example when the group realises that in order to maintain itself, members need to think more about group processes. It is a much more fluid and organic project. Learning opportunities arise from the task (developing a dance group and putting on a performance), rather than learning itself providing its basis. In Case Study 1 the worker is asking: how can I enable learning to arise from the task? In Case Study 2 the workers are asking: what tasks can we devise which will enable learning to take place?

From this discussion it should be clear by now that in pursuing projects we are likely to use a range of educational interventions, and that these will be reflected in any project plan we devise. There may be an educator-led or learner-led emphasis, but we will wish to pursue approaches which offer as much opportunity for learner autonomy as possible, consistent with our intentions and purposes. This has implications for the approach we take to planning: the extent to which we can engage people in the devising of the project, or setting the objectives.

Each of the six questions we used in creating a plan can be approached so that group members take primary responsibility for following them through. Or the educator may do the planning, with learner influence designed to occur at a later stage. So, in planning the project we can ask:

Who will:

1) identify need and examine whether or how this can or should be met?
2) decide whether meeting the need identified fits the purposes of the agency?
3) decide whether meeting this need is a priority when compared with other work?
4) draw up a draft project plan including the objectives to be met, the time-scale and the success criteria?
5) identify and obtain the resources which will be required to implement the plan?
6) gain agreement for the project plan?

And *how* will we assist them?

Asking these questions at the planning stage says much about whose project this is and the educative role we are adopting.

Managing the project

Much of this section of the chapter has been about thinking through purpose, role and task: what we are attempting to do, and how we will approach it. Managing the project is about following these through, paying attention at each stage to the same questions. Just as in project planning, we are attempting to build mutuality – shared ownership – into the process, so we will wish to do this in project management.

Of course we want to ensure that projects are completed satisfactorily, but not at the expense of people's learning, growth and autonomy. We will want to adopt a role which reflects what we are trying to achieve, including learning about core values of virtue, equality and fairness, caring for others, identity and self-esteem. That means striking a careful balance between completing the project task and paying attention to questions of process and learning: *how* the task will be completed. We are reminded of the triangle mentioned earlier (p. 126) – the balance between maintaining the *task*, the *group* and the *individual*. An enabling role does not mean paying less attention to task completion, but thinking through how it can be achieved in ways which build confidence and maximise learning for those involved. This is the balance between what Herschel Prins referred to as the *enabling* and *ensuring* functions (in Marken and Payne, 1987: 37), and there are potential conflicts between them.

The chart opposite summarises this balance.

The left side of Table 11.1 shows a simple management process. Although it appears as a series of linear steps, in reality we may need to revisit earlier steps as the project proceeds. So for example, questions raised about resources may mean going back to adjust the objectives. Or if we discover that problems are arising for some members of the group, we may need to stop one part of the task while we pay attention to process.

Each of the steps on the left is necessary for a project to be managed successfully. Depending upon its nature, time-scale and complexity, some may be more important than others, but all will need to be present in one form or another, even in simple projects. Think of a relatively straightforward project such as running a workshop on 'young women and the media'. You might expect it to take quite a bit of *planning*, but there may be few opportunities to *monitor and adjust*. Nonetheless, when participants begin to show signs of boredom, or an unanticipated issue emerges, the project managers will need to make a quick decision about how to respond. In more long-term projects, monitoring and adjusting will take place regularly and may result in revising plans and possibly even rethinking the purpose.

We must not assume, however, that for management to take place, we (informal educators) must do all, or indeed any, of the managing. Again, it is

Table 11.1 The balance between enabling and ensuring

Ensuring function	Enabling function: think about
Clarify purpose	Whose need? How is it to be defined, and by whom?
	What benefits? Whose perceptions will inform our intentions?
	How will the project fulfil the purpose?
	How does the project purpose fit with informal education principles?
	What values are reflected?
	Who needs to own the project? How can I act to enable their ownership?
	Have I negotiated a clear role for myself/my agency? How will my role support the group's learning?
	How will policies, e.g. equality, confidentiality, health and safety, be enacted?
Set objectives	What objectives? Who will set them and how? Who else needs to be involved, and how?
	Do they reflect the right balance between task and learning-related objectives?
	Are they achievable? By when? Can we develop a useful learning framework or curriculum?
Identify resources	What resources will be needed? What resources are available?
	What resources does the group have? How can these be enhanced, e.g. through supporting group learning?
	How can I help the group to use its own resources? How can I help it to identify what further resources will be required?
	What do they need from me?
Plan	What steps are required in order to complete the project? How can I support the group to do its own planning?
	Does the group make clear, shared decisions?
	What decisions might I need to reserve for myself? Can these be negotiated?
	How does the plan allow for learning to take place?
Organise and develop	What skills in organising does the group have?
	Are the group's own roles clear and helpful?
	Are relationships in the group helping it to achieve?
	In what ways are power issues being dealt with?
	Is the group communicating well?
	How best can I support them?
Monitor and adjust	How will the group measure its progress and make decisions about next steps?
	Is the group on track?
	Is the group creating space for itself to reflect?
	Can mistakes, issues and problems be aired?
	In what ways can I assist?
Evaluate	How will the group know what it has achieved?
	Is there a clear end-point in sight?
	How can I assist the group to gain a sense of achievement? How can individual and group learning be recognised and acknowledged?
	What next? How can I help them to build on their achievements and to move on?
	What next for me and my agency? What have we learned? What impact on the need? What should we do as a result?

a question of role: what responsibility are we to take for the project's success? Can we fulfil the ensuring function without taking control and undermining the core principles and purposes of informal education? How best can we perform our educational role?

The right side of the chart suggests some of the questions we might ask of ourselves in planning and running a project. The key idea is simply this: ensuring (a management function) does not have to mean *doing*. I can choose to ensure by *enabling* instead of controlling. In doing so I do not relinquish my responsibility to try to make things happen successfully, but choose a role for myself which gives the group as much control over its own destiny as I can. I support group members' growth and development most by recognising that:

> People … learn social and political responsibility only by experiencing that responsibility … by actively participating.

> (Freire, 1974: 36)

When we work with people we become part of the complex web of roles within the group. The role we adopt as informal educator sits alongside and interacts with their roles. If the educator's management role is to be complementary, it must enable group members to assume responsibility for what happens, to take as much control as possible. We can then attend primarily to the opportunities for learning which the project presents: by encouraging group members to reflect upon and learn from and about themselves, other group members, and the task in which they are engaged. In that way we build in the mutuality and reciprocity that we seek.

References

Argyle, M. (1972) *Social Relationships.* Buckingham: Open University Press.

Argyle, M. (1991) *Cooperation. The Basis of Sociability.* London: Routledge.

Brookfield, S. (1986) *Understanding and Facilitating Adult Learning.* Buckingham: Open University Press.

Brown, A. (1992) *Groupwork,* 3rd edn. Aldershot: Ashgate Publishing Ltd.

Butler, S. and Wintram, C. (1991) *Feminist Groupwork.* London: Sage.

Davies, B. (1975) *The Use of Groups in Social Work Practice.* London: Routledge and Kegan Paul.

Dewey, J. (1916) *Democracy and Education.* New York: Macmillan.

Freire, P. (1974) *Education: The Practice of Freedom.* London: Writers and Readers Publishing Cooperative.

Gibson, A. and Clarke, G. (1995) *Project-Based Group Work Facilitator's Manual: Young People, Youth Workers and Projects.* London and Bristol, Pennsylvania: Jessica Kingsley Publishers.

Hare, A. P. (1962) *Handbook of Small Group Research*. New York: Free Press, quoted in Douglas, T. (1976) *Groupwork Practice*. London: Tavistock/Routledge.

Harris, V. (ed.) (1994) *Community Work Skills Manual*. Newcastle: Association of Community Workers.

Jeffs, T. and Smith, M. (1996) *Informal Education: Conversation, Democracy and Learning*. Derby: Education Now Publishing Co-operative Ltd.

Kunstler, P. (1955) *Social Group Work in Great Britain*. London: Faber and Faber.

Marken, M. and Payne, M. (eds) (1987) *Enabling and Ensuring*. Leicester: National Youth Bureau/Council for Education and Training in Youth and Community Work.

Mullender, A. and Ward, D. (1991) *Self-Directed Groupwork*. London: Whiting and Birch Ltd.

Payne, C. and Scott, T. (1985) *Developing Supervision of Teams in Field and Residential Social Work*. London: National Institute for Social Work.

Payne, M. and Merton, B. (2000) *Louder Than Words: Youth Work and Learning for Sustainable Development*. Leicester: Youth Work Press.

Smith, M. (1994) *Local Education: Community, Conversation, Praxis*. Buckingham: Open University Press.

Vernell, B. (1994) *Understanding and Using Groups*. London: Whiting and Birch Ltd.

Young, K. (1999) *The Art of Youth Work*. Lyme Regis: Russell House Publishing.

12

A social theory of learning

Etienne Wenger

Our institutions, to the extent that they address issues of learning explicitly, are largely based on the assumption that learning is an individual process, that it has a beginning and an end, that it is best separated from the rest of our activities, and that it is the result of teaching. Hence we arrange classrooms where students – free from the distractions of their participation in the outside world – can pay attention to a teacher or focus on exercises. We design computer-based training programs that walk students through individualized sessions covering reams of information and drill practice. To assess learning we use tests with which students struggle in one-on-one combat, where knowledge must be demonstrated out of context, and where collaborating is considered cheating. As a result, much of our institutionalized teaching and training is perceived by would-be learners as irrelevant, and most of us come out of this treatment feeling that learning is boring and arduous, and that we are not really cut out for it.

So, what if we adopted a different perspective, one that placed learning in the context of our lived experience of participation in the world? What if we assumed that learning is as much a part of our human nature as eating or sleeping, that it is both life-sustaining and inevitable, and that – given a chance – we are quite good at it? And what if, in addition, we assumed that learning is, in

This is a revised version of the original text which appeared as 3–17 in *Communities of Practice* by Etienne Wenger. First published in 1998 by Cambridge University Press.

its essence, a fundamentally social phenomenon, reflecting our own deeply social nature as human beings capable of knowing? What kind of understanding would such a perspective yield on how learning takes place and on what is required to support it? In this chapter, I will try to develop such a perspective.

A conceptual perspective: theory and practice

There are many different kinds of learning theory. Each emphasizes different aspects of learning, and each is therefore useful for different purposes. To some extent these differences in emphasis reflect a deliberate focus on a slice of the multidimensional problem of learning, and to some extent they reflect more fundamental differences in assumptions about the nature of knowledge, knowing, and knowers, and consequently about what matters in learning.

The kind of social theory of learning I propose is not a replacement for other theories of learning that address different aspects of the problem. But it does have its own set of assumptions and its own focus. Within this context, it does constitute a coherent level of analysis; it does yield a conceptual framework from which to derive a consistent set of general principles and recommendations for understanding and enabling learning.

My assumptions as to what matters about learning and as to the nature of knowledge, knowing, and knowers can be succinctly summarized as follows. I start with four premises.

1) We are social beings. Far from being trivially true, this fact is a central aspect of learning.
2) Knowledge is a matter of competence with respect to valued enterprises – such as singing in tune, discovering scientific facts, fixing machines, writing poetry, being convivial, growing up as a boy or a girl, and so forth.
3) Knowing is a matter of participating in the pursuit of such enterprises, that is, of active engagement in the world.
4) Meaning – our ability to experience the world and our engagement with it as meaningful – is ultimately what learning is to produce.

As a reflection of these assumptions, the primary focus of this theory is on learning as social participation. Participation here refers not just to local events of engagement in certain activities with certain people, but to a more encompassing process of being active participants in the *practices* of social

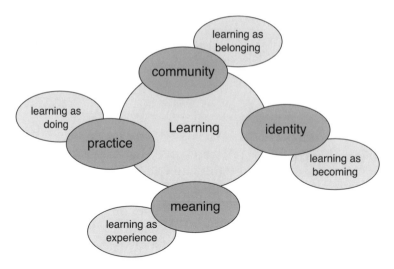

Figure 12.1 Components of a social theory of learning: an initial inventory

communities and constructing *identities* in relation to these communities. Participating in a playground clique or in a work team, for instance, is both a kind of action and a form of belonging. Such participation shapes not only what we do, but also who we are and how we interpret what we do.

A social theory of learning must therefore integrate the components necessary to characterize social participation as a process of learning and of knowing. These components, shown in Figure 12.1, include the following.

1) *Meaning:* a way of talking about our (changing) ability – individually and collectively – to experience our life and the world as meaningful.
2) *Practice:* a way of talking about the shared historical and social resources, frameworks, and perspectives that can sustain mutual engagement in action.
3) *Community:* a way of talking about the social configurations in which our enterprises are defined as worth pursuing and our participation is recognizable as competence.
4) *Identity:* a way of talking about how learning changes who we are and creates personal histories of becoming in the context of our communities.

Clearly, these elements are deeply interconnected and mutually defining. In fact, looking at Figure 12.1, you could switch any of the four peripheral components with learning, place it in the center as the primary focus, and the figure would still make sense.

Therefore, when I use the concept of 'community of practice' […], I really use it as a point of entry into a broader conceptual framework of which it is a constitutive element. The analytical power of the concept lies precisely in that it integrates the components of Figure 1 while referring to a familiar experience.

Communities of practice are everywhere

We all belong to communities of practice. At home, at work, at school, in our hobbies – we belong to several communities of practice at any given time. And the communities of practice to which we belong change over the course of our lives. In fact, communities of practice are everywhere.

Families struggle to establish an habitable way of life. They develop their own practices, routines, rituals, artifacts, symbols, conventions, stories, and histories. Family members hate each other and they love each other; they agree and they disagree. They do what it takes to keep going. Even when families fall apart, members create ways of dealing with each other. Surviving together is an important enterprise, whether surviving consists in the search for food and shelter or in the quest for a viable identity.

Workers organize their lives with their immediate colleagues and customers to get their jobs done. In doing so, they develop or preserve a sense of themselves they can live with, have some fun, and fulfill the requirements of their employers and clients. No matter what their official job description may be, they create a practice to do what needs to be done. Although workers may be contractually employed by a large institution, in day-to-day practice they work with – and, in a sense, for – a much smaller set of people and communities.

Students go to school and, as they come together to deal in their own fashion with the agenda of the imposing institution and the unsettling mysteries of youth, communities of practice sprout everywhere – in the classroom as well as on the playground, officially or in the cracks. And in spite of curriculum, discipline, and exhortation, the learning that is most personally transformative turns out to be the learning that involves membership in these communities of practice.

In garages, bands rehearse the same songs for yet another wedding gig. In attics, ham radio enthusiasts become part of worldwide clusters of communicators. In the back rooms of churches, recovering alcoholics go to their weekly meetings to find the courage to remain sober. In laboratories, scientists correspond with colleagues, near and far, in order to advance their inquiries. Across a worldwide web of computers, people congregate in virtual spaces and develop shared ways of pursuing their common interests. In offices, computer users count on each other to cope with the intricacies of obscure systems. In neighborhoods, youths gang together to configure their life on the street and their sense of themselves.

Communities of practice are an integral part of our daily lives. They are so informal and so pervasive that they rarely come into explicit focus, but for the same reasons they are also quite familiar. Although the term may be new, the experience is not. Most communities of practice do not have a name and do not issue membership cards. Yet, if we care to consider our own life from that perspective for a moment, we can all construct a fairly good picture of the communities of practice we belong to now, those we belonged to in the past, and those we would like to belong to in the future. We also have a fairly good idea of who belongs to our communities of practice and why, even though membership is rarely made explicit on a roster or a checklist of qualifying criteria. Furthermore, we can probably distinguish a few communities of practice in which we are core members from a larger number of communities in which we have a more peripheral kind of membership.

In all these ways, the concept of community of practice is not unfamiliar. By exploring it more systematically [...] I mean only to sharpen it, to make it more useful as a thinking tool. Toward this end, its familiarity will serve me well. Articulating a familiar phenomenon is a chance to push our intuitions: to deepen and expand them, to examine and rethink them. The perspective that results is not foreign, yet it can shed new light on our world. In this sense, the concept of community of practice is neither new nor old. It has both the eye-opening character of novelty and the forgotten familiarity of obviousness – but perhaps that is the mark of our most useful insights.

Rethinking learning

As I will argue [...], placing the focus on participation has broad implications for what it takes to understand and support learning.

- For *individuals*, it means that learning is an issue of engaging in and contributing to the practices of their communities.
- For *communities*, it means that learning is an issue of refining their practice and ensuring new generations of members.
- For *organizations*, it means that learning is an issue of sustaining the interconnected communities of practice through which an organization knows what it knows and thus becomes effective and valuable as an organization.

Learning in this sense is not a separate activity. It is not something we do when we do nothing else or stop doing when we do something else. There are times in our lives when learning is intensified: when situations shake our sense of familiarity, when we are challenged beyond our ability to respond, when we wish to engage in new practices and seek to join new communities. There are also times when society explicitly places us in situations where the issue of learning becomes problematic and requires our focus: we attend classes, memorize, take exams, and receive a diploma. And there are times when learning gels: an infant utters a first word, we have a sudden insight when someone's remark provides a missing link, we are finally recognized as a full member of a community. But situations that bring learning into focus are not necessarily those in which we learn most, or most deeply. The events of learning we can point to are perhaps more like volcanic eruptions whose fiery bursts reveal for one dramatic moment the ongoing labor of the earth. Learning is something we can assume – whether we see it or not, whether we like the way it goes or not, whether what we are learning is to repeat the past or to shake it off. Even failing to learn what is expected in a given situation usually involves learning something else instead.

For many of us, the concept of learning immediately conjures up images of classrooms, training sessions, teachers, textbooks, homework, and exercises. Yet in our experience, learning is an integral part of our everyday lives. It is part of our participation in our communities and organizations. The problem is not that we do not know this, but rather that we do not have very systematic ways of talking about this familiar experience. [...]. An adequate vocabulary is important because the concepts we use to make sense of the world direct both our perception and our actions. We pay attention to what we expect to see, we hear what we can place in our understanding, and we act according to our world views.

Although learning can be assumed to take place, modern societies have come to see it as a topic of concern – in all sorts of ways and for a host of different reasons. We develop national curriculums, ambitious corporate training programs, complex schooling systems. We wish to cause learning, to take charge of it, direct it, accelerate it, demand it, or even simply stop getting in the way of it. In any case, we want to do something about it. Therefore, our perspectives on learning matter: what we think about learning influences where we recognize learning, as well as what we do when we decide that we must do something about it – as individuals, as communities, and as organizations.

If we proceed without reflecting on our fundamental assumptions about the nature of learning, we run an increasing risk that our conceptions will have misleading ramifications. In a world that is changing and becoming more complexly interconnected at an accelerating pace, concerns about learning are certainly justified. But perhaps more than learning itself, it is our *conception* of learning that needs urgent attention when we choose to meddle with it on the scale on which we do today. Indeed, the more we concern ourselves with any kind of design, the more profound are the effects of our discourses on the topic we want to address. The further you aim, the more an initial error matters. As we become more ambitious in attempts to organize our lives and our environment, the implications of our perspectives, theories, and beliefs extend further. As we take more responsibility for our future on larger and larger scales, it becomes more imperative that we reflect on the perspectives that inform our enterprises. A key implication of our attempts to organize learning is that we must become reflective with regard to our own discourses of learning and to their effects on the ways we design for learning. By proposing a framework that considers learning in social terms, I hope to contribute to this urgent need for reflection and rethinking.

The practicality of theory

A perspective is not a recipe; it does not tell you just what to do. Rather, it acts as a guide about what to pay attention to, what difficulties to expect, and how to approach problems.

- If we believe, for instance, that knowledge consists of pieces of information explicitly stored in the brain, then it makes sense to package this information in well-designed units, to assemble prospective recipients of this information in a classroom where they are perfectly still and isolated from any distraction, and to deliver this information to them as succinctly and articulately as possible. From that perspective, what has come to stand for the epitome of a learning event makes sense: a teacher lecturing a class, whether in a school, in a corporate training center, or in the back room of a library.

  But if we believe that information stored in explicit ways is only a small part of knowing, and that knowing involves primarily active participation in social communities, then the traditional format does not look so productive. What does look promising are inventive ways of engaging students in meaningful practices, of providing access to resources that enhance their participation, of opening their horizons so they can put themselves on learning trajectories they can identify with, and of involving them in actions, discussions, and reflections that make a difference to the communities that they value.
- Similarly, if we believe that productive people in organizations are the diligent implementors of organizational processes and that the key to organizational performance is therefore the definition of increasingly more efficient and detailed processes by which people's actions are prescribed, then it makes sense to engineer and re-engineer these processes in abstract ways and then roll them out for implementation.

But if we believe that people in organizations contribute to organizational goals by participating inventively in practices that can never be fully captured by institutionalized processes, then we will minimize prescription, suspecting that too much of it discourages the very inventiveness that makes practices effective. We will have to make sure that our organizations are contexts within which the communities that develop these practices may prosper. We will have to value the work of community building and make sure that participants have access to the resources necessary to learn what they need to learn in order to take actions and make decisions that fully engage their own knowledgeability.

If all this seems like common sense, then we must ask ourselves why our institutions so often seem, not merely to fail to bring about these outcomes, but to work against them with a relentless zeal. Of course, some of the blame can justifiably be attributed to conflicts of interest, power struggles, and even human wickedness. But that is too simple an answer, and unnecessarily pessimistic. We must also remember that our institutions are designs and that our designs are hostage to our understanding, perspectives, and theories. In this sense, our theories are very practical because they frame not just the ways we act, but also – and perhaps most importantly when design involves social systems – the ways we justify our actions to ourselves and to each other. In an institutional context, it is difficult to act without justifying your actions in the discourse of the institution.

A social theory of learning is therefore not exclusively an academic enterprise. While its perspective can indeed inform our academic investigations, it is also relevant to our daily actions, our policies, and the technical, organizational, and educational systems we design. A new conceptual framework for thinking about learning is thus of value not only to theorists but to all of us – teachers, students, parents, youths, spouses, health practitioners, patients, managers, workers, policy makers, citizens – who in one way or another must take steps to foster learning (our own and that of others) in our relationships, our communities, and our organizations.

13

Trouble and tribes: young people and community

Jeremy Brent

In Southmead, an area in which I have worked and researched over a number of years, young people are persistently seen as a major problem that stands in the way of the formation of community, which itself is seen as an almost magical solution to the ills of the area. It is as if young people are held responsible for holding the area back. However, young people too continually engage in collective activities that bear certain strong resemblances to what is generally labelled 'community', except that their activities are not approved of, and are not given the accolade of having this term applied to them.

For me, this leads to a difficult question, 'What is community, anyway?', which I have explored more fully elsewhere (Brent, 2004). In this article I want to look at young people in relation to ideas of community, including issues of sociality, collectivity, locality and power. I give examples of adult views of young people, followed by accounts of young people's own communal actions, and relate these to theories of community, including that of 'neo-tribes' described as unstable 'effervescent communities' (Maffesoli, 1996: 66), that challenge the nostalgic idea of community as 'warm togetherness' (Bellah, 1997: 388).

This is a revised version of the original text which appeared in *Youth and Policy, the journal of critical analysis* edited by Ruth Gilchrist, Tony Jeffs and Jean Spence. Published by The National Youth Agency.

Southmead itself is a large housing estate on the northern edge of Bristol. No thumbnail sketch can do the area justice, and even exacerbates the problem of pathologisation from which the area, like others like it, suffers. However, to show the context of the argument, here are some bare facts and figures.

Southmead has a population of over 10,000. It was primarily developed over a twenty five year period between 1930 and 1955, with later infill. The housing is low density – the vast majority of it being three-bedroom houses with gardens. Ever since it was built Southmead has had a reputation for trouble and poverty. It was the subject of a major action research study by the Bristol Social Project in the 1950s, and in one of the papers from that project, tellingly entitled *Difficult Housing Estates*, it is described as:

> containing areas of bad reputation which caused the whole neighbourhood to be held in low esteem.

> (Wilson, 1963: 3)

Three decades later a survey stated that:

> Throughout its history, Southmead has received attention in the media as a problem estate where crime, lawlessness and anti-social behaviour are rife. Riots and fire bombings in the early and late 1980's and the problem of joyriding, which recently received national coverage, have all seemed to firmly establish Southmead as 'Bristol's trouble-plagued estate'.

> (Safe Neighbourhoods Unit, 1991: 7)

In the 1999 *Audit of Crime and Disorder in Bristol*, Southmead was named as a major 'crime hot-spot' in the city, the only area with as many as five entries out of eight police priority categories (Bristol Community Safety Partnership, 1999). The 'problem' tag therefore has a long history – from at least 1952, when the Bristol Social Project research was set up, until at least the end of the 1990s.

Southmead has also always featured as one of the poorest areas in the city in the *Poverty in Bristol* reports that Bristol City Council issue, with the 1996 report stating that the estate falls within the 'highest' fifth of the five indicators used to measure deprivation in Bristol. In 1998 the Southmead ward was scored as having the third worst quality of life out of 34 Bristol wards, and in DETR statistics it figures among the worst 10% of wards in England (Bristol City Council, 1996, 1999; DETR, 1998).

Southmead is not alone as an area with such statistics. There are some 2000 such estates throughout Britain, the main feature of Southmead being its size – four to nine times larger than the '20 of the most difficult' that were surveyed in a Joseph Rowntree Foundation study (Power and Tunstall, 1995). Nor is it alone as being seen as an area where, despite all the figures of poverty, it is young people that are seen as the major social problem.

[...]

Rather than attempting to make a formal definition of youth, I will in this article be using other people's 'common sense' [...] definitions of young people, not because common sense is right, or even consistent, but because it is this common sense that leads to attitudes and responses to young people's behaviour and actions.

There is one distinction often made between different young people – the 'good' versus the 'bad', or 'disaffected' – which needs to be treated with care, if not scorn. This distinction is far too neat, bears little close examination, and is even 'wicked' in the way that it is used (Piper and Piper, 1999). Certainly in my experience some young people that are involved in 'bad' activities, are, in other circumstances, categorised as 'good' (as can be seen in my examples later). The argument as to whether young people are *either* bad *or* good is finally a sterile approach to looking at the issues involved in young people living in a 'community', and puts all the onus of good behaviour on to them.

Adult views of young people and community

Like many poor areas, Southmead has been exhaustively researched and surveyed. Without fail, all the various official surveys of Southmead cast young people as a, even *the*, major problem of the area. The very first research into community in the area was set up because of the problem of young people: 'Juvenile delinquency was the initial problem and starting point for the project' (Spencer et al., 1964: 24). Later reports continually reiterate that theme. Out of the blue, with no lead up of argument or evidence, a 1983 report states that: 'youth problems [are] a major factor in Southmead' (Bristol City Council, 1983). A report written in 1991 is full of disparaging references to young people, including the one that states: 'There was almost universal agreement that those largely responsible for crime in Southmead are young people' (Safe Neighbourhoods Unit, 1991: 46). The final sentence in the section on Southmead in the 1996 poverty report, again after no previous discussion of, or data on, young people, and with no reference to the relevance to a poverty analysis, states: 'The area is *dominated* by young people and families with dependent children living in local authority housing' (Bristol City Council, 1996: 54). The 1999 *Audit of Crime and Disorder in Bristol* gives as one of the reasons for Southmead being a priority ward for crime and disorder that there are more than 25% young people in the population (Bristol Community Safety Partnership, 1999: 28).

In all the reports young people are seen as a cause of crime, their behaviour a problem. The Crime Audit answers its own question about Southmead, 'Who are the offenders and why are they offending?' thus:

In keeping with the largest concentrations of young people in the city the area has high levels of truancy and youth unemployment. A minority of young people on the estate experiment with drugs and some have become addicted to hard drugs. Many burglaries and thefts are committed to fund drug habits. There is boredom and a lack of prospects amongst young people leading to crimes such as criminal damage.

(Bristol Community Safety Partnership, 1999: 33)

Throughout the reports on Southmead, young people are the *only* group that are identified as criminal, their large concentration seen as a problem. Even in discussion of domestic violence, men are not named as the major responsible group.

In the 1991 survey, there was a separate section in which under-18 year olds were surveyed. They were asked questions that the adults were not asked. Had they ever played truant? Had they been involved in crime? And 'During the last year have you had an alcoholic drink or taken any drugs?' (Safe Neighbourhoods Unit, 1991). Asking these questions shows clearly how surveys create a perception of young people as a problem and manufacture data that maintain this perception; the questions asked in surveys are not themselves innocent. This process occurred again two years later in a survey of drug mis-use which also concerned itself exclusively with young people – the only adults questioned were those who worked with young people, and adult drug use was not mentioned at all (Monaghan, 1993).

The 1991 survey had two answers for the problem of young people. One was to offer better facilities and support. The other was, through housing allo-cation policy, to reduce the numbers of families with children moving into the area, and 'avoid concentrating households with children of the same age on the same street', cleansing of the area of this 'problem', an idea with chilling overtones (Safe Neighbourhoods Unit, 1991: 65–67).

[…]

That there is a problem of the behaviour of some young people in Southmead can not be denied. F—, a long-time youth worker with a strong commitment to young people in Southmead told me:

Walking around the estate on Saturday I was so ashamed. The kids were being really horrible. I saw them attack X—, and another old woman who used to work in the Post Office. They were throwing bricks at buses, and opening and closing the bus doors. Wherever I went on the estate there were kids behaving badly. They were collecting penny-for-the-guy. When people refused to give them any money, they followed them into the shops and pestered them. I feel that it is getting so bad that it can't get better. I was gutted and ashamed that I knew these kids. With this old lady they were jostling her in the street, and almost hit her.

[...]

Much of the conflict between adults and young people is about behaviour in public space. [...] A noticeable facet of Southmead life is the number of young people using the public space of the streets; in common with many poor areas, young people are a high proportion of the population. Their use of the street is not unusual, as is pointed out in a work on the geographies of youth culture: 'Studies on teenagers suggest that the space of the street is often the only autonomous space that young people are able to carve out for themselves' (Valentine et al., 1998: 7). This attempt at autonomy brings them into conflict with other street users, challenging adult rules of sociality. In Brown's research, in place of a reciprocal sociality between young people and adults, there was a 'perpetual, never ending conflict over space which characterises much of the relationship between the generations in public' (Brown, 1995: 40).

In these descriptions of conflict, young people are always mentioned in the plural. There are always more than one of them. The behaviour is collective. Melucci writes that collective behaviour is 'never a purely irrational phenomenon. It is always to a degree meaningful to its participants [...]' (Melucci, 1989: 191). I want to use his insight to examine this behaviour, as collectivity is another important facet of the idea of community. Used with the idea of public space, it is closely linked to another idea often used as an ingredient of community: that of control over locality. In looking at examples of young people's collective actions in Southmead, and their relation to public space and locality, wider issues of community are raised than just that of the behaviour of young people.

Youth behaviour may be seen as destructive to community, but nostalgia for past youth is one aspect of community building. People love the shared history of remembering themselves as young. In 1993 there was an exhibition, called '40 Years of Youth Work in Southmead.' This was extremely popular, much more popular in the area than the exhibitions of contemporary work done by young people, and led to more people bringing in their even older photographs, and eventually the compilation of the book *Alive and Kicking!*, full of memories of youth (Truman and Brent, 1995). As Stuart Hall has put it: 'organic community was just always in the childhood you left behind.' (Hall, 1991: 46). Shared memories of youth can be an important ingredient of adult community. Now, though, I want to give examples of the communal activities created by young people themselves.

Young people, collective action and neo-tribes

One of the features of the social life of young people in Southmead is the way certain sites – street corners, park areas, shops – by some mysterious way become the place where crowds of young people congregate and socialise. These places become young people's space for a time, with their own shorthand titles (over the years 'Greystoke', 'the woods', 'the bollards', and so on), until eventually the police are called, and the crowds dispersed until, a few weeks or months later, a new site emerges as that place to be. One area, 'the Green', was used so often as a gathering place and centre of joyriding and battles with the police, that in 1996 it was built over. 'They've taken *our* green away', I was told by young people at the time. Three months later the crowds met up again at 'the woods', as described below. These gatherings are comparable to the concept of 'neo-tribes'. Neo-tribes have been characterised as 'recently invented communities involving some membership choice', which occur in '"wild zones" ... where aesthetic and other resources are thin on the ground' (Lash and Urry, 1994: 318). They are arguably a modern version of 'community' in a mass society, with young people in Southmead being active and creative inventors of their own such communities.

The sight of large numbers of teenagers meeting together and enjoying themselves should be a cause for celebration for all those interested in their welfare. Especially when the young people feel 'empowered' enough to organise all their own activities –sitting around campfires, cooking food in the open, chatting, laughing, playing games, all with no adult supervision. However the headline in one local newspaper was: *'BIKER GROVE! Beauty spot is ravaged by teen hoodlums'.* The story went on:

> Police and park rangers are joining forces to clamp down on teenage motorcyclists who have turned a woodland beauty spot into an off-road race track.
>
> The move follows complaints from residents walking their dogs at Badocks Wood, in Southmead, about noise and dangerous driving.
>
> ... The area has been plagued by gangs of youths in recent months, who meet up on mopeds and use the wooded slopes and paths as an off-road adventure circuit.
>
> (Bristol Observer 4 April 1996)

Despite its sensationalism the newspaper coverage missed the full dramatic importance of the events in Badocks Wood for young people. The newspaper's perspective was that of the outraged adults, and in no way reflected young people's perspective of pleasure as that area was taken over and used for a carnival of collective action and transgression (that this transgression worked was confirmed by the affronted tone of the article).

Badocks Wood runs along the valley of the River Trym, here a stream. The plateau to one side of the valley is rough parkland, with long grass and young trees. It is on the borders of Southmead and the wealthier areas of Henleaze and Westbury; as well as being suitable terrain for the activities that took place, being border country maybe gives greater scope for breaking social rules. While during the day it is the province of dog walkers, at night through early spring 1996 large groups of young people congregated there. This area had become the place for them to be.

Going around the area in the day (at night I would have been out of time and out of place; even as a youth worker, I am excluded from young people's communities), I could get a sense of the excitement that the young people must have felt, as well as seeing the destruction caused. It was like a scene after a carnival. I could almost hear the shrieks of delight from the evening before. On a long stretch of grassland one could see the marks of wheels running up and over a dip. The ground in the woods was covered in skid marks from racing around amongst the trees and slopes. There were the remains of bonfires and food wrappers, and burnt out wrecks of cars. Branches had been pulled off trees for firewood. There was the dramatic sight of a burnt out Metro on top of the old burial mound. The fence around the mound and the post with its Ancient Monument information had gone, the wood used for fires.

Entry to the area was through a hole in the fence. The hole was small, so only small cars (hence the Metro) were being used. In the course of one week there were eight wrecks in the area. The motorbikes were taken home at night.

The authorities cleared the area of this activity by a concerted operation; the aftermath of this was extreme anger amongst young people and antagonism to the police and all other adults. It was a difficult time for staff at the Youth Centre, as angry young people moved there and vented their rage. The community police team felt the antagonism – they had a meeting with me to discuss the events, and struck me as being totally frustrated. They saw the issue as a matter of the law, as shown by this piece they put in the community newspaper:

> Once again, as spring approaches, the problem of off-road motorcyclists has re-surfaced in Badocks Wood … Offences include dangerous riding and riding without due care and attention, for which fines of up to £1,000 can be levied … One youth was arrested

recently for theft of a bike. We hope in the coming months to counter this danger to lawful users of the parks.

(Southmead Community News May 1996)

All this illicit activity had resulted in a total of one arrest. The events were virtually unpoliceable, with the collective activity of the young people leaving the police powerless until they used semi-military tactics.

At around the same time there was a minor collective event which I witnessed directly. One evening young people started to pull up brick pavers from the courtyard in front of the Youth Centre. Once one was loose, they could all be pulled up. This turned into a tremendous group effort, pulling up the bricks and loading them into trolleys taken from the local shops, wheeling them up to the side of the Youth Centre and building a wall from them – a proper wall, with the headers and stretchers of proper brickwork, if no mortar. I was struck by the immense enjoyment this collective activity brought, the creativity of the wall building, the great effort being put into a 'meaningless' activity – for the wall did virtually nothing, in fact a gap was left at one end for people to walk through. K __ in particular was working hard and enjoying it – calling for people to help her push the loaded trolley. It did greatly annoy – because of its meaninglessness? – and of course its destructiveness of the yard. It frightened old people, who took another way to walk through. It unsettled place, made people unsure whether the path was blocked or not, safe or not.

Both these examples show a challenge to accepted modes of sociality, but also display an alternative, transgressive form of collective social behaviour. These are not orderly forms of community which might offer solutions to problems of neighbourhood crime, but are transgressive – deliberately breaching boundaries, pushing the limits and challenging the law – crucially establishing a different kind of community, one which belongs to these young people. This transgressive impulse leads groups of young people to embrace and celebrate (and even extend) the negative labelling of the area that respectable community activity is working hard to overturn. [...]

Only, of course, for a short time. These were not sustainable communities. Even without police action, their transgressive moment would have passed, even if reappearing in other guises at other times (as has happened since). These short-lived communal gatherings have been described as: 'the efflorescence and effervescence of neo-tribalism ... whose sole *raison d'être* is a preoccupation with the collective present.' (Maffesoli, 1996: 75). They are not stable: 'neo-tribalism is characterized by fluidity, by punctuated gathering and scattering', like a ballet, 'the arabesque of sociality' (Maffesoli, 1988: 148). The basis of neo-tribalism (Maffesoli and others who use this term ignore any racial/racist or primitive connotations of the word tribe – they see them as thoroughly modern and universal phenomena) is sensation, touch, performance, not causality or utilitarianism: 'the communal ethic has the simplest of foundations: warmth, companionship – physical contact with one another' (Maffesoli, 1996: 16). This is not a description of community as being necessarily good – in fact, Maffesoli uses the phrase 'group egoism' to describe such groups. He sees neo-tribes as being aesthetically, not ethically or politically, based, though he argues that an ethics may develop from those aesthetics (1991, 1996).

[...]

This description by a joy rider from Southmead, being interviewed for *The Place We're In*, a multimedia project at Southmead Youth Centre (www. bristol. digitalcity.org/community/southmead.htm), has a similar aesthetic quality.

> *How do you get into a car?*
> You need a good screw driver ... right ... flat head ... make sure the end bits nice and thin bit ... fit in the door lock ... put in ... put in the door lock ... turn in round whatever open the door ... door open ... climb inside ... put your foot inside the steering wheel, someone else grabs the other end ... turn it round ... snaps – steering wheel snaps ... grab the casing from the back of the steering column ... rip it off ... get the ignition barrel head – file it down, put a screw driver in the back of it, pop the black box off, put something in the black box that'll fit in it – turn it, start it, drive off.
>
> *What happens next?*
> Drive round, drive it round, spin it round, kill it off – burn it out.
>
> *So last night, how many people would you say were on the street?*
> Thirty, twenty, thirty.
>
> *Do you get a really big rush when you get it together?*
> Yeh, sound funny ... watching the cars getting spun round, smoked whatever.
>
> *How do you manage to get the tyres to smoke?*
> Foot down, handbrake up – put your foot down really fast, let the clutch off fast and it smokes on the spot for ages, or some times you put a brick on the accelerator ... leave it on its own ... just goes round ... smokes on its own.

Accounts like these, with their disobedient, errant view of what is 'good', puncture the worthiness of much community rhetoric. [...] These examples of collective behaviour have a romantic edge to them – in witnessing them and describing them there is a sense of the strong desire for shared, communal excitement. Freie writes that we are highly susceptible to what he calls counterfeit community: 'lacking genuine community, yet longing for the meaning and sense of connectedness that it creates – the feeling of community – people become vulnerable to the merest suggestion of community,' (Freie, 1998: 2).

[...]

The desire for connectedness can also be more vicious than this expansive, if destructive longing. Forms of collective organisation are concerned with inclusion, exclusion and control, as in this episode I witnessed of control in a girl gang:

> E__ came to club, asked for Y__, told her about party. Y__ said she wasn't going. Later a group of girls came up, all done up, hair especially, carrying cans of lager and cider. E__ and E__ (12), L__ and R__ (15), J__ (16). Called Y__ out. Went around side of building, then J__ dragging Y__ by hair to front of building, where all could see – punching her, kicking her, banging her head against railing. I went over, stopped fight. Y__ kept asking for J__ to stop. Y__ went off, cut under left eye. Blokes standing round took no part in it – not even to stop it when it became unfair. Consensus – J__ showing her power – do not leave my group, do what I want you to do – was the message. People predict that Y__ will toe the line.

My very strong impression was of the establishment of an alternative power structure making sure that no one left the gang, maintaining itself very deliberately in public in the rawest possible way.

By contrast here is an example of forceful public exclusion. One evening the H__s, a family living down the road from the Youth Centre, were driven out by young people. On the evening it happened there was a whole crowd in front of the house, hurling missiles and attacking the police even as they escorted the family away. I was told ferociously by young people to keep away, that 'This is the way we do things'. There was a strange sense of righteousness about this riot, despite its viciousness. Several were arrested. A few weeks later, in a quieter conversation that took place while young people were creating large paintings for an exhibition (a 'good' communal activity), I discovered what some of the girls involved saw as their reasons for the attack:

> The atmosphere was relaxed, and they started to talk about the H__s. They had a lot of stories to tell – to each other, to O__ [another girl], and by proxy to me, though they did not seem certain as to what I should know. They were amused at how they had welcomed the H__s, and taken R__ (girl of their age) under their wing, as she seemed so naive. In the light of what subsequently happened, 'We were the naive ones!'

They obviously went round to the H__s' house a lot, and were there on the birthday of the father. There was drink, so they knew that they were doing forbidden things that their parents would not allow. The father then invited them to play strip poker, wanted them to sit on his lap, give him a birthday kiss, locked the door and wanted them to stay the night, helped in all of this by his sons. The daughter had gone to bed. The only way they got out was by pretending to be ill. They were laughing about all this as they talked about it, in the way one laughs about something that had been frightening at the time.

[…]

Though Maffesoli sees neo-tribes as aesthetic rather than political groupings, they can also be formed to political effect. In the autumn of 1996 there was a campaign against cuts to the Bristol Youth Service. K__, whom we last met destroying a pavement to build a useless wall, became a leader of the campaign amongst young people in Southmead. The young people assembled a mass petition, made up of their hand prints, each signed with a statement as to why they liked the Youth Centre. K__ met with councillors, and presented this document to Bristol City Council, being the first person under 18 to be allowed to address a full Council meeting, thereby taking part in an approved form of community activity. The collective had been turned to a partially successful political purpose – the cuts in Southmead were less than originally proposed.

Young people and place

A major ingredient in the make-up of these moments of collective activity by young people has been that of place. Southmead itself can feel very bleak, a landscape in which aesthetic resources are sparse. This is felt strongly by young people: 'spaces send messages to young people about how an external world values or fails to value the quality of their lives.' (Breitbart, 1998: 308). Young people in Southmead told the youth worker discussing a survey they had done (Kimberlee, 1998) that 'Southmead is a shithole'. Lefebvre argues that […] it is only by way of revolt that adolescents 'have any prospect of recovering the world of difference – the natural, the sensory/sensual, sexuality and pleasure' (Lefebvre, 1991: 50). In the events around Badocks Wood, this was a suitable space, in terms of size and potential for such revolt, such a recovery of an aesthetic enjoyment of life.

In some ways, the issue is simple. Place is important for young people who have not the qualifications or other resources to move away […]. Locality therefore becomes recognised by young people as their 'community of destiny' (Maffesoli, 1996: 125). […]. This relationship is much stronger than that of communities of choice. […]

Local, known place has its own security. France and Wiles relate the creation of 'locations of trust – small bubbles of security in an insecure world' (France and Wiles, 1998: 68/9) as a reaction to the risks of late modernity. These locations are created by big business in, for example, secure guarded shopping malls that so often exclude young people. As spatiality is controlled against young people, it is no surprise that young people create counter-locations for themselves, their own bubbles where they, if no-one else, feel allowed. However, while for some young people this may create a security, for others it creates terror. 30% of young people surveyed in Southmead in 1998 said that they felt unsafe, and the discussions after the survey highlighted the desire of many young people for safe places to go (Kimberlee, 1998). The rough and transgressive actions of some young people terrify others. The constitutive attachment to place is coupled with acts that are destructive of that very place, an everlasting conundrum: why are young people destroying their own? Piven and Cloward, in their work on poor people's movements, point out that people rebel at what is around them as they do not know what the outside forces are that are affecting their lives, nor how to reach them. Without strategic opportunities for defiance, people attack what is around them, act where they are located and with people that they know. The very powerlessness of their situation explains why their defiant behaviour can appear to be so inchoate. They conclude that 'it is difficult to imagine them doing otherwise' (Piven and Cloward, 1977: 18–22). The combined anger and zest of young people are often not *directed* towards a goal, but are emotions that are *expressed* where they live. Only when there are clear cut issues, like cuts to the Youth Centre, is anger directed at a political decision affecting their lives.

However, despite actions often being aggressively local (young people in Southmead have their own symbol, the Southmead 'S', and fight against young people from other areas), the cultural symbols of youth are global. The youth culture of Southmead is not a closed culture, similar to the way the youth culture of Yucatec Maya investigated by Massey, where romantic preconception might lead one to expect a local 'authenticity', is also not 'a closed, local culture'. She writes:

> all youth cultures … are hybrid cultures. All of them involve active importation, adoption and adaptation. This challenges the idea that 'local cultures' are understood as locally produced systems of social interaction and symbolic meaning.
>
> (Massey, 1998: 122/3).

Young people in Southmead probably play the same electronic games she found in Mexico. As the action of young people is about giving a centrality to their own existence, so they will wear the designer clothes of the global market. Campbell observed in the early 1990s: 'All over peripheral estates across Britain teenagers were wearing designer casuals that signified their refusal to be peripheral, to be on the edge of everything.' (Campbell, 1993: 271).

In a photograph in *The place We're In* exhibition, the Nike swoosh is highly visible amongst those crowding around a stolen car. The Nike slogan, 'Just Do It' does summon up an impulse of rebellion, even if from the safety of corporate headquarters thousands of miles away. There is a continual interplay between the global and the local elements of youth culture, with both having major effect. Locality is not an easy autonomy, not separation from the rest of the world, but is still an important stage for collective formations.

Conclusion: young people and questions of community

The various examples I have given of communal activity amongst young people may be disruptive to a peaceful sociality of Southmead, yet contain many of the elements associated with community – solidarity, collective action, boundary enforcement, and control of space – and indicate a central component left out of more utilitarian descriptions of community – a strong aesthetic desire for connection. What they do not do is provide community as a solid and stable entity.

The neo-tribes, or micro-groups, formed and re-formed by young people give a speeded up version of the way a range of different ingredients are used, similar to that used in ideas of the construction of communities, though without the approbation that the term provides. As Raymond Williams has famously written, community as a term is one that 'seems never to be used unfavourably'. It is always 'warmly persuasive' (Williams, 1983: 76). To say that what young people are doing when joyriding is building community appears to be a contradiction in terms, but I would argue that this is what they are doing, and also what is being done with even more controversial activities, like heroin use, another collective activity that ties people into a group. Others too have questioned whether strong community does lead to lower crime rates, as criminal activity can be part of an oppositional collective culture (Warner and Rountree, 1997). This means that community is not, of itself, an *answer* to these activities, though thinking about the needs and desires expressed through them might provide fruitful material for forming less destructive forms of collectivities (to use a less loaded term than community). These would have to take into account the issues of identity, activity, aesthetics, control, and place, that these collectivities raise.

- *Identity.* The formation of young people's collectivities is connected to the formation of their identity as young people, as opposed to being children or adults. The joy rider who gave such an open interview said that, in five years time he would not be doing the same kind of stuff; he would be 'Probably working an' shit.' It is the uncertainty of the identity 'youth' that leads young people to form such dramatic tribal groupings.

The lack of solidity in their lives leads to a search for it. […] This solidity is also what drug addiction promises, when choice is surrendered to an external force. Identity is craved for when it is least stable.

- *Activity.* This identity is achieved by activity and involvement, working together to be part of something, not being left on the sidelines as a mere spectator. All the examples given are active, even involving hard work, and in the case of joy riding, a range of different skills. Neo-tribes flourish in areas without resources: the reasons for collective activities being mostly illicit may not only be about the joys of transgression, but reflect the paucity of licit skilled activity for young people to be involved with.

- *Aesthetics.* A major spur to these activities was to gain pleasure from otherwise barren physical and social landscapes. The activities were not utilitarian, are even a shock to a narrow idea of what is useful; there is often a popular horror that cars are not stolen to sell for cash, but for the pleasure of driving and destroying them. Theatricality and performance are major factors in these activities, with the spectacle being the substance, a performance of community with strong similarities to adult community rituals.

- *Control.* Control can, of course, also be a pleasure, and all these activities involved some form of control, taking power over place and people. These forms of control can be violent, the forms used by rebellious groups countering the ways that they feel controlled. Control both by and against these groups can be raw, but that itself is part of the pleasure, part of the aesthetics. […]

- *Place.* The connection of community to place in these activities is both clear and obscure. There are strong reasons for emphasising the importance of place, both social and geographical, in all the events described. They always happen in place, each activity is very localised, and could not be otherwise. However, they are not unique to specific places – such activities are replicated over Britain, and further afield. Specific locality does not create these activities, but it is the milieu in which they are created, and a milieu that they create. The activities themselves are used to create the meaning of localities, using any cultural and physical means available.

How does this leave us with an idea of community? While I have identified these ingredients in young people's collective action, they are also used in adult community action (Brent 2004). There are several things that these actions are not: not necessarily utilitarian; not conformist; not lacking conflict; not permanent; and finally, not necessarily 'good', in the way that many modern communitarian arguments are about its necessity as a social good (e.g. Atkinson, 1994; Bellah, 1997; Etzioni, 1995). […]

Community, or lack of it, is not the only factor involved in young people's behaviour. There are issues of power involved, issues that communitarians too often ignore (Phillips, 1993; Frazer and Lacey, 1993). All the activities described are gendered, even if they challenge traditional ideas of gendered behaviour. The behaviour is related to Southmead being a place of class and poverty. It involves the power position of young people, in terms of their rights, in terms of the resources available to them, and in terms of the way power is exercised upon them. The punitiveness of many adults would like to achieve, in Foucault's words, 'docility and utility' (Foucault, 1977: 218). However, it is this very negative use of power that strengthens transgressive resistance. The most successful adult initiatives with young people in the area have been based on tolerance and reciprocity, and have generated their own excitement and feelings of connectedness (Greenhalgh, 1999; Kimberlee, 2000). The proponents of discipline as the major tool to be used with young people have not understood the dictum that 'If power were never anything but repressive, if it never did anything but to say no, do you really think anyone could be brought to obey it?' (Foucault, 1980: 119). Any community building that wants to include young people needs to be creative and exciting, not disciplinary and forbidding, and has to recognise those strong aesthetic desires for excitement and connectedness amongst young people as well as amongst adults.

Jeremy Brent is Senior Youth Worker in Southmead, Bristol.

References

Amirou, R. (1988) 'Sociability/"Sociality"'. In *Current Sociology* 36.

Atkinson, D. (1994) *The Common Sense of Community*. London, Demos.

Bauman, Z. (1996) 'On Communitarianism and Human Freedom. Or, How to Square the Circle.' In *Theory, Culture & Society* 13(2): 79–90.

Bellah, R. N. (1997) 'The Necessity of Opportunity and Community in a Good Society.' In *International Sociology*, Vol. 12(4): 387–393.

Breitbart, M. M. (1998) '"Dana's Mystical Tunnel". Young people's designs for survival and change in the city.' In Skelton & Valentine 1998.

Brent, J. (1997) 'Community without unity' in P. Hoggett (ed.), *Contested Communities*. Bristol, Polity Press.

Brent, J. (2004) 'The desire for community: Illusion, confusion and paradox', in *Community Development Journal* Vol. 39, No. 3, 213–223.

Bristol City Council (1983) *Southmead Report – Report of Southmead Working Group*.

Bristol City Council (1996) *Poverty in Bristol 1996 – an update*.

Bristol City Council (1999) *Indicators of Quality of Life. Sustainability Update 1998/1999*.

Bristol Community Safety Partnership (1999) *Audit of Crime and Disorder in Bristol*.

Brown, S. (1995) 'Crime and Safety in Whose "Community"? Age, Everyday Life, and Problems for Youth Policy'. In *Youth & Policy* 48.

Campbell, B. (1993) *Goliath. Britain's Dangerous Places*. London, Methuen.

Department of Environment, Transport and the Regions (1998) *Index of Local Deprivation*.

Etzioni, A. (ed.) (1995) *New Communitarian Thinking. Persons, Virtues, Institutions, and Communities*. Charlottesville, University of Virginia Press.

Foucault, M. (1977) *Discipline and Punish. The Birth of the Prison*. London, Allen Lane.

Foucault, M. (1980) *Power/Knowledge. Selected interviews and Other Writings 1972–77*. (ed.) C. Gordon. London, Harvester.

France, A. and Wiles, P. (1998) 'Dangerous Futures: Social Exclusion and Youth Work in Late Modernity.' In Finer, C. J. and Nellis, M. (eds), 1998, *Crime & Social Exclusion*. Oxford, Blackwell.

Frazer, E. and Lacey, N. (1993) *The Politics of Community. A Feminist Critique of the Liberal-Communitarian Debate*. Hemel Hempstead, Harvester Wheatsheaf.

Freie, J. P. (1998) *Counterfeit Community. The Exploitation of Our Longing for Connectedness*. Lanham, Rowman & Littlefield Publishers Inc.

Greenhalgh, D. (1999) *Southmead Slamming*. VHS video, Bristol City Council.

Hall, S. (1991) 'The Local and the Global: Globalization and Ethnicity' and 'Old and New Identities, Old and New Ethnicities.' In King, A. D. (ed.) 1991, *Culture, Globalization and the World System. Contemporary conditions for the representation of identity*. Basingstoke, Macmillan.

Kimberlee, R. H. (1998) *Young People's Survey of Southmead 1998*. Bristol, Southmead Youth Centre.

Kimberlee, R. H. (2000) *'Champions and Challenges'. An Evaluation of the Southmead Youth Sports Development Initiative*. Bristol City Council.

Lash, S. and Urry, J. (1994) *Economies of Signs and Space*. London, Sage.

Lefebvre, H. (1991) *The Production of Space*. Oxford, Blackwell.

Maffesoli, M. (1988) 'Jeux De Masques: Postmodern Tribalism.' In *Design Issues* IV.

Maffesoli, M. (1991) ' The Ethics of Aesthetics.' In *Theory, Culture & Society* 8.

Maffesoli, M. (1996) *The Time of the Tribes. The Decline of Individualism in Mass Society*. London, Sage.

Massey, D. (1998) 'The Spatial Construction of Youth Culture.' In Skelton & Valentine 1998.

Melucci, A. (1989) *Nomads of the Present. Social Movements and Individual Needs in Contemporary Society*. London, Hutchinson Radius.

Monaghan, G. (1993) *Drug Misuse on the Southmead Estate*. Bristol, Bristol Drugs Prevention Team.

Phillips, D. L. (1993) *Looking Backward. A Critical Appraisal of Communitarian Thought*. Princeton, Princeton University Press.

Piper, H. and Piper, J. (1999) '"Disaffected Youth". A wicked issue: a worse label.' In *Youth & Policy* 62: 32–43.

Piven, F. F. and Cloward, R. A. (1977) *Poor People's Movements. Why they succeed, how they fail*. New York, Pantheon Books.

Power, A. and Tunstall, R. (1995) *Swimming against the tide. Polarisation or progress on 20 unpopular council estates, 1980–95*. York, Joseph Rowntree Foundation.

Safe Neighbourhoods Unit (1991) *The Southmead Survey 1991*. Prepared for Bristol City Council and Bristol Safer Cities Project.

Skelton, T. and Valentine, G. (1998) *Cool Places. Geographies of Youth Culture*. London, Routledge.

Spencer, J., Tuxford, J. and Dennis, N. (1964) *Stress and Release in an Urban Estate*. London, Tavistock.

Truman, J. and Brent, J. (1995) *Alive & Kicking! The Life and Times of Southmead Youth Centre*. Bristol, Redcliffe Press.

Valentine, G., Skelton, T. and Chambers. D. (1998) 'Cool Places: an introduction to Youth and Youth Cultures.' In Skelton & Valentine 1998.

Warner, B. D. and Rountree, P. W. (1997) 'Local Social Ties in a Community and Crime Model: Questioning the Systemic Nature of Informal Social Control.' *Social Problems* Vol. 44, No. 4.

Williams, R. (1983) (Revised edition), *Keywords. A vocabulary of culture and society*. London, Fontana.

Wilson, R. (1963) *Difficult Housing Estates*. London, Tavistock.

14

Anti-discriminatory practice

Neil Thompson

Introduction

[...] 'Valuing diversity' is the moral and professional requirement to recognize and respond to the significant differences of culture, language, gender and so on. These differences are important aspects of interpersonal interactions for, without due sensitivity to their differences, the potential for effective and appropriate interactions is seriously reduced.

[...]. Instead of concentrating on diversity as a factor in interpersonal interactions, I shall address the question of how the discrimination and oppression associated with diversity can be tackled in and by the process of intervention. That is, I shall examine some of the ways in which our practice in people work can:

- Recognize the impact of discrimination and oppression on people's lives;
- Avoid the pitfall of reinforcing or exacerbating such discrimination and oppression; and
- Challenge and undermine the oppressive structures, attitudes and actions that disadvantage certain groups in society.

This is a revised version of the original text which appeared as Chapter 17 in *People Skills, second edition* by Neil Thompson. First published in 2002 by Palgrave Macmillan. Reproduced with permission of Palgrave Macmillan.

The basic starting point is that developing anti-discriminatory practice is an *essential* part of good practice. If we are not sensitive to issues of discrimination, we run the risk of condoning, reinforcing or even amplifying the oppression to which such discrimination leads. If we practise in ways that take no account of discrimination, we may find that we are actually doing more harm than good. That is, instead of our work empowering people and promoting equality, it can actually have the opposite effect by taking away people's power and control and reinforcing, or even exacerbating, existing inequalities. For example, if a worker does not take account of racism in working with black service users, then the actions and attitudes of the worker may make the service user feel even more devalued and alienated in a white-dominated society.

The chapter is divided into three main parts. The first looks at ways in which, as individual practitioners, we can move in the direction of anti-discriminatory practice. The second part outlines the organizational context and considers aspects of organizational policy and culture that are significant. The third part explores ways in which groups of practitioners can work together to influence the direction of change for both individual practice and the organizational context. In this way, part three links together parts one and two.

Individual practice

There is a strong element of professionalism in people work, in the sense that people workers tend to have a degree of autonomy in terms of decision-making, choosing how we tackle problems and so on. This gives us a considerable degree of responsibility for our actions, and so it is very important that we consider the likely consequences of our actions. As people workers, we are generally in a position of power in relation to the people we seek to help, and so we have to make sure that such power is used positively and constructively, and is not abused, or used irresponsibly.

In view of this, we need to look carefully at the use of power in society and its effects on disadvantaged or minority groups. I shall do this by addressing three sets of issues: recognizing oppression, power-sharing through partnership and participation, and empowerment.

Recognizing oppression

Many aspects of oppression are so deeply ingrained in everyday life that many people do not notice them at all – they become taken for granted. For example, many disabled people are seriously disadvantaged by access difficulties due to environmental barriers. This problem is clearly visible for all to see but, unless we are 'tuned in' to issues of discrimination and oppression, we are unlikely to notice. A key task, then, is to become more aware of discrimination so that we are able to recognize oppression and its consequences.

There are a number of processes that are associated with discrimination and oppression. These include:

- *Marginalization*   Many people are pushed to the margins of society and excluded from the mainstream where important decisions are made. Consider, for example, the predominance of white, able-bodied men in positions of power, and the predominance of black people, women and disabled people in low-paid work and the unemployment figures. This can also be seen at a micro level. For example, it may be assumed by a worker that the man is the 'head of the household'. Another example would be forms that ask for the person's 'Christian' name, rather than first name, thereby marginalizing people of other religious backgrounds or indeed no religious background at all.
- *Group closure*   This is a process similar to marginalization in so far as it hinges on an 'us–them' mentality. The term refers to situations whereby people define themselves as a group and, in so doing, exclude other people unfairly. For example, many clubs seek to exclude women in order to maintain an all-male membership.
- *Stereotyping*   Rigid views of what particular individuals or groups are like are not helpful in people work, as they reflect and reinforce the discrimination some groups of people experience. As Jones (1985) comments:

  > Stereotypes are usually defined as oversimplified, and often biased, conceptions of reality that are resistant to change. The term is primarily used with reference to conceptions of particular categories of people, conceptions that are often negative in tone and linked to prejudiced attitudes and behavioural discrimination. (in Kuper and Kuper, 1985, p. 827)

  We therefore need to ensure that we do not allow our own thinking to rely on oppressive stereotypes, and that we challenge them in the thinking of others.
- *Stigmatization*   Some individuals or groups tend to be 'stigmatized'. That is, they are automatically seen in negative terms because of who they are or some aspect of their circumstances. For example, people living on a housing estate with a higher than average crime rate may all be 'tarred with the same brush' and assumed to be untrustworthy and unreliable. Stigma is therefore closely associated with stereotyping.

- *Scapegoating*   An individual within a family or group can become the person who takes the blame for the problems of that family or group. Often it is a relatively powerless person within a group who bears the brunt of the group's difficulties. He or she becomes a valve for releasing group tensions. This can also apply at a macro level. A group of people can become the scapegoat for a whole society. For example, black people in Britain are sometimes seen as the cause of social problems, rather than the victims.

Case study 1: Practice focus

Malik was the only black youngster who attended the centre. At first, he seemed to be well liked and accepted by the rest of the group. However, when the group went through a period of tension and conflict, the situation changed quite markedly. Some of the more influential members of the group began to take out their frustrations on Malik. The situation very quickly accelerated into one of open conflict, with Malik being blamed for a variety of problems. This clear example of scapegoating gave the staff a major challenge to face, but one that they had to tackle because of the gross unfairness of the situation.

These are just some of the negative and destructive processes that reflect and illustrate experiences of oppression arising from misuses of social power. They are part and parcel of everyday life, and so we can so easily fail to notice them if we do not make the effort to bear them in mind and consider their implications for the people we work with, and for our own practice.

Partnership

[…] partnership is an essential feature of good practice in people work. This is because a failure to work in partnership is likely to result in:

- *Resentment and non-co-operation*   If people are not involved in planning what is to happen, or not consulted about what they want or need, we should not be surprised when they respond with resentment and/or a low level of co-operation. An approach based on partnership, by contrast, is likely to produce a much higher level of commitment. A lack of consultation only serves to reinforce existing inequalities and power imbalances.

- *Mystification*   Partnership is based on openness and sharing of information and plans. If people are kept in the dark, the work becomes shrouded in mystery. This tends to have the effect of creating suspicion and mistrust, and therefore creates barriers to positive interactions and effective practice. Once again, this serves to reinforce existing inequalities.
- *Dependency*   If service users are not involved in partnership, then they will have little or no control over what is happening to them. This is a situation that is likely to increase, rather than decrease, the likelihood of dependency. Dependency, in turn, increases a sense of powerlessness.
- *Short-lived success*   Even if some degree of success is achieved without partnership, in many cases it is unlikely to be sustained over a period of time. This is because, unless the person or persons concerned have played an active part in solving the problem, they are unlikely to understand what made the difference, and will therefore be less well equipped to deal with the situation in future. Similarly, if someone has co-operated with change due to the pressure we have put them under, it is likely that old patterns and old habits will be resumed, once we are no longer involved.

Partnership not only avoids these, and related problems, it also provides a much firmer foundation for practising in ways that play a part in countering discrimination and oppression. Indeed, partnership helps to lay the foundations for empowerment.

Empowerment

The basic idea underpinning empowerment is that people should be helped to gain power and control over their own lives and circumstances. This is important for all individuals, but it is particularly so for members of oppressed groups in order to counter the negative effects of discrimination and marginalization. For example, the effects of sexism are such that women have to fight harder to make their voices heard in a male-dominated world.

Indeed, one important aspect of empowerment is to help people have a voice, to have opportunities for putting forward their point of view. This is a key element of user participation and a point to which I shall return later.

Other aspects of empowerment include:

- Working in partnership to avoid creating dependency;
- Boosting confidence and self-esteem, where necessary;

- A collective approach – bringing together people with similar problems, concerns and strengths; and
- Consciousness-raising – helping people to see their problems in their broader context, with less emphasis on 'personal failings' and more on the destructive effects of the way society is organized.

Of course, a central feature of work geared towards empowerment must be that we do not, in any way, contribute to the discrimination and oppression people experience. That is, we must ensure that our own attitudes and actions, including the language we use, are not discriminatory or oppressive. This involves a degree of self-awareness, use of supervision, continuous professional development, understanding of diversity and reflective practice. Tackling discrimination and oppression, then, is not a discrete activity in its own right. Rather, it is a part of most, if not all, of our activities as people workers. In view of this, we need to recognize that empowerment is not a simple skill, but rather a complex set of activities linked into a wide range of aspects of people work.

It is also important to note that empowerment has become a fashionable concept that receives a lot of attention. As Gomm (1993) acknowledged, it is now something of a 'buzzword'. However, we should be careful not to allow this to distract us from its central importance as an essential feature of good practice in people work. Empowerment is indeed fashionable, but this is not to say that it is nothing more than a fashion.

The organizational context

Anti-discriminatory practice is not simply a matter of individual practice. The organizational context in which such practice takes place is also vitally important in terms of the success or otherwise of our efforts to challenge and undermine discrimination and oppression. There are ways in which this context can facilitate anti-discriminatory practice, and ways in which it can hinder it.

In considering the organizational context, there are some fundamental questions that need to be asked:

- Are there equal opportunities policies in place?
- If so, do they relate only to staffing, or also to service delivery?
- Are such policies simply 'paper' policies, or are they actually implemented at an operational level? and
- Are senior managers committed to organizational change, or are they resistant to it?

These are important questions that have a significant bearing on the extent to which anti-discriminatory practice will be supported or facilitated. Answers to these questions will help to provide a picture of the organizational context.

An important concept in this regard is that of organizational culture, which Johannsen and Page (1990) define as:

> Values, beliefs and customs of a group or type of people. In a company or co-operation, its culture is demonstrated by its management style, including the degree of autocracy or participation practised, and the expectations of employees. (p. 79)

An organization's culture strongly influences 'the way we do things round here.' That is, common working practices, attitudes and approaches are shaped to a large extent by dominant cultural expectations within the organization concerned.

Such a culture will also be a significant issue in terms of tackling discrimination. Some cultures are strongly rooted in tradition, and are therefore unlikely to be responsive to equality initiatives. Other cultures, by contrast, are more flexible, and are therefore amenable to change in the direction of anti-discriminatory policy and practice. In order to promote anti-discriminatory practice, it is therefore important to get to know the organization in which we work, particularly in terms of cultural norms and expectations. That is, if workers are to influence the direction of change positively in an organization, we must first understand how that organization works.

However, we must also understand the context in which organizations operate, namely the legal context. There are a number of Acts of Parliament that outlaw discrimination and provide a basis from which to tackle inequality. For example, the Race Relations Act 1976:

> places a statutory duty on local authorities to ensure that their functions are carried out with due regard for the need to eliminate unlawful discrimination and to promote equality of opportunity and good relations. (Woolfe and Malahleka, 1990, p. 5)

A knowledge of legal requirements with regard to discrimination and equality can prove very useful in seeking to influence an organization that is reluctant to embrace the importance of equality and diversity. It can be used to influence policy and practice within an organization. However, such attempts to bring influence to bear are likely to be far more potent when undertaken collectively, at the level of the group.

Group influence

The impact a single individual can have on an organization's approach to discrimination is inevitably quite limited. However, groups of people working collectively can be far more effective in promoting change. It is therefore worth considering some of the ways in which groups can influence both the organization at a macro level and individual practice at a micro level. These include:

- *Staff meetings* Some staff groups promote anti-discriminatory practice by including it as a standing item on team meeting agendas. This can be used to enhance practice within the team, and issues can also be fed through management channels to express concerns and make suggestions.
- *Training* Staff groups can apply pressure to have appropriate anti-discrimination training provided. Also, such training can be used to identify organizational changes that need to be made, and again these can be fed back through management channels. Indeed, training can be an important vehicle for promoting organizational development.
- *Support groups* Members of staff with a particular background can usefully come together to support each other and act as a pressure group. For example, many organizations have a black workers' support group and/or a women's group. Such groups can be of benefit not only to the members of those groups, but also to other workers and the organization by providing important insights into the experience of discrimination and oppression.
- *Development groups* There is much to be gained from like-minded people banding together to discuss, and implement, possibilities for developing anti-discriminatory practice. Such groups can play a valuable role by identifying problems to be addressed, exploring potential solutions and generally raising awareness of the need to work within an anti-discriminatory framework. Development groups can be specific (for example, addressing a specific form of oppression, such as racism or ageism) or general (addressing all forms of oppreassion).
- *User participation* The notion of partnership discussed earlier involves the participation of service users in the assessment of their needs and the attempts to meet them. However, participation can also apply at a broader level. Where service users are empowered to contribute their views on planning, developing and evaluating services, the result can be a very

positive one in terms of ensuring responsiveness to need and identifying barriers to good practice, including aspects of discrimination and oppression.

Case study 2: Practice focus

After attending a course on anti-discriminatory practice, a group of colleagues decided it would be very useful to create a support group to work together on issues of inequality, discrimination and oppression. They agreed to meet on a monthly basis to compare notes, support one another and seek to influence practice and policy. Within a year some managers were using the group as a source of advice and consultation on important matters relating to equality and diversity. The group were delighted that their collective approach had achieved far more than any individual actions could have done.

Each of these group strategies for promoting anti-discriminatory practice can be instrumental in raising awareness and making positive progress towards challenging oppression. However, in addition to this, the very fact of working in groups can, in itself, be a tremendous source of empowerment.

Group-based approaches to anti-discriminatory practice can be very effective in influencing both individual practice and the organizational context. Consequently, each individual worker can make a positive contribution by playing a part in forming groups and supporting existing groups. Each worker can be part of a network geared towards challenging discrimination, an anti-oppressive alliance.

Conclusion

A commonly held value in the helping professions is the recognition of the uniqueness of the individual. This is clearly a value that has an important part to play in ensuring that people are treated with dignity, with their rights as individuals respected. However, there is also another side to this coin, namely the need to recognize the significance of broader social factors in shaping the experience of the individual:

> Whilst ['individualisation'] clearly has distinct advantages and much to commend it, it also has the disadvantage of discouraging practitioners from seeing clients in their broader social context – specifically within the context of membership of oppressed groups. For example, in dealing with a woman experiencing depression, the significance

of gender can be highlighted (Brown and Harris, 1978) and aspects of depression can be related to expectations of female roles in society. In this way, the classic mistake of encouraging women to be more 'feminine' can be avoided. They can be helped to understand their feelings in the context of finding a positive thread of meaning rather than simply slotting into an accepted social role – especially when it may very well be that such oppressive gender expectations played a significant part in the onset of the depression, for example in terms of domestic violence, restricted opportunities for personal fulfilment, or sexual abuse. (Thompson et al., 1994, pp. 17–18)

In a way, this point captures a basic feature of anti-discriminatory practice – a valuing of the uniqueness and individuality of the person, but set in the context of structured inequalities, discrimination and oppression.

That is, if we do not take account of social factors such as sexism, racism, ageism and disablism, we will be able to do justice to only those individuals who are fortunate enough not to be subject to any form of oppression. For those who do experience oppression, we shall be ill-equipped to respond appropriately to the reality of their experience, and will therefore run the risk of actually adding to their oppression.

We can conclude, then, that all practice needs to be anti-discriminatory practice, in so far as approaches that are not sensitive to discrimination will not only miss significant aspects of the situation, but may actually do a great deal of harm.

References

Brown, G. W. and Harris, T. (1978) *The Social Origins of Depression*, London, Tavistock.

Gomm, R. (1993) 'Issues of power in Health and Welfare', in Walmsley et al. (1993).

Johannsen, H. and Page, G. T. (1990) *International Dictionary of Management*, 4th edn, London, Guild Publishing.

Jones, E. E. (1985) 'Stereotypes', in Kuper and Kuper (1985).

Kuper, A. and Kuper, J. (eds) (1985) *The Social Science Encyclopaedia*, London, Routledge.

Thompson, N., Osada, M. and Anderson, B. (1994) *Practice Teaching in Social Work*, 2nd edn, Birmingham, Pepar.

Walmsley, J., Reynolds, J., Shakespeare, P. and Woolfe, R. (eds) (1993) *Health, Welfare and Practice: Reflecting on Roles and Relationships*, London, Sage.

Woolfe, S. and Malahleka, B. (1990) 'The Obstacle Race: The Findings of the BASW Report on an Action Research Project into Ethnically Sensitive Social Work', Birmingham, BASW.

15

Thinking about direction

Mark Smith

In conversation we can never be sure of the way things will turn out. People appear with something on their mind that they 'just have to talk about'; events occur which alter the subject. Above all, as we engage with ideas and situations our understandings and feelings change. If we are to begin with situations rather than subjects (Lindeman, 1989: 6), what guides our thinking and acting? How do we make decisions about the direction that encounters are taking?

Thinking things through

The local educators I talk with, like schoolteachers, do not appear to think things through in the linear way proposed by 'scientific curriculum-makers' such as Tyler (1949) and the 'problem-solvers' such as Priestley et al. (1978).

> The rational 'formulate objectives, identify appropriate learning activities and evaluate the achievement of objectives' is a favourite ... approach in teachers' initial training; but there is little evidence that it reflects the thinking of practising teachers.
>
> (Brown and McIntyre, 1993: 18)

Workers have to 'improvise, contemplate and prepare' (Yinger, 1990: 85). In this, 'purpose and intention may not ... always be marked by closely specified

This is a revised version of the original text which appeared as Chapter 4 in *Local Education* by Mark Smith. Published in 1994 by Open University Press. Reproduced with the kind permission of the Open University Press/McGraw-Hill Publishing Company.

goals' (Brookfield, 1983: 15). However, while much learning may at first seem to be incidental it is not necessarily accidental: actions are taken with some purpose. The specific goal may not be clear at any one time, either to educators or learners, yet the process is deliberate. Educators in these situations can seek to foster an environment in which conversation can take place.

This process of thinking things through, of practical reasoning, still needs clear reference points. The talk of local educators can be littered with links to these. Words like 'aim', 'role', 'values' and 'tactics' are used to describe why workers did this or took that decision.

> My style of work involves reaching out to young people who normally don't have contact with the service … which is why I go out to them rather than them coming to me … It's about creating new opportunities for them, giving them new experiences and having a chance to participate – I know the word is thrown about rather a lot – in different activities. And then once they are doing those things, I think my agenda is certainly a lot about looking at their lives; looking at the influences in their lives; looking at all the different issues that affect them; and creating time and space to talk to them about some of those things … looking at all the processes that happen there.

In these few sentences this worker uses a number of organizing ideas: the impact of her style of work; the concern with participation; the desire to create space so that people may reflect on their lives; the focus on process; the wish to enable people to be themselves. These are common concerns and the pivotal place they occupy indicates the beginnings of a framework for thinking about direction.

Creative participation

The starting point for this worker, and many others I talk with, is a picture of the relationships and activities that they want to see in a situation. While this varies according to situation and worker, for most it boils down to an emphasis on participation in 'meaningful' activities (see, for example, DES, 1982). Central to this, as the worker suggests, is space to talk about experiences. As another put it, 'you look to create environments where something can happen'. Much like the teachers in Brown and McIntyre's (1993: 54–61) study, this worker seeks to establish and maintain a 'normal desirable state of activity'. For local educators I suggest this state is 'creative participation'.

Given the significance of choice, setting, experience and conversation to local educators, the emphasis on creative participation is hardly surprising.

When people are not involved and things do not appear to be 'happening' this triggers various interventions to move things on or to address a particular worry or question. Where people are involved, workers have the chance to 'get alongside them', to join in activities and conversations, and to encourage creative participation.

This way of describing the state of relationships and activities in a situation brings out a number of motifs in workers' thinking. First, it highlights involvement – and for youth workers, community workers and community educators this is one of the most enduring of concerns (see, for example, Thomas, 1983: 66). Second, 'creative' carries the notion of possibility; people's engagement allows for the chance of becoming something more (Rosseter, 1987: 52). Third, the label expresses a desire for agency – that people should be encouraged to be creators rather than consumers of situations (Smith, 1980). Last, the idea of participation carries a social dimension.

> As an aspect of social practice, learning involves the whole person; it implies not only a relation to specific activities, but a relation to social communities – it implies becoming a full participant, a member, a kind of person. In this view, learning only partly – and often incidentally – implies becoming able to be involved in new activities, to perform new tasks and functions, to master new understandings.
>
> (Lave and Wenger, 1991: 53)

Agency, involvement, the sense of being part of a group, and the chance to be something more – before going much further it is worth looking at these and rehearsing the other themes concerning purpose that can emerge from the way that workers may talk about their work.

Aim or purpose

Once we recognize that the nature of people's participation may be the first port of call for local educators, it is then possible to approach the 'larger' purposes in their labours. Here I want to highlight seven themes that have emerged from my conversations with local educators.

[...]

1) Much of the practice I have heard described has been directed at identifying and challenging assumptions: developing an understanding of the context in which people act and how this has helped to shape their thinking; imagining and exploring alternatives; and developing what Brookfield (1987: 9) describes as a 'reflective scepticism'. In short, it has been concerned with developing the ability to think

critically. Some seem to approach this as a skill, but, more accurately, it is a disposition or frame of mind.

[...]

2) Overlapping with the desire to foster critical thinking can be a wish to give people a chance to experience new sensations; to do things that they would not normally do. This concern is often linked to a desire to get away from the neighbourhood. This can be eagerly taken up by workers in the forms of residentials, trips and events. The hope is that getting people away from their immediate neighbourhood and doing different things might help them to develop a more critical perspective on their situation and to have some sense of alternative possibilities in their lives.

[...]

3) A third key theme concerns the promotion of mutual respect and fairness. Some workers use organized, structured programmes in this area, some look mostly to matters arising out of everyday interactions – someone mouthing off about 'blacks' in the drop-in; young women being pushed off the pool table in the pub by young men; people jumping the queue at the bingo hall; a member of the community association committee getting free drinks in the bar; and so on. One form of intervention made is in the shape of a question: 'Is that fair?'

[...]

4) Some workers have a concern with wholeness, a desire to work for the development of the whole person. This has several dimensions, including such things as valuing yourself; being in touch with your capacities; working to integrate different parts of yourself.

[...]

5) A fifth theme concerns thinking about others – what they might be experiencing, what their needs are. Clearly this overlaps with the wish to cultivate mutual respect, but it was also doing something more. Underlying this may be a concern that people should not always put their needs first, that they should think of others.

[...]

6) There is also some talk of the importance of creating an environment in which people feel they belong, and of people being part of

something greater than the immediate groups to which they belong. This feeling or sense may be given many labels – for example, neighbourliness, solidarity, sisterhood, brotherhood and comradeship.

[…]

7) The last key theme is that of working with people so that they may work and act together both to organize activities and groups for their own satisfactions, and to understand and act on the institutions and processes that significantly affect the lives of people in particular neighbourhoods or communities. The orientation is to community development and organization: an emphasis on 'self-help, mutual support, the building up of neighbourhood integration, the development of neighbourhood capacities for problem-solving and self representation, and the promotion of collective action to bring a community's preferences to the attention of political decision-makers' (Thomas, 1983: 109). As Barr's (1991: 65–72) study of community work shows, 'community development' is the preferred and dominant model informing practice.

Different workers have different emphases – for example, youth workers may stress the first themes; community workers the last two themes in particular. This 'difference' is not something that should be pushed too far. It is not very clear-cut and, anyway, all these statements of overall aim involve coming to some understanding of what makes for human well-being or human flourishing. They have within them an implicit or explicit view of the good, or what makes for the good life. This is then reflected in the picture workers have of the relationships and processes that they feel characterize a good session or desired state of activity.

Role

[…]

Attention to role is particularly important in the case of local educators. They are not able to draw on a strong public understanding of their work. People are less sure about what behaviour to expect. A common view of youth workers, for example, is as ineffectual leftovers from 1960s hippydom such as Rick Lemmon in Townsend's (1984) *The Growing Pains of Adrian Mole*. Another sees them as social workers. Indeed, in one study of adolescents' views of social work it was found that there were fewer differences between the perception of social workers and youth workers than between social workers and other occupations (Jones, 1987: 198–9).

This inability to draw on a coherent set of public expectations concerning local educators' behaviour is not simply to do with the public's lack of knowledge. People's identities as workers are bound up with local networks and practices. Local educators operate within fluid settings. Within these social interaction generally follows less explicit rules and conventions than, say, in a classroom. These have to be learnt, and different behaviours negotiated that are specific to the situation. As Banton has commented:

> A loosely textured social structure in which roles are less clearly defined offers less resistance to change but can also give less protection to the people that have to play roles in it.
>
> (Banton, 1968: 198)

The relative openness to change and the lack of protection contributes to a considerable amount of uncertainty concerning role and purpose within the various professional groupings examined here (Smith, 1988: 75–84). It is not only that the public are not clear about what local educators do (or should do). Practitioners may lack a fully worked-through understanding of their role and purpose.

Being in a position where less can be taken for granted, practitioners have to pay special attention to role-making; to explore how expectations about their behaviour are reworked in the interactions they have with people. This tentative process (Turner, 1962) involves changes both in the practitioner and the person worked with. Roles have to be made and accepted by the various parties. Practitioners cannot simply say 'I am a community worker' and expect those with whom they work to accept it. The role of local educator requires the existence of another role: that of local learner. Thus, people have to accept workers as workers, and understand themselves as in need of being 'worked with' before a full working relationship can be established.

Much of the interaction that follows is then concerned with the testing of roles; with participants looking at the other's behaviour and as a result maintaining or modifying their own actions in role. When engaged in conversation, one of the key aspects of our performance concerns staying in touch with our capacities and our understanding of our role in the situation.

[…]

When it comes to the practice of education within local networks and everyday settings, matters are rarely what they appear to be. For example, the casual conversation of workers is not primarily about socializing and spending a pleasant half hour (although it may involve these things). It is work. It has further purpose. The danger in this situation […] is that we can be fully taken in by our own act and so lose touch with the reality of our performance; or that we may have no belief in our 'act' and no ultimate concern with the beliefs of our 'audience'. In other words, we become so distanced from our behaviour that it becomes false, or involves the cynical manipulation of those with whom we are working.

There is much more to pull local educators off course. The 'testing', the impact of changing circumstances, and the difficulty of operating for long periods of time can all act to fog their sense of themselves in the situation. There is also the continuing likelihood of roles being defined differently by people in the situation. While we may understand ourselves as 'educators', those we are attempting to work with might stubbornly define us as 'friends'. This may be a try-on, the result of misreading the situation, or a statement of fact, but until roles are defined and accepted there is likely to be conflict and drift. We may, for example, seek to retrieve the ethical notion of local education as 'friends educating each other' (Collins, 1991: 48–9).

It is also misleading to talk of 'role' in the singular in these circumstances. While there may be an overarching concept of the role of the educator, there are associated with it a number of sub-roles or behaviours which are specific to situations. For example, in order to undertake their educational function, many local educators have to be able to organize play schemes, drive minibuses, mend inflatables and so on. It is often when these different behaviours do not fit with one another, when they are not experienced as coherent, that workers begin to pay deep attention to their role and purpose.

Agenda and tactics

In what our worker had to say about her aims another concept appears important: agenda. […]

> I use the word 'agenda'. Is the way I use it different to the aim?…The aim is something much bigger; the agenda might be something that varies from hour to hour or day to day. It's something that is determined by what is going on at that moment in time to some extent.

On the whole, 'agenda' seems to be used in relation to particular situations, although it does sometimes find its way into broader statements of aim, such as in the original statement by the worker. It is something that moves with the situation. Items are dealt with, forgotten or deemed not to be appropriate. In contrast, some local educators, perhaps working within a narrow brief, will have fairly fixed agendas. For example, those specifically promoting 'drugs awareness' may seek to confine their interventions to these areas, but this can be a source of tension as conversations are not that neat and tidy (see Fisher, 1993).

There is no way of knowing how 'agenda' has come into common usage by practitioners, but the way workers conduct their meetings and their group sessions does appear to have been influential. Sessions often begin with a period of agenda-setting and some negotiation about order and emphasis. People are seen as bringing their own agendas and as having some rights in how sessions are conducted and what business is done. More than that, in encounters there may be a common wish to bring these out into the open; a hope that hidden agendas could be eliminated or at least minimized. This is not to say that there is not some 'smuggling' of items going on – but as Lindeman (1987: 130) said, the methods are ones that everyone can understand: 'No conspiracy. No manipulation about this'. In conversation there has to be some agreement as to subject. However, as Taylor (1993: 77) has shown in relation to Freirian approaches to literacy, even where there is an explicit commitment to dialogue, the hidden or personal agendas of educators can easily have a controlling influence over key aspects of the encounter.

Another idea was commonly associated with agenda by more than one worker: a concern for employing the right tactics.

> One of the interesting things for me about having conversations and discussions is trying to change your tactics in terms of how you bring up conversations ... Yes, you have got to get your tactics sorted out. It can be quite interesting being in a difficult situation with a group, when you feel the atmosphere building up, thinking to yourself, 'Right I have got to bring them down a little bit, how am I going to do it?' [...]

'Tactics' as used here appears to refer to the moves workers make in order to address items on their agenda or to connect what is happening with their overall aims. There is attention to detail and to the particular. In this last comment by the worker we can also see 'role' appearing again, but here in connection with the behaviour of others in the situation. It is a key element in the decisions she makes about which tactics to employ.

Framing direction

These four ideas, when linked to a concern for creative participation, provided the beginnings of a framework for thinking about direction in dialogue (Figure 15.1). What seems to be of importance here is the way practitioners frame situations. This framing allows workers to make sense of their practice and the experiences and situations they encounter. At any one time we may apply several frameworks or schemes of interpretation (Goffman, 1986: 25). What separates the two boxes in Figure 15.1 is the extent to which their contents changed with the situation. In other words, practitioners appeared to have an overarching understanding of their aims and roles as workers. While these altered over time, they

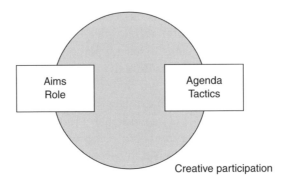

| Aims
Role | | Agenda
Tactics |

Creative participation

Figure 15.1   The beginning framework

were nowhere near as fluid as the content of their agendas or the tactics they employed. Thus, when working, the local educator on whom we have been focusing takes stock of the situation, and reasons her way through to what is the best course of action. In this she is guided by her understanding of what makes for well-being, and what is the proper way of working. The notion of 'creative participation' provides a picture of the interactions involved and connects with all elements. [...]

[Nevertheless] workers can oscillate between the general and the particular in relation to aim. For this reason, it is important to free up the concept: to leave 'aim' as a way of thinking about intentionality at all levels and to find another way of describing what might be called 'general aims'. Here, 'purpose' seemed a suitable replacement. Thus purpose, the reason for which the work exists and is done, found its way into the first of the two boxes.

Repertoire

I then overlaid a further element: repertoire (see Figure 15.2). The idea of repertoire came from Schön (1983). He argued that practitioners build up a catalogue of examples, images, understandings and actions. This repertoire includes the whole of their experience in so far as it is accessible to them for understanding and action (1983: 138). It is by drawing on some aspect of repertoire that workers are able to make sense of the situations they encounter:

> When a practitioner makes sense of a situation he perceives to be unique, he *sees* it *as* something already present in his repertoire. To see *this* site as *that* one is not to subsume the first under a familiar category or rule. It is, rather, to see the unfamiliar, unique situation as both similar to and different from the familiar one, without at

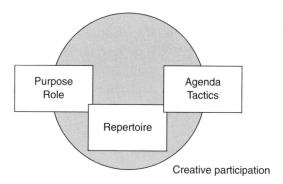

Figure 15.2   Repertoire

first being able to say similar or different with respect to what. The familiar situation functions as a precedent, or a metaphor ... for the unfamiliar one.

(Schön, 1983: 138)

In working with individuals and groups, things occur, an expression, a word, that evoke previous experiences or bring an image to mind. We might then use that image or experience to develop an understanding of the new situation. We can draw on other responses or ideas so that we may act on our new understanding, testing it, seeing if it works. In so doing we have to try to ensure that our sense of what is happening now is not overpowered by the past or by the image or metaphor that has been evoked.

The idea that practitioners carry with them a catalogue of ideas, images, understandings and actions, and that they draw upon this constantly in action is a powerful one. Thus, in Figure 15.2 thinking is structured by reference to creative participation and our understanding of role, purpose, tactics and agenda. We are then able to draw upon our repertoire in making sense of both the particular (tactics, agenda, the situation) and the general (role and purpose).

Issues

When thinking about this framework it was clear that there was something missing. For example, a number of practitioners use the notion of 'issues' when discussing the direction of their work. The worker we are focusing on here was no exception.

> For me [pregnancy] is really such a crucial issue … The lack of discussion about contraception is absolutely shocking … But there are then much wider issues about relationships, contraception, that sort of thing, which nobody is dealing with at the moment. There is this massive myth that the school is doing such wonderful work really.

At one level the introduction of issues was obvious, there being a desire to promote 'issue-based' approaches within some quarters. Such approaches take a specific dimension such as sexism, racism, unemployment or drug abuse and then use the phenomenon as the basic rationale for prioritizing and directing interventions and resources (Jeffs and Smith, 1990b 16). However, the way 'issues' is used by many of the workers I talk with does not fall in line with what might be expected from an issue-based model. Issues are things to look out for rather than the basis for allocating resources or the major reason for intervention – although there is some prioritization on the basis of people's experiences. For example, several workers have talked of looking for, and working with, 'burning issues', those concerns which were felt to be especially important or critical by participants.

The final clue as to where to place issues came around where 'pregnancy' fitted into our worker's scheme of things when working with young people. How did it relate to aim (purpose) and agenda? She described it as a crucial issue. What became clear was that something called 'issues' existed in her framework somewhere between aim and agenda. Issues are more flexible than aims, but do not change as much as the content of her agendas. In working with young people she could predict what 'issues' were likely to come up in conversation:

> If I was to look at all the residentials I do then I could name all the issues that I know will crop up over that weekend … The first ones … are sexism and racism. Drugs crop up quite a lot, but one of the most important things is relationships between the group. […] There is probably another one – growing up, talking about pressures. Families. I know that in the course of spending time with young people we are going to touch on all of those.

She linked these issues into her overall aim (purpose), which was getting young people to question and to look at why they respond to situations in the way they do. She also translated them into specific agenda items when working with particular groups or individuals. For her a number of issues would always be around when working with young people, but they had to be made sense of within her overall aim. (Her list closely matches the concerns which subsequently emerged in the major study of 16–19-year-olds by

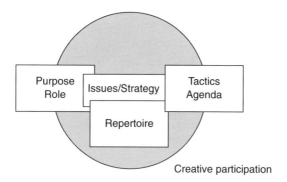

Figure 15.3   Introducing strategy and issues

Banks et al. (1992).) The community workers I talk with are usually similarly able to reel off a list of potential issues: for example, housing, community relations, transportation, schooling, shopping, and local social facilities. What we have here is not 'issue-based' work, but work organized around creative participation in conversation, and through which certain issues are identified and perhaps worked on. We are therefore able to introduce a fourth box overlapping and bridging those containing purpose/role and agenda/tactics (see Figure 15.3).

Strategy

A further dimension has also entered the fourth box: strategy. With the original two boxes we had, on the one hand, an overarching understanding of role and purpose, and on the other, the working out of tactics and agenda items for the specific situation. Missing from this was the middle-range activity of planning:

- *Target groups.* Which are the main groups that local educators should seek to make contact with and develop work with? Local educators may have a brief to work with specific groups (for example, young women), or may have identified people sharing certain learning needs that accord with the main concerns of their work (for example, officers of tenants' associations needing briefing about new housing legislation).
- *Primary places for work.* In which neighbourhoods and institutions should the work be concentrated? Once the basic neighbourhood or area is identified, decisions about specific places of work, such as how

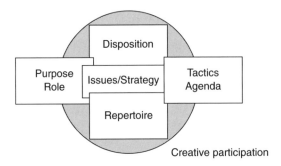

Figure 15.4　Disposition and interaction

> much time should be spent in schools, on the streets or in people's homes, will be largely dependent on the other elements discussed here.
>
> - *Main times for work.* This is really just a case of making bets as to when people will be around and wanting to be involved in the work; and then matching this up with what is reasonable, and what is possible from the educator's point of view.
> - *Basic approaches.* What are the central methods; what is the broad balance between the approaches?

This is an unexceptional list. Most of the projects I come across have some statement concerning target groups, methods and so on. Just about all the workers I talked with for this research had a work plan for the next three months or more. It is this middle-range planning that I am calling 'strategy'.

The idea of 'strategy' has come into progressive use in the field. It dovetails with the use of tactics by the workers studied here (tactics being elements of strategies). Three immediate influences have been at work in this respect. First, there has been the import of business management thinking and practice into the organization of fieldwork. Within that sphere, with increasing scale and the need for forward planning, strategic thinking has developed (Knight and Morgan, 1990). Second, and in relation to community work in particular, there has been a long-standing concern with influencing political processes and an explicit interest in building strategies of influence (see, for example, Francis and Henderson, 1992: 36–52). Last, and a little speculatively, within youth work I suspect that the notion of 'strategy' has also been promoted by the popularity of sports and games as means of working. [...]

Disposition

The framework is still incomplete. In my earlier work on informal education (Smith, 1988; Jeffs and Smith, 1990a) it become clear that practitioners were going beyond elements such as have been assembled here. When reflecting-in-action they were appealing to wider values and appreciations.

[...]

Here, I am suggesting that they are broadly guided in this by their understanding of what makes for the 'good'; of what makes for human well-being (Jeffs and Smith, 1990a: 17–18). This mode of thinking comes very close to what Aristotle describes as 'prudence' or 'practical wisdom' (*phronēsis*):

> It is thought to be the mark of a prudent man to be able to deliberate rightly about what is good and advantageous for himself; not in particular respects, e.g. what is good for health or physical strength, but what is conducive to the good life generally.
>
> (Aristotle, 1976: 209)

Phronēsis involves the disposition to act truly and justly (Carr and Kemmis, 1986: 33). It entails an orientation to 'good' or 'right' rather than 'correct' action. This frame of mind allows people to break a rule or convention if they judge that to follow it would not promote 'the good', either generally, or of those involved in specific situations (Grundy, 1987: 62). [...] Phronēsis, unlike more technical forms of reasoning, involves an understanding of other human beings:

> The person who is experienced in the world, the man who knows all the tricks and dodges and is experienced in everything there is, does not have the right understanding that the person who is acting needs; he has it only if he satisfies one requirement, namely that he too is seeking what is right, i.e. that he is united with the other person in this mutual interest.
>
> (Gadamer, 1979: 288)

[...]

Where educators are committed to working out the meaning of the universal in situations, and to exploring how actions may further that which is just and good, this can only happen in interaction with those with whom they are working. The action we seek to take is informed and committed. All of the elements interact, are open to change and are constructed and reconstructed in particular situations and contexts [...]. So it is that a fifth box enters our diagram (see Figure 15.4). In some respects, I could have included 'disposition' in with 'repertoire' – but its orientating role indicated that it may be of a different order for workers.

It should be noted that disposition is not simply temperament or personality. It is about a particular orientation. Obviously the intimate and dialogical nature of what we are examining here focuses attention on the person of the educator (Foreman, 1990). However, the defining features of the orientation involved in informed, committed action matter, too.

Direction, curriculum and context

Emerging here from the activity of local conversations, walking around neighbourhoods, visiting council offices and working with groups is a particular way of conceptualizing direction in education. It is some distance from curriculum models. Those models which focus on the use of behavioural objectives (curriculum as product) can be immediately ruled out as can those that centre on a body of knowledge-content and/or subjects, 'which are then "transmitted" or "delivered" to pupils by the most effective means' (Blenkin et al. 1992: 23). This leaves us with process/praxis approaches to curriculum-making to consider (Stenhouse, 1975; Grundy, 1987).

Process/praxis approaches are driven by general principles and emphasize judgement and meaning-making. The main difference between them is that the process approach does not make explicit statements about the interests it serves; the praxis model brings these to the centre of the process and makes an explicit commitment to emancipation (Grundy, 1987). At its centre is praxis: informed, committed action.

[...]

References

Aristotle (1976) *The Nicomachean Ethics* (trans. J. A. K. Thomson; revised H. Tredennick). London: Penguin.

Banks, M., Bates, I., Breakwell, G., Bynner, J., Emler, N., Jamieson, L. and Roberts, K. (1992) *Careers and Identities*. Milton Keynes: Open University Press.

Banton, M. (1968) *Roles. An Introduction to the Study of Social Relations*. London: Tavistock.

Barr, A. (1991) *Practising Community Development. Experience in Strathclyde*. London: Community Development Foundation.

Blenkin, G. M., Edwards, G. and Kelly, A. V. (1992) *Change and the Curriculum*. London: Paul Chapman.

Brookfield, S. D. (1983) *Adult Learning, Adult Education and the Community*. Milton Keynes: Open University Press.

Brookfield, S. D. (1987) *Developing Critical Thinkers. Challenging Adults to Explore Alternative Ways of Thinking and Acting*. Milton Keynes: Open University Press.

Brown, S. and McIntyre, D. (1993) *Making Sense of Teaching*. Buckingham: Open University Press.

Bruner, J. (1977) *The Process of Education*. Cambridge, MA: Harvard University Press.

Carr, W. and Kemmis, S. (1986) *Becoming Critical. Education, Knowledge and Action Research*. Lewes: Falmer.

Collins, M. (1991) *Adult Education as Vocation. A Critical Role for the Adult Educator*. London: Routledge.

Department of Education and Science (1982) *Experience and Participation. Review Group on the Youth Service in England* (Thompson Report). London: HMSO.

Fisher, E. (1993) 'A health education project' in M. K. Smith (ed.), *Youth or Adult? The First Five Years*. London: YMCA National College/Rank Foundation.

Foreman, A. (1990) 'Personality and curriculum' in T. Jeffs and M. Smith (eds), *Using Informal Education*. Buckingham: Open University Press.

Francis, D. and Henderson, P. (1992) *Working with Rural Communities*. London: Macmillan.

Gadamer, H.-G. (1979) *Truth and Method* (2nd edn). London: Sheed and Ward.

Goffman, E. (1986) *Frame Analysis. An Essay on the Organisation of experience*. Boston: Northeastern University Press. First published in 1974.

Grundy, S. (1987) *Curriculum: Product or Praxis*. Lewes: Falmer.

Jeffs, T. and Smith, M. (eds) (1990a) *Using Informal Education. An Alternative to Casework, Teaching and Control?* Buckingham: Open University Press.

Jeffs, T. and Smith, M. (1990b) 'Taking issue with issues', *Youth and Policy*, 28: 16–19.

Jones, R. (1987) *Like Distant Relatives. Adolescents' Perceptions of Social Work and Social Workers*. Aldershot: Gower.

Knight, D. and Morgan, G. (1990) 'The concept of strategy in sociology: A note of dissent', *Sociology*, 24(3) 475–83.

Lave, J. and Wenger, E. (1991) *Situated Learning. Legitimate Peripheral Participation*. Cambridge: Cambridge University Press.

Lindeman, E. (1987) 'Building a social philosophy of adult education' [1951] in S. Brookfield (ed.), *Learning Democracy. Eduard Lindeman on Adult Education and Social Change*. Beckenham: Croom Helm.

Lindeman, E. (1989) *The Meaning of Adult Education*. Norman: Oklahoma Research Centre for Continuing Professional and Higher Education. First published in 1926.

Priestley, P., McGuire, J., Flegg, D., Helmsley, V. and Welham, D. (1978) *Social Skills and Personal Problem Solving. A Handbook of Methods*. London: Tavistock.

Rosseter, B. (1987) 'Youth workers as educators' in T. Jeffs and M. Smith (eds), *Youth Work*. London: Macmillan.

Schön, D. A. (1983) *The Reflective Practitioner. How Professionals Think in Action*. London: Temple Smith.

Smith, M. (1980) *Creators not Consumers. Rediscovering Social Education*. Nuneaton: National Association of Youth Clubs.

Smith, M. (1988) *Developing Youth Work. Informal Education, Mutual Aid and Popular Practice*. Milton Keynes: Open University Press.

Stenhouse, L. (1975) *An Introduction to Curriculum Research and Development*. London: Heinemann.

Taylor, P. V. (1993) *The Texts of Paulo Freire*. Buckingham: Open University Press.

Thomas, D. N. (1983) *The Making of Community Work*. London: George Allen & Unwin.

Townsend, S. (1984) *The Growing Pains of Adrian Mole*. London: Methuen.

Turner, R. H. (1962) 'Role taking: process versus conformity' in A. H. Rose (ed.), *Human Behavior and Social Processes*. Boston: Houghton Mifflin.

Tyler, R. W. (1949) *Basic Principles of Curriculum and Instruction*. Chicago: University of Chicago Press.

Yinger, R. J. (1990) 'The conversation of practice' in R. T. Clift, W. R. Houston and M. C. Pugach (eds), *Encouraging Reflective Practice in Education. An Analysis of Issues and Programs*. New York: Teachers College Press.

PART 3

Professional development

16

Reflective practice

Neil Thompson

Introduction

The concept of reflective practice is one that is closely associated with the work of Donald Schön (Schön, 1983, 1987, 1992). It is an approach to professional practice that emphasizes the need for practitioners to avoid standardized, formula responses to the situations they encounter. Reflective practice involves coming to terms with the complexity, variability and uncertainty associated with human services work.

This chapter therefore explores the implications of developing reflective practice. It begins by addressing the basic question of: 'What is reflective practice?' From this we move on to consider the process of applying theory to practice. This involves clearing up some misunderstandings about the relationship between theory and practice, and establishing why it is important for practice to be based on theory. Finally, I shall explore the role of creativity in facilitating both systematic and anti-discriminatory practice.

What is reflective practice?

Reflective practice begins from the premise that human problems cannot be solved by the simple application of technical solutions. People's problems

This is a revised version of the original text which appeared as Chapter 24 in *People Skills, second edition* by Neil Thompson. First published in 2002 by Palgrave Macmillan. Reproduced with permission of Palgrave Macmillan.

are far too complex and 'messy' to be resolved in this way. Schön draws a distinction between the 'high ground' of theory and research and the 'swampy lowlands' of practice. He describes this as follows:

> In the varied topography of professional practice, there is a high, hard ground which overlooks a swamp. On the high ground, manageable problems lend themselves to solution through the use of research-based theory and technique. In the swampy lowlands, problems are messy and confusing and incapable of technical solution. The irony of the situation is that the problems of the high ground tend to be relatively unimportant to individuals or to society at large, however great their technical interest may be, while in the swamp lie the problems of greatest human concern.
>
> (Schön, 1983, p. 54)

One significant implication of this is that practitioners cannot sit back and wait for 'experts' to provide them with solutions on a plate. Workers have to engage with the complexities of practice and navigate a way through them. That is, reflective practice is an active process of constructing solutions, rather than a passive process of following procedures or guidelines.

In order to do this, we must first undertake what Schön (1983) calls 'problem setting'. The messy situations workers encounter do not come with clearly defined problems ready made for the practitioner to start working on. Consequently, the first task the worker faces is to make sense of the situation, to develop a picture of the problem(s) to be tackled. This, then, is the process of 'problem setting'. As Schön (1983) puts it: 'Problem setting is a process in which, interactively, we *name* the things to which we shall attend and *frame* the context in which we will attend to them' (p. 40). Problem setting is part of the process of assessment and illustrates the point that assessment should not be seen as routine or mechanical – it is an active process of forming a picture, identifying problems and mapping out a way forward.

In this way, we can see that the 'high ground' of theory is not going to provide 'off the peg' solutions. Rather, what needs to happen is for the overview we gain from the high ground to be combined and integrated with the specific insights we gain by being 'close to the action' within the actual situations we are dealing with. That is, workers need to use their experience and expertise in such a way that it comes to be 'tailor-made' for the specific situation they are working with at any particular time.

A reflective practitioner, then, is a worker who is able to use experience, knowledge and theoretical perspectives to guide and inform practice. However, this does not mean applying ideas in a blanket form, unthinkingly and uncritically, regardless of the circumstances. Reflective practice involves cutting the cloth to suit the specific circumstances, rather than looking for ready-made solutions.

To inexperienced workers, this may sound very difficult and daunting. However, it is based on a set of skills that can be developed with experience, and offers a sound basis for high-quality practice and high levels of job satisfaction.

Relating theory to practice

Reflective practice involves being able to relate theory to practice, drawing on existing frameworks of ideas and knowledge so that we do not have to 'reinvent the wheel' for each new situation that arises. I shall therefore address some of the key issues relating to the application of theory to practice. I shall begin by outlining two common misunderstandings concerning the relationship between theory and practice.

First, we need to recognize that the relationship is not a simple or straightforward one. Theory influences practice in a number of subtle and intricate ways, but practice can also influence theory (Thompson, 2000). These are important points to recognize, as they help to dispel the myth that theory and practice are separate, unconnected domains. I shall discuss below the dangers of driving a wedge between theory and practice. Second, it is also important to realize that theory does not provide hard and fast answers or clear, simple solutions to problems. To see it otherwise is to misconceive the part that theory plays in guiding practice.

These two sets of issues represent the two extremes of a continuum. At one extreme, the tendency to separate theory from practice is problematic in terms of cutting off an important resource for understanding practice situations. At the other extreme, it is unhelpful to have unrealistic expectations of what theory can or should offer, as this too can have the effect of driving a wedge between theory and practice.

The middle ground between these two extremes is where reflective practice operates. It involves recognizing the ways in which the general principles offered by theory can be adopted and 'tailored' to fit the specific circumstances of each situation dealt with. The tendency to divorce theory from practice is a dangerous one in so far as it leaves us open to a number of possible difficulties. These should become clear by considering why we should integrate theory and practice as effectively as possible.

In a previous text (Thompson, 2000), I identified the following six reasons for relating theory to practice. I shall comment briefly on each of the six.

Anti-discriminatory practice

[...] Discrimination and oppression are inherent in the way society is organized. We therefore need to pay attention to theories of discrimination and oppression if we are to challenge their destructive effects. A reliance on 'common sense' is likely to reflect, rather than challenge, dominant discriminatory attitudes.

The fallacy of theoryless practice

Even if a framework of ideas is not used deliberately or explicitly, it is inevitable that our actions will be guided by sets of ideas and assumptions. The idea that we can have practice without theory is therefore a fallacy. A theory does not have to be a formal or 'official' theory as found in books or academic journals. Theory can refer to any ideas or frameworks of understanding that are used to make sense of our everyday experience and practice situations.

Theory is therefore inevitably applied to practice, but, if we do not apply such theory explicitly or deliberately, we are relying on untested assumptions and therefore leaving a lot to chance.

Evaluation

Evaluating our practice gives us useful opportunities to learn from our experience by identifying what worked well and what was problematic [...]. In order to do this we have to draw on a theory base. For example, in evaluating a particular approach that was adopted, we need to have at least a basic understanding of the ideas on which that approach is based.

Continuous professional development

[...] A commitment to continuous professional development [...] depends on a theory base. The process involves avoiding 'getting into a rut' of unthinking, uncritical routines. Continuous professional development rests on our ability and willingness to adopt a reflective approach, to think creatively and critically about our work.

Professional accountability

As professionals, people workers are accountable for their actions. Consequently, we need to be able to explain and justify the decisions we make and the steps we take. It is difficult, if not impossible, to do this without reference to a theory base. Professional accountability demands reasoned arguments to justify our actions, and this, of course, involves drawing on a set of concepts that guide and inform our practice.

Inappropriate responses

If we rely on 'common sense' responses to the problems we encounter, there is a serious danger that our actions may not only prove ineffective but actually make the situation worse:

> A failure to draw on theoretical knowledge may lead to an inappropriate response on the part of the worker. We may misinterpret what is happening and react in a way which is not helpful or which even makes the situation worse. For example, a person experiencing a bereavement may express considerable anger towards the worker. If the worker does not recognise such anger as a common part of the grieving process, he or she could easily misread the situation and interpret the anger as a rejection of the worker's help. (Thompson, 2000, p. 35)

Reflective practice, as these six examples illustrate, owes much to a purposeful application of theory to practice. This goes far beyond an implicit, uncritical use of theory, and involves a proactive approach to using theoretical ideas and knowledge as a framework for maximizing effectiveness.

This brings us to the question of how can we apply theory to practice – what needs to be done to draw on the benefits that theory can offer? This is a vast topic and so, in the space available, I shall limit myself to outlining the following six steps that can be taken to promote reflective practice:

- *Read* For theory to be used to best effect it is important that we break down the barriers by challenging the assumption that reading is for students or staff in training and not for fully-fledged practitioners. Unfortunately, it is commonly assumed by many people that reflecting on theory is a task for students but not for practitioners. For example, an experienced social worker once told me that he missed being a student as he had enjoyed reading widely on the subject of social work and related topics. When I asked him what was stopping him from continuing to do so, he struggled for an answer. In the end, he replied that it was because it was 'not the done thing'. It is important, then, that such a 'reading is for students only' culture is broken down. Some may argue that they do not have enough time to read. However, there are two points that need to be made in response to this. First, time spent reading is an *investment* of time and can, by enhancing our practice, save time in the long-run. Second, reading can increase our levels of job satisfaction by giving us a broader perspective and greater insights into people work. In view of this, I feel it is worth devoting some of our own time, outside of working hours, to read about subjects related to our work.
- *Ask* 'Asking' can apply in two ways. First, in relation to reading, much of the people work literature base is written in a jargonistic academic

style that makes it difficult to understand. It can be helpful, then, to ask other people about such issues so that you can get past this barrier. The danger is that some people may give up on reading because they feel uncomfortable with the style of writing being used. Second, we can learn a great deal from other people's practice. Students often learn a great deal by asking questions like: 'Why do you do it that way?' or 'Have you any ideas how I might tackle this situation?' There is much to be gained from creating an open, inquiring, mutually supportive atmosphere in which all staff, not just students, can learn from each other.

- *Watch*   There is much to be learned from developing an enhanced level of awareness in terms of observational skills. Much of the time we may miss significant issues because we treat situations as routine and commonplace. We need to remember that every situation is unique in some ways, and so we need to be attuned to what is happening and not make blanket assumptions. Practising in a routine, uncritical way can mean that we are, in effect, going around with our eyes closed, oblivious to significant factors that could be very important in terms of how we deal with the situation. Theoretical knowledge can help us understand and explain our experience, but if our experience is closed off by a failure to be sensitive to what is happening, then we will not notice that there is anything to be explained. Reflective practice relies on developing a sensitivity to what is happening around us.

- *Feel*   The emotional dimension of people work is [...] a very important one. Our emotional responses can, at times, be painful and difficult to deal with. At the other extreme, using theory can sometimes be seen as cold and technical. However, this does not mean that the two – thinking and feeling – cannot be reconciled. Thought can help us understand (and therefore deal with) feeling, and feelings can help bring theory to life, turn concepts into working tools, and thereby develop a reflective approach.

- *Talk*   Sharing views about work situations and how these can be dealt with encourages a broad perspective. It provides opportunities for people to learn from each other's experience, to find common ground and identify differences of approach. Constructive dialogue about methods of work, reasons for taking particular courses of action and so on can be an excellent way of broadening horizons, deepening understanding and enhancing skills. Such dialogue also helps to create an open and supportive working environment, and this, in itself, can be an important springboard for reflective practice.

- *Think*   There are two main barriers to a thoughtful approach to practice. These are routines and pressure. A routinized approach amounts to working 'on automatic pilot' and is clearly a dangerous way of dealing with the sensitive issues. As I mentioned earlier, dealing with situations in a routine, unthinking way leaves us very vulnerable to mistakes. Pressure can also stand in the way of thinking about our practice. If we are very busy we have to be wary of allowing ourselves to be pressurized into not thinking about what we are doing. We need to remain in control of our workload [...] so that we are able to think about our actions. Thinking time should be seen as an essential part of good practice, rather than a luxury that has to be dispensed with when the pressure is on.

These steps are not the only ones that can be taken to develop reflective practice but they should provide a good 'launch pad' for working out patterns of practice that can draw on the benefits of a reflective approach. One further important step towards reflective practice is the development of creative approaches, and it is to these that we now turn.

Creative approaches

Students training to enter the human services are often anxious to be presented with ready-made techniques to use in practice, a toolbox of methods that can be applied in a simple or straightforward way. Such expectations, although understandable, are both unrealistic and unhelpful.

They are unrealistic because there are only a limited number of techniques that can be applied across a range of situations, and these will not be enough, in themselves, to provide an adequate repertoire for people workers. They are unhelpful because they are based on an inappropriate model of professional development. The worker should be seen not as a receptacle or storehouse to be 'stocked up' with methods and techniques, but rather as a generator of ideas and potential solutions.

There will be common themes across the situations encountered (and this is where theory can be of great value) but there will also be features unique to each situation. People workers therefore have to be equipped to deal with novel situations by generating novel solutions. It is therefore worth considering, albeit briefly, how a creative approach can be developed.

De Bono is a writer closely associated with the notion of creativity through his writings on 'lateral thinking': 'Lateral thinking is specifically associated with the ability to escape from existing perceptual (and conceptual) patterns in order to draw up new ways of looking at things and doing things' (1986, p. 114). Creativity, then, involves moving away from the tramlines that lock us into routine practices and narrow perspectives.

A major barrier to developing creativity is an attitude that says: 'I can't. I'm not the sort of person who's creative'. [...] This is a defeatist attitude that confuses skills with qualities. This is particularly significant with regard to creativity, as it is sometimes seen as having an almost magical quality, as if it were a 'special gift'. However, de Bono's comments on this are again helpful: 'There is a great deal of rubbish written about creativity because – like motherhood – it is automatically a good thing. My preference is to treat creativity as a logical process rather than a matter of talent or mystique' (1986, p. 114).

Creativity, then, can be learned; it can be developed through deliberate effort and experience. To promote this type of development, I shall present five strategies for stimulating a creative approach. These are:

- *Changing angle*   Have you ever noticed how different a room looks if you sit in a different position from your usual one? Changing our 'angle' on a situation can give us a new perspective, with fresh insights. It can therefore pay dividends to switch position, metaphorically, so that we see the situations we are dealing with from different angles. This is also an important part of working in partnership, learning to see situations from other people's points of view so that we can more effectively work together.
- *Developing a vision*   Having clear objectives [...] involves developing a vision of where we want to be, the point we want to reach. This type of vision can also stimulate creativity. If we know where we are now and where we want to be in future, then we can map out the various routes for getting there, different 'modes of transport' and so on. By generating such options we are avoiding the narrow focus of seeing only one way forward.
- *Stepping back*   Sometimes we can get so close to a situation that we 'cannot see the wood for the trees', and we therefore get bogged down or lose our sense of direction. By 'stepping back', we can put some distance between ourselves and the situation that we are tackling. Stepping back from a situation gives us a breathing space and helps us develop a fresh perspective.
- *Letting go*   The technique of brainstorming can be a very helpful one by allowing people to make lots of suggestions without having to worry about whether they are sensible, logical or workable. In this way, the strait-jacket of conventional thinking can be thrown off and the potential for creative solutions is released. By 'letting go' in this way we generate a wide range of possibilities, many of which will have to

be rejected as unsuitable. However, amongst these, there may well be a veritable nugget of gold.

- *Provocation*   This is another concept from de Bono, and he explains it in the following terms:

  > A patterning system like the mind creates patterns which we then continue to use. Most of our thinking is concerned with fitting things into these patterns so that we can act usefully and effectively. But to change patterns and to unlock those 'insight patterns' which are readily available to us (only after we have found them) we need something entirely different. Provocation is the process. With provocation we do not describe something as it is or as it could be. With provocation we look at the 'what if' and 'suppose' ... Provocation creates an unstable idea so that we may move on from it to a new idea. (1983, p. 200)

Conclusion

Reflective practice involves drawing on theory, in so far as this represents the accumulated experience and expertise of others. In this way, we can use the theory base to avoid the need to 'reinvent the wheel'. However, theory does not come tailor-made for practice – the cloth has to be cut to fit the circumstances. The reflective practitioner therefore has to *engage* with theory, to use it and shape it creatively in a constructive and positive way, rather than simply wait passively for theory to provide ready-made solutions.

Reflective practice is, then, a creative and proactive practice, one that casts the practitioner in an active role. This is an approach to practice that is entirely consistent with people work, a form of work where the situations we deal with have many common themes, but are also, in some ways, special and unique. Reflective practice offers the use of a theory base to help us understand the common themes, and a focus on creativity to help us deal with the unique aspects of each situation we encounter.

References

Bono, E. de (1983) *Atlas of Management Thinking*, Harmondsworth, Penguin.

Bono, E. de (1986) *Conflicts*, Harmondsworth, Penguin.

Schön, D. A. (1983) *The Reflective Practitioner*, New York, Basic Books.

Schön, D. A. (1987) *Educating the Reflective Practitioner*, San Francisco, Jossey Bass.

Schön, D. A. (1992) 'The Crisis of Professional Knowledge and the Pursuit of an Epistemology of Practice', *Journal of Interprofessional Care*, 6(1).

Thompson, N. (2000) *Theory and Practice in Human Services*, 2nd edn, Buckingham, Open University Press.

17

'The sum of the parts' – exploring youth working identities

Stan Tucker

A sense of identity

There are many ways in which we define ourselves or others define us. Through our religious beliefs, social class, education, family experiences, occupational status, to name but a few. What we are and how we see ourselves is the product of a range of opportunities and life chances (Goffman, 1959; Giddens, 1991). Sometimes we make conscious choices to follow a particular path and on other occasions our 'options' can be restricted by the actions of others – parents, teachers, social workers, etc. On occasions we are able to express our autonomy and a sense of freedom, at other times powerful external forces may gently (or sometimes not so gently) move us in a particular direction.

Within this chapter the opportunity is provided to explore how different forces, factors and demands can shape the occupational identities of those who work with young people in today's society. To understand what youth working involves is to understand how expectations about the kind of work that needs to be carried out with the young come together (Tucker, 2004). The argument is made here that those working with young people have some degree of autonomy as to how they might carry out their work. Yet at the same time there are a range of influences – social, economic, educational, political and occupational that are important to understand when it comes to exploring what those working with young people do and why they do it.

Here, the term 'youth working' is deliberately used as a form of shorthand to cover the range of occupational activities involved in the areas of education, social care and health. These occupational areas are brought together in this way for a very specific reason. For it will be argued that those working with the young enter their respective fields of work with a range of common pressures and issues shaping their day-to-day practices. Such pressures and issues come in a range of shapes and sizes but they are consistently filtered through the policies that govern work with the young, the kind of services that are created for them, education and training opportunities, and priorities and visions for different kinds of work.

In turn, occupational identities are constructed out of much more than the skills, knowledge and status that individuals and groups possess. For identities are also the product of attitudes and values that are held by a particular occupational group; the way those attitudes and values are shaped; the external pressures that are able to influence both attitudes and values and priorities for practice. Understanding how people view themselves and the ways in which such images are accepted, modified or rejected by others assists in clarifying what can be considered to be professional practice. Specifically it will be asserted that the youth working identity is the 'sum of various parts' and it is how these parts come together that determines the responses that are made to the perceived needs of young people.

It's all in 'the game'

How we see young people, the ways in which those working with them respond to their 'needs', what are defined as 'legitimate' ways of working, are all crucial to that which is carried out in the name of youth working. For it is important to remember that while a range of professions and occupations claim the possession of specific and sometimes-unique skills to work with young people (Esland, 1980), at the same time their long-term credibility can depend on the ability to respond to wider social problems, issues and policies (Wilding, 1982). For example, the youth justice worker is expected to 'turn young people away from crime', the Connexions worker to improve the employment prospects of 'marginalized' young people, the Residential social worker to care for and control those deemed to be 'at risk'. Targets for activity are frequently externally generated, often through government departments and their agents. The ability to meet such targets may influence the longer-term survival prospects of particular organisations and groups or at the very least influence the level of resources offered to them. For it is more likely that governments, for example, will feel better disposed to those occupational groups who are willing to pursue their priorities.

Crucially, specific policies and practices are consistently promoted and used to define some of the key parameters for youth working activity. To understand these parameters there is a need to comprehend the key policy ideas and forms of practice that underpin them. For many of those working with the young would rightly claim that they do their best to provide high quality and relevant services that meet the real needs of young people and in doing so have the ability to prioritise, organise and structure their work. The concept of 'professional autonomy' (Finlay, 2000) is frequently advanced as a crucial element in defining the nature of professional work. The idea being that those involved in such activity have a significant amount of freedom to shape their activities in the workplace. But how free are individuals and groups to determine approaches to work, their priority audiences, how resources are to be distributed, etc.?

This is certainly a contentious area for debate. For it is advocated here, that to really understand current agendas and priorities for work with the young there is a need to dig below the level of what might be usefully described as occupational intentions and practices. In order to achieve this it is possible to use the analogy of a 'game' to demonstrate the range of factors that serve to shape day-to-day practice (Tucker, 2004). The 'game' then, varies according to the demands being made on young people and those working with them. Those demands can be potentially empowering: to promote rights and responsibilities; to engage young people in decision-making; or to assist them to voice their opinions. The demands, however, can also be constraining: concerned with control, regulation and conformity. Sometimes the demands point in one direction, sometimes in another and sometimes potentially competing demands are placed alongside each other. The arena for the 'game' also changes, be it education, health or social care with such arenas often advancing congruent and sometimes very different representations of youth working. The players in the 'game' are young people, those working with them, politicians, parents, and so on. There is also the issue of equality of treatment in the 'game' to consider. There exist various divisions or leagues of young people, principally constituted around notions of 'race', gender, disability or social class. In turn, professionals are assigned the task of controlling, gatekeeping, guiding and educating these particular groups.

Yet, the boundaries of the 'game' do not stop there insofar as particular concepts of youth and youth working permeate the very foundations upon which services for the young are created – they influence 'game plans', tactics and strategies. Griffin (1993) provides a framework for better understanding the forces that are in fact highly instrumental in shaping, prioritising and determining the nature of services offered to young people and their parents within society. The lives of the young are consistently viewed as being 'problematic' by wider society. Various labels are used to describe the actions and activities of the young – 'deviant', 'mad', 'bad', 'perverted', 'diseased', and so on. In this way specific 'representations' of the period of youth are constructed and sustained. It is argued, however, that these views are so dominant (they permeate media accounts of young people's lives, government reports, approaches to professional education and training, research reports, etc.) that they significantly influence practice approaches. Young people need to be 'contained', 'controlled', 'educated', 'diverted', and so on – in turn such practice approaches come to dominate the youth working agenda and forms of service delivery.

There is also a price to pay for poor performance in the 'game'. For like young people, those who work with them who fail to respond to wider agendas and concerns can soon become the target for criticism and sanction – their 'tactics' can become a focus for government scrutiny, their attitudes labelled as inappropriate or 'dangerous' (Tucker, 1999). For example, claims have been made by the state, through both political and employer channels that the skills and knowledge possessed by many of those working with young people fail to meet the demands of today's society. The importance of this kind of action should not be underestimated. For in questioning the approaches of those working with young people, a climate is created whereby it is possible to legitimise different kinds of state-sponsored interventions – the development of new approaches to training via a system of National Vocational Qualifications, the introduction of school league tables and national testing, the transferring of services from the statutory to the voluntary and private sectors, etc. Sometimes overtly and sometimes covertly the rules of the 'game' can be transformed.

Adapting identities to circumstances

There can be no doubt that the world of youth working is changing at a rapid rate. Alongside this, individuals and groups are left to make sense of emerging government policies, changes in funding regimes, the need to target services, etc. The impact of external pressure, particularly around the requirements of government, can cause anxiety and stress for those working with young people. Indeed, it would appear that those groups who want to hold on to their professional status must acknowledge, and at least in part embrace, the constraints and controls applied by external groups (Abbott and Wallace, 1990).

Perhaps this has always been the case that no occupational group is ever completely free to 'do its own thing'. Yet the climate for work with young people (particularly in the public sector) has changed so fundamentally, that there is a need to understand not only the nature of that change, but also how it impacts on professional work and the identities adopted by individuals and groups. Think for a moment about how the welfare state has changed in recent times. No longer is the public sector the sole provider of services for the young. We have 'purchasers' (sometimes local authorities) and 'providers' (sometimes the voluntary or private sectors) of services. Projects are often only supported if a range of partners is willing to work together to offer services and support. Indeed, the advent of what the government often describes as 'joined up' services means that interprofessional activity is required to meet multiple objectives – improvements in health, education, social care, etc. (Mittler, 2001). Professionals are expected to work together and share their expertise and skills. At one level this can have positive outcomes in that new ways of working may be developed. At the same time some may feel that the 'unique' skills they possess are effectively downgraded or lost through such relationships.

How, then, do such factors combine to influence the professional identities of those involved in youth working? The argument being made here is that how we speak about young people, research into their needs, develop services for them, etc. is essentially underpinned by the views that are expressed by policy makers. For those who hold sway in powerful institutions, the enforcers of legislation, professional groupings, etc. are able to influence and shape views and perspectives about young people. One intention of this kind of activity is to influence the boundaries and priorities of professional work. In this way youth can be variously seen as a period for fostering and developing ambitions; as a time of transition; as a period where the 'problematic' behaviour of some must be regulated and controlled. The important point to make is that the power to define youth and youth working often rests with those who are seen to have invested in them knowledge, power and the ability to make their voices heard (Griffin, 1993).

Changing youth working

Much of that described above is encapsulated in government pronouncements during the late 1990s and early 2000s concerning the need to develop multidisciplinary and interprofessional work with the young. This agenda, though, is about much more than the promotion of 'joined up' services to improve quality (Blakemore, 1998). The government has used a variety of public concerns, with a particular focus in this instance being placed on a continuing failure to 'safeguard' children from abuse, to bringing forward a radical agenda for altering service structures, work priorities and approaches to education and training for those working with the young.

The 'safeguarding' children agenda consistently reflects a range of concerns around the ability of particular professional groups i.e. social workers, teachers, health personnel etc. to offer appropriate support to those considered to be 'at risk' of abuse (Laming, 2003). We see presented through the media, representations of work with children and young people that is variously described as inefficient, ineffective, badly co-ordinated and of poor quality. In part these themes are extracted from many of the reports inquiring into the deaths of children in abusive circumstances. In part they are the product of ongoing media-influenced concerns that serve to fuel public pressure about the need to reform social work, teaching, etc. In turn, we witness a level of 'panic' in the media that is transmitted to the public and politicians. Now, it is not being suggested here that many of the complaints made about work in this area aren't justified – although media-inspired policy pronouncements need to be carefully scrutinised. However, what happens with these kinds of complaint: how they are reported and constructed; the 'evidence' that is cited in support; who is deemed to be 'responsible'; can assist in providing a justification for radical change to be introduced to work with young people.

Following on from the publication of the report 'Every Child Matters: The Next Steps' (DfES, 2004a) (a product of Lord Laming's inquiry into the death of Victoria Climbié) the government introduced changes to both the structure and organisation of services for the young and the way individuals and groups are trained. The Children Act (2004) requires increased levels of co-operation at a local level. New 'safeguarding' children services are in place. Local authorities are required to make a directorate level appointment to co-ordinate health, social care and education policy and service delivery. Joint inspections will be undertaken of work. The post of national Children's Commissioner has been introduced. These changes will undoubtedly have a major influence in practice terms and influence how services, occupational groups and individuals organise, prioritise and deliver their work.

At the same time the government has constructed a set of core competencies, skills and abilities that those working with children and young people need to possess when it comes to the safeguarding of children (DfES, 2004b). Whether such skills are 'appropriate' or 'inappropriate' is not the subject of this discussion. The important connection to make is that the government is attempting to influence what constitutes the necessary skill and knowledge mix within this area. Crucially, it will ultimately be this range of skills and knowledge that occupational groups are expected to take on board within the context of education and training activities.

In looking at this particular example we begin to see that the process of professional identity construction does not take place in a uniform way. The formation of an identity may be the product of a change in policy, practice, structural organisation or education and training. The formation of an identity takes place in different arenas of activity, at different times and in a variety of ways. If we take for example the area of education and training, the important point to grasp is that those in positions of power have the ability to shape and influence the knowledge base of an occupational group. The control of the content and delivery of education and training can be seen as one of the important ways that professional identities can be modified or changed.

At the same time it is important to note that such changes are not necessarily received in an uncritical fashion. What is delivered, how a nationally prescribed training programme is interpreted, the way that changes are discussed, analysed and presented are important factors to consider. Different parties – government, educators, fieldwork practitioners, trade unions, managers, employers, etc. contest the professional education and training curriculum. For Apple (1993, p. 43) such a curriculum should be viewed as a 'site of political struggle'. It is used in a variety of ways, sometimes to promote change and sometimes to resist it. It is, however, important to recognise that there is not a 'grand narrative' to which all parties are willing to subscribe. Indeed Apple promotes the view that the knowledge and skills agenda of any profession will be contested and debated at almost every level. In turn there is resistance by some and acceptance by others. Resistance for example might come in the form of the challenging of 'problematising' perspectives of the young by trainers. Acceptance may come from employers who want to move towards competency-based work that increases levels of occupational accountability.

What can be said with a high degree of certainty is that the way professional identities are constructed, organised, developed and delivered is subject to a range of factors. In looking at any occupation there is a need to audit its activities and priorities from a variety of positions. Specific consideration should be given to:

- Government priorities for particular areas of work – looking at policies, reading and listening to political speeches can usefully reveal these
- Media representations of the work of particular occupational groups – sometimes these emerge as specific responses to youth related problems, perceived 'failure' to respond to the needs of the young, etc.
- Resistance to changes in education and training – this might come from trade unionists, trainers or professional bodies
- Employer driven demands for change – often the product of concerns about the suitability of education and training programmes to deliver appropriately skilled workers
- Changes to the structure and organisation of services and the way these can be used to create new patterns of working
- Control of resources and their distribution to direct practice and work priorities
- How dominant representations of the period of youth can be highly influential in shaping service delivery

Identity as a 'sum of the parts'

The major concern within this chapter has been to demonstrate that to understand how professional youth working identities are developed, it is important to understand the factors that influence their construction. In essence the occupational identity of anyone working with young people is the sum of a variety of different parts. It is the way that these parts can combine, as well as the way that one part may be more influential than another, that shapes both how those working with young people see themselves and the way others perceive them.

This form of analysis is important in the sense that it moves us away from seeing professional work as being solely underpinned by a high degree of individual or collective autonomy. Individuals and groups enjoy a significant degree of influence over the work they do but crucially the story does not end there. If we see the construction of an occupational identity as part of a much wider 'game' then our ability to understand the nature of the work carried out with young people is significantly expanded.

In essence the construction of any occupational identity should be viewed as a 'site of struggle' (Foucault, 1991). For the reality is that a variety of groups use different strategies in an attempt to determine the nature of the work that is carried out with the young. The 'struggle', however, is not just concerned with the methods employed to intervene – the debate runs much deeper than that. At the heart of the 'struggle' other forces and factors can be seen to be at work. Young people, it has been argued here, are viewed in particular ways within society. The labels that are applied to them are so powerful it can be asserted that they dominate public perceptions and media representations of the period of youth. Yet more than this, the representations of the period of youth employed shape the kind of services that are provided for them. Reflect on this issue for a moment for the statement has a profound significance on the construction of occupational identities. If you have the power to define the period of youth and if such definitions come to dominate societal perceptions then how we see young people and how we talk about them become that much more important.

The terms 'competing discourse' and 'dominant discourse' are useful ones to employ in order to capture the complexity of the situation. Imagine a range of conversations (discourses) being conducted in society about young people. Some may have a positive agenda – the central concern could be about promoting young people's rights, extending opportunities for participation and empowerment, etc. Alongside this other conversations (discourses) may pursue the 'problematic' agenda of youth – influenced by demands to control and regulate their activities (Griffin, 1993). And crucially these conversations do not unfold in a simple linear way; there may be elements of both discourses in for example a government policy about crime prevention. What decides the main thrust of work with the young, however, is the discourse or discourses that come to dominate public, professional, government and crucially media perceptions. Individuals, groups, organisations and governments struggle to dominate the discursive agenda. Dominant discourses are also challenged and some may attempt to subvert or change them.

Youth working takes many forms within society. It has been likened here to a game where a variety of players attempt to influence tactics, 'win' resources and dominate the ideas and practices of others. Crucially, what emerges from this analysis is that the field of play is far from equal. Groups, institutions and governments use various means at their disposal in an attempt to control the game. Yet at the same time those working with young people possess a degree of autonomy to interpret the rules of the game and in some instances modify or adapt them.

The youth working occupational identity can be usefully described as 'the sum of the parts'. Those parts are shaped and determined by a range of factors. Here an attempt has been made to demonstrate how those parts come together to influence work with the young. Yet the parts are not fixed in any absolute sense. Ways of working with young people and the priorities attached to such work change over time – to meet new demands, uncertainties, problems, etc. To understand the youth working identity is to understand the complex issues that underpin and influence occupational identity construction.

References

Abbott, P. and Wallace, C. (1990) *The Sociology of the Caring Professions*, London: Falmer.

Apple, M. (1993) 'What post-modernists forget: cultural capital and official knowledge', *Curriculum Studies*, 1(3).

Blakemore, K. (1998) *Social Policy: an introduction*, Buckingham: Open University Press.

Department for Education and Skills (2004a) *Every Child Matters: The Next Steps*, Nottingham: DfES Publications.

Department for Education and Skills (2004b) *Building a Children's Workforce – A Common Core of Skills, Knowledge & Competence* (Issue 2), London: DfES.

Esland, G. (1980) 'Professions and Professionalisation', in Esland, G. and Salaman, G. (eds), *The Politics of Work and Occupations*, Milton Keynes: Open University Press.

Finlay, L. (2000) 'The Challenge of Professionalism' in Brechin, A., Brown, H., and Eby, M. A. (eds), *Critical Practice in Health and Social Care*, London: Sage.

Foucault, M. (1991) *Discipline and Punish: the Birth of the Prison*, Harmondsworth: Penguin.

Giddens, A. (1991) *Modernity and Self-Identity: Self and Society in the Late Modern Age*, Cambridge: Polity Press.

Goffman, E. (1959) *The Presentation of Self in Everyday Life*, New York: Doubleday Anchor.

Griffin, C. (1993) *Representations of Youth: the Study of Adolescence in Britain and America*, Cambridge: Polity Press.

Lord Laming (2003) *The Victoria Climbié Inquiry*, Norwich: HMSO.

Mittler, P. (2001) *Working Towards Inclusive Education Social Contexts*, London: David Fulton.

Tucker, S. (1999) 'Making the Link: dual 'problematization', discourse and work with young people', *Journal of Youth Studies*, 2(3).

Tucker, S. (2004), 'Youth Working: Professional Identities Given, Received and Contested', in Roche, J., Tucker, S., Thomson, R. and Flynn, R. (eds), *Youth in Society*, London: Sage.

Wilding, P. (1982) *Professional Power and Social Welfare*, London: Routledge and Kegan Paul.

18

Using line management

Annmarie Turnbull

This chapter begins by defining what we mean by line management supervision. It places this in the wider context of learning organisations and personal and organisational change. Your individual needs as a supervisee are then considered, prior to a more detailed outlining of the purposes and processes of managerial supervision. The chapter ends by asking you to evaluate your own existing arrangements for line management supervision and to plan any changes you need to make in them.

What is line management supervision?

To answer this question, we need to look at the two terms, 'supervision' and 'line management' separately.

Supervision

What is supervision? What does it mean to supervise? One dictionary definition says that it is 'to superintend, oversee the execution of a task etc. and to

This is a revised version of the original text which appeared as Chapter 18 in *Principles & Practice of Informal Education* edited by Linda Deer Richardson and Mary Wolfe. First published in 2001 by RoutledgeFalmer.

oversee the actions or work of a person'. […] For the moment let us use the term in its generic, everyday meaning.

[…]

When asked how it felt to be supervised in the way described by the definition some responses to the question were:

> When I was about seven my mother let me make some scones. I felt a bit frightened but excited and very proud when I'd made them.

> If I get stuck with something I go to my boss and ask for her views. It makes me feel supported and responsible.

> My boss went through a weekly checklist on my work every Monday. I hated it. It was so cold and seemed to be about getting things off the list, not the hows and whys of the work. It was unreal.

> I was about ten and my dad supervised my painting a figurine. I felt we were a team achieving something together.

> A friend who's a DIY buff checked each stage when I tried to assemble a wardrobe. At first it annoyed me, it seemed so slow, but I really needed it. It showed me what I usually do wrong and made me a bit more confident.

You might have found that […] being supervised, [has] strong feelings associated with it, both negative and positive. It is helpful to monitor your own feelings about supervision in a wide range of contexts, as this can have a powerful effect on how useful the line management supervision you receive at work can be to your learning, and to the learning of the organisation for which you work.

Line management

Line management responsibility is represented by vertical lines, joining managers and those for whom they are accountable, on what is often called an organisation chart. The chart diagrams the roles of the people within the organisation and the formal avenues of accountability that exist. While ultimately the head of the organisation, whether called the Director, Principal or Manager, is responsible for what happens in the work place, line management produces a chain of responsibility. A sensible organisation will ensure that measures are in place that enable the work to be done both efficiently, for example with clear boundaries of responsibility, and effectively, for example to the standard the agency has set itself. Line management is one method of strengthening these measures. It enables all workers to be clear about whom in the organisation they must answer to about their work performance.

[…]

If line management supervision is linked to responsibility for a person's work, as it usually is, its primary purpose is to help to manage the work and achieve the organisation's goals. Effective managerial supervision provides an opportunity for an organisation to get the best from its staff, who, after all, are its major resource. But it is also concerned with your development as an individual professional worker. We will consider the purposes of line management supervision, for the organisation, the worker, and the manager, next.

The learning organisation

All the people in an organisation are potential resources for learning. Knowles' comment on learning in organisations draws attention to the potential of every work setting for learning.

> No educational institution teaches just through its courses, workshops and institutes; no corporation teaches just through its in-service education programs; and no voluntary organisation teaches just through its meetings and study groups. They all teach by everything they do, and often they teach opposite lessons in their organisational operation from that which they teach in their educational program.
>
> (quoted in Hughes and Pengelly, 1997: 77)

From this perspective, it is apparent that line management needs to be evaluated to ensure that it constantly meets the needs of the participants. How far and in what ways your work place is meeting its obligations to its clients can, in part, be discovered by assessing what is happening in supervision. Are the needs of all the participants (employee, manager, client(s)) being met appropriately?

In 1967, Joan Tash described a project that aimed to train the supervisors of youth workers. Her book is every bit as valuable today as it was [over] three decades ago, because it looks in detail at the processes of supervision at work and measures their outcomes. Tash concluded that supervision was a valuable learning forum. Among the sorts of learning it facilitated were: learning to use theories (that is, to relate theories to practice); learning to use feelings; learning to use values; learning from practical situations and learning to manage time better. But Tash also acknowledged that the supervisory relationship often has limitations. Mistakes were made within supervision and it was not a panacea for bad practice elsewhere in organisations.

One of the key thinkers on learning in organisations, Argyris (1982), pointed out that we only learn in environments where we are encouraged to be responsible, productive and creative, and where errors are seen as the vehicle for learning. A good learning culture needs to provide opportunities for risk taking and for experiential, practical and reflective learning; and this is what we want to enhance, not only in our line management supervision, but through-out the organisations we work for.

Supervision and the informal education worker

As Christian and Kitto have recognised, the work of informal education offers particular challenges:

> The worker functions in relative isolation, often alone and in the evenings when other professionals are at home; works within a framework where there are few restrictions on the kind of activity; and meets situations charged with emotions. All this means that the worker is more prone to confusion, and more subject to chaos, than those working in more structured ways.

> (Christian and Kitto, 1987: 1)

This potential for isolation and lack of clarity in the work of many people, including adult educators, youth and community workers, advice and health education workers, teachers and social workers, is reason enough for making the best use of any available line management supervision.

It is also an opportunity to broaden or deepen your professional skills. In fact, the activities involved in line management supervision can make this one of the most useful learning forums in our working lives.

It may be that you have only a baseline knowledge and experience of some areas of work. Perhaps you have helped people in distress and have used some rudimentary counselling techniques. Your manager could help you to identify different levels of expertise in helping those in distress and increase and deepen the repertoire of knowledge and skills you use.

Again, if you have never acted for and on behalf of young people and your job requires you to work as an advocate, you will inevitably lack all the knowledge and skills you need to undertake that role proficiently. Managerial supervision is the arena in which to specify and evaluate your learning goals.

Finally, while some people think that a professional qualification magi-cally bestows the ability to operate successfully at work without feedback from your manager, this is rarely the case. As individuals we are constantly changing as we age and gain new experiences. We are also frequently working in settings which themselves are, as Christian and Kitto remind us, demanding and con-fusing. Our agencies may be undergoing profound changes in terms of their values and orientation, their priorities or their operating systems. And of course all this is set within a constantly changing wider society which impacts constantly on our selves and our work. All these changes are the backdrop to the line management supervisory relationship.

[...]

The manager's aims for supervision

Line management supervision can be a microcosm of the wider management of the agency or it can operate in apparent isolation or even conflict with the organisation as a whole. It may be regulated by rigid policies and procedures, by form-filling and checklists, just as the wider work of the agency is. It can be an apparently unstructured and informal activity within an agency that prides itself on non-hierarchical structures and easy-going, non-judgemental working relationships. Or, in contrast, a vague commitment to managerial supervision may operate in a highly regimented work place and a careful, regularly monitored supervision process may exist in an apparently chaotic work place. Ideally, however, this relationship at work needs to be part of a wider management strategy to enhance the support, learning and individual accountability of all the agency's staff and, by extension, of its clients.

In managerial terms, the overall aim of the relationship is to maximise your competence and confidence in order to help you to be more proficient and self-determining as a worker in the organisation. Kadushin (1976) has developed a model of supervision for social workers, but it is equally applicable in many fields of 'people' work. He identifies three distinct managerial goals for supervision.

1. To share responsibility for work standards and practice

The line manager has to protect the reputation of the agency in relation to your work. This entails ensuring that you understand the agency's philosophies, policies and priorities and are using them successfully in your practice. The norms that operate in the organisation in relation to culture, values, boundaries, control, accountability, planning, objective setting and standards are all involved in this goal. Line managers also have to ensure that work is correctly resourced and that staff are informed of and, where appropriate, involved in, changes within the organisation.

2. To develop skills, knowledge and attitudes in relation to the work

Managerial supervision also has a role in facilitating learning at work. To meet this goal, line managers need to discover how you learn best and what motivates and demotivates you. They need to be aware of the specific skills needed for your work and, if these are absent, to find ways of developing them.

3. To support workers in their work

Line managers are one source of support for you at work. They can give clear feedback on your work and help you to develop realistic work programmes

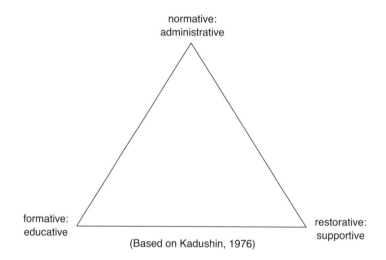

(Based on Kadushin, 1976)

and time management systems. The work we do is sometimes stressful. The supervisor needs to understand your stressors and offer appropriate assistance. This might mean giving you uninterrupted time and space to talk, sending you home to sleep, or insisting that you take the risk of trying a new piece of work.

These three goals can be summarised as normative/administrative, formative/educative and restorative/supportive. The three are connected and interdependent in practice, however, and Kadushin represents them as three corners of an equilateral triangle.

[…]

The line management supervisory relationship

In your work place, an important concern will be how the relationship with your manager can work successfully. The supervisor/supervisee relationship is just one aspect of the relationship you have with your manager. Both of you will have expectations of that relationship, which need to be clarified. Managers will need to be clear on the extent to which they agree with the triangular model of supervision presented above, or the version of it which they wish to use.

Research on the qualities of an 'ideal supervisor' has produced awesome lists which it would be impossible for anybody to display consistently. You may not have a clear idea whether you see the role of line manager supervisor as that of a tutor, teacher, counsellor, colleague or boss. It is important to clarify your own expectations of this relationship.

[…]

The relationship contains a number of implicit duties and obligations for both parties. You will need to be able to describe your work fully and accurately and to identify issues with which you need help. This will mean preparation. You will need to be able to ask for guidance and support and to be open to feedback. Here you will have to be mindful of any tendencies you have to justify, explain or defend your actions needlessly. The relationship also works best when you adopt an active role. You may want to challenge assumptions and restrictive thinking you face in your work or in managerial supervision itself. You need to be able to assess what feedback is useful to you, to implement and monitor changes agreed, and, over time, to identify areas where your work has improved. You also need to be able to take action if you receive inadequate supervision from your manager.

Managerial supervisors usually acknowledge a responsibility to find a space where you can talk freely about work and to negotiate sufficient time for supervision. They usually help workers to explore, clarify and improve their work practices and share their own knowledge, experience and skills. Because of their normative role, they must challenge work they judge incompetent, inappropriate or unethical. But they will also acknowledge change and progress in work proficiency.

[…]

Line management supervision is inevitably a dynamic process. As one of its key functions is to facilitate change for the workers, the clients and ultimately for the organisation, its content and processes themselves need to develop over time. Both you and your manager have to be aware of the range of knowledge and skills necessary to operate as competent reflective professionals.

Setting boundaries

It is impossible to be prescriptive about a relationship which, as you will see, can be so variable. There is no set pattern for line management supervision. But it is worth clarifying some of the boundaries of a supervisory relationship, with regard to some simple practical matters, as soon as possible.

[...]

Lack of clarity about the limits can be a powerful deterrent to a productive learning relationship.

In examining purposes, your previous experiences and current expectations can usefully be discussed with your manager Any agency documents dealing with staff support and development will also be valuable. Your organisation might have appraisals and performance reviews, but these have different purposes and need to be distinguished carefully from the supervisory process. Whether you work with, or near, your manager on a day-to-day basis may have an important impact too. The more managers see staff at work, the more accurate their assessments and observations are likely to be.

Clear arrangements for the site, frequency and timing of programmed sessions are important, but there may also be a need for brief, unplanned contact. Confidentiality is of critical importance. Vague assumptions about the boundaries here are inadequate; apparent breaches of confidentiality are a frequent criticism of poor managerial supervision.

[...]

While [you may believe that confidentiality should ...] cover issues such as keeping personal matters, disclosed failings and the opinions of colleagues confidential, it is not always possible to ensure the confidentiality we would wish. In managerial supervision, the supervisor has a responsibility for good practice in the agency and may therefore have to pursue issues disclosed in confidence, on a 'need to know' basis. Managers may also need to discuss their supervisory practices with their own supervisors. They may have taken notes of your meetings. Who will have access to these and what is their status within the organisation? The bounds of confidentiality are complex and therefore need to be discussed early on in the relationship.

Contracts

One way of helping to systematise and formalise managerial supervision is to contract for effective supervision meetings. Specific work situations will require different contracts, but perhaps at the initial meeting with your line manager, and at regular reviews, you can develop an explicit contract. This might usefully cover agreements about your agenda, the meeting space and notes of the meetings. Will you use an agenda? Who will set it and when will it be set? Will there be any regular items appearing on it? Will the meeting space be private? Will there be interruptions? When will dates and length of meetings be established? Who will make notes? Will they be signed? Who will have access to them, and what happens when you or your manager move on?

Making line management supervision work

However carefully planned, the process of managerial supervision may encounter various blocks. If you and your manager are aware of these, they can be more easily avoided. Possible blocks include organisational factors (for instance, overwork); misunderstandings caused by differing backgrounds or management styles; restrictive thinking and assumptions; and perceptions of power and authority.

[…]

The three goals of managerial supervision are difficult to manage. It is often the case that the triangle becomes skewed, with more emphasis placed on one aspect of the process than on the other two. It may not be feasible or even desirable to always keep the weighting of emphasis equal across all three areas, but beware of a situation which gets stuck in one corner of the triangle. […]

Styles of line management supervision

You may be working with someone whose background, training and experience are markedly different from your own. For example, managers may have been trained in a particular form of counselling or in formal education, and this will inevitably influence the style of their supervision. It is also likely that their style will be affected by the character of the rest of their work. Whether they are practitioners or simply managers, for example, may influence how they operate in supervision.

While you need to share enough of a common language and value system to be able to learn together, diversity need not be a hindrance. Indeed, the more conscious you are of the diverse experiences both of you bring to the relationship, the richer the process can be. Ideological, cultural, sex, sexual orientation, class and personality differences all inevitably complicate managerial supervision, but if they are recognised and acknowledged, they can also enrich it enormously. But it is true that both participants will have to work much harder if aspects of their background and attitudes are affecting their work adversely. Sometimes our own patterns and behaviours prevent us from seeing situations clearly. Or it may be that we are ignorant of what it means to be in the position of those we work with. For example, we may not understand what it means to be homosexual or to have a disability.

[…]

Many unspoken assumptions might hamper relationships. They include stereotyping on the basis of ethnicity, the expectation that management must involve a powerful and assertive authority figure, the confusing of teaching or coaching with supervising. […]

Power

It is also important to acknowledge the power dynamics of the supervisory relationship. In line management supervision, the authority of supervisors is underlined by the legitimate power they hold in the organisation. However, other power dynamics often operate as well.

[…]

[…] [sometimes] both are insecure in the relationship and […] stuck in an impasse over who holds what kinds of power or authority, these dynamics can be very destructive. The supervisor [might] try to be supportive and encouraging, but is not helping the supervisee, who doesn't need a father figure, but some concrete professional development. It is inevitable that our individual attitudes to authority will impinge on the process. If, for example, you have an internal image of an authority figure you respect, you may seek for that image in supervision and judge the supervisor accordingly. Try to be aware of this possible dynamic to prevent it from affecting the relationship adversely.

It's also worth remembering that a core aim of line management supervision is to enhance your self-directedness. The development of your own personal authority is therefore at the heart of supervision.

Managerial supervision as dialogue

The most important aspect of line management supervision is the dialogue between you and your manager. For this to be as fruitful as possible, you will need to develop the skills of active listening and giving and receiving feedback.

There are all sorts of methods for protecting ourselves from the negative impact of failing. Perhaps you try to cover up, blaming problems, events or other people. Perhaps you minimise the failing and try to focus on what you regard as your compensating successes. Maybe you justify the failure as part of the plan, a necessary step to success. Or perhaps you admit it and try to learn from it. You would not be very usual if you typically used the last method, but by receiving feedback skilfully you can avoid evading your responsibility for failings and you are more likely to have your strengths recognised. Feedback may be uncomfortable to hear, but that may be less of a disadvantage than not knowing what others think and feel. Your manager will have opinions about you as well as perceptions about your behaviour, and it can help to be aware of them. However, it is important to remember that you are entitled to your opinion. You may choose to ignore information if it is of little significance, irrelevant or refers to behaviour you wish to maintain for other reasons.

When receiving feedback, it is useful to listen carefully to precisely what is being said about your work performance and your professional judgement. Ask your manager to explain anything that is not clear. Later, if possible, check the comments with observations made by others – to see whether the feedback has general agreement.

If you do not receive feedback at all, you may have to ask for it and, indeed, help your manager to provide useful feedback to you. Sometimes you may get feedback restricted to one aspect of your behaviour and may need to ask for comments on other areas of your work. Providing feedback, whether positive or negative, can be uncomfortable and difficult for managers; they may need help from you.

Having received feedback, it is important to assess its value, the consequences of ignoring it or of using it. Then you can decide what to do as a result of it. It will be wasted if you don't make active decisions. Your objective is to communicate constructively with someone who is offering you feedback on something that you need to consider doing differently. In that way line management supervision can become a vibrant part of your professional development.

Mapping your support needs

You should now have some of the tools to evaluate your own experiences of managerial supervision. How far is this process currently helping you to monitor your practice and to develop proficiency? To what extent is it supporting and encouraging you? If it is not meeting your learning goals and support needs, you need to assess the situation and take some action.

One possibility is to look for sources of professional supervision outside the line management relationship.

[…] The normative aspects of supervision diminish in non-managerial supervision. This has advantages and disadvantages. It may be that involvement in a different model of supervision will enable you to shift the focus from work performance to exploration of personal needs and goals. However, you should recognise that, without line management supervision, your work is not being managed directly. This leaves both you and the organisation in a vulnerable position, with no-one taking responsibility for you and your work when difficulties arise.

Consider if there is the potential to change or develop your supervisory relationships at your work place. If you cannot alter the current arrangements, you may need to look towards colleagues or role models within the organisation for support. Are there potential mentors, or colleagues, who could work with you in a supervisory relationship? If there are, ask them. Look carefully at your methods for self-supervision. Perhaps you can now see ways that these can be improved. If you can see that there are still barriers to getting what you need, or gaps in its provision, you will have to look beyond your organisation towards the wider professional networks in which you operate. As we learn best by doing, look for activities and organisations where you can become directly involved. You owe it to yourself as a professional worker to start to make time and space for supervision.

References

Argyris, C. (1982) *Reasoning, Learning and Action*. San Francisco: Jossey Bass.

Briscoe, C. (1977) 'The consultant in community work', in C. Briscoe and D. N. Thomas (eds) *Community Work: Learning and Supervision*. London: George Allen and Unwin Ltd.

Clough, R. (1995) 'Taking supervision work in residential care', in J. Prichard (ed.), *Good Practice in Supervision. Statutory and Voluntary Organisations*. London: Jessica Kingsley Publishers Ltd.

Christian, C. and Kitto, J. (1987) *The Theory and Practice of Supervision. Occasional Paper 1*. London: YMCA National College.

Hawkins, P. and Shohet, R. (1989) *Supervision in the Helping Professions. An Individual, Group and Organizational Approach*. Milton Keynes: Open University Press.

Hughes, L. and Pengelly, P. (eds) (1997) *Staff Supervision in a Turbulent Environment. Managing Process and Task in Front-line Services*. London: Jessica Kingsley Publishers Ltd.

Kadushin, A. (1976) *Supervision in Social Work*. New York: Columbia University Press.

Tash, M. J. (1967) *Supervision in Youth Work*. London: YMCA National College (reprinted 2000, YMCA George Williams College).

Index